MILEY CYRUS

GOOD GIRL / BAD GIRL

MILEY CYRUS

GOOD GIRL / BAD GIRL

CHLOÉ GOVAN

OMNIBUS PRESS
London / New York / Paris / Sydney / Copenhagen / Berlin / Madrid / Tokyo

Cover designed by Fresh Lemon.

ISBN: 978.1.78305.546.3
Order No: OP55803

Exclusive Distributors
Music Sales Limited,
14/15 Berners Street,
London, W1T 3LJ.

Music Sales Corporation
180 Madison Avenue, 24th Floor,
New York,
NY 10016,
USA.

Macmillan Distribution Services,
56 Parkwest Drive
Derrimut, Vic 3030,
Australia.

Every effort has been made to trace the copyright holders of the photographs in this book but one or two were unreachable.
We would be grateful if the photographers concerned would contact us.

Printed in the EU.

A catalogue record for this book is available from the British Library.

Visit Omnibus Press on the web at www.omnibuspress.com

Introduction

IT was August 2013 – the night of the MTV VMAs – and all hell was about to break loose in Brooklyn, New York. From demure Disney princess to defiantly debauched fallen angel, this was the moment when chameleonic Miley Cyrus would formally come of age.

Fittingly, she was just a few months short of her 21st birthday – although in showbiz, the trademark of reaching legal majority was less about age and more about the moment of the first onstage twerk.

Duly, performing with fellow vocalist Robin Thicke for a medley of her number one hit 'Can't Stop' and his chart-topping track 'Blurred Lines' – she would writhe provocatively, get up, close and personal with some life-size teddy bears, simulate masturbation with a giant foam finger and finally bend over in front of Robin and deliver what would soon become her trademark twerk.

The fact that her lewdness extended even to teddies – traditionally children's toys – made the message abundantly clear: she was ceremonially shedding the skin of her squeaky clean Hannah Montana TV persona and becoming her own woman.

However the vocal partnership was far from music to Robin's mother, Gloria's, eyes. Apparently oblivious to the already abundant and ever-present sexual content in his songs and videos, she would place the blame for the scandal squarely on Miley, claiming damningly, "I was *not* expecting her to put her butt that close to my son!" "The trouble is," she'd shuddered in revulsion, as though Miley had been a predatory sex pest and Robin a traumatised and unwilling victim, "now I can never unsee it!"

Miley was unapologetic – controversial or not, it was called showbiz for a reason, and true to form, this young multimillionaire was going to put on a show. As it turned out, Mrs Thicke Senior was the least of her worries – when it came to condemning Miley, she was at the back of a very long queue.

During her performance, Twitter had almost crashed under a never-ending stream of outraged tweets – at the record-breaking rate of over 300,000 per minute. Not only did the scandal far surpass Mother Monster Lady Gaga's shenanigans – which that night had included dressing as a priest – but the tweet count had been almost a third greater than the time Justin Timberlake had 'accidentally' ripped down Janet Jackson's top at the 2009 Superbowl to reveal a pre-watershed bare nipple. Plus it also almost topped that of the USA's recent presidential election night. Not only had the 2013 VMAs attracted more than triple their maximum tweet per minute rate from the previous year, but it seemed Miley was now a hotter topic than Barack Obama. Robin had surely been right when he'd delivered a conspiracy-laced wink to his onstage ally and asserted, "You know, tonight, we're going to make history."

Yet the furore that ensued was part PR genius and part beautiful night-mare. The headlines the following morning screamed that "misguided" Miley was incapable of computing the difference between sexy and slutty, that she was on the verge of a mental breakdown and that the performance was a cry for help from a troubled young woman. Why else, the world asked accusingly, would anyone want to get onstage, gyrate and – shock, horror – enjoy herself?

Even one of Miley's backing dancers, Hollis Jane, reported that the experience that night had been the most "degrading and dehumanising" of her life. By her rather dramatic account, she had left the venue "shaking and crying".

In that moment, a newcomer to Planet Earth might have been forgiven for assuming that New York was not the heartland of liberty that its iconic statue suggested, but in fact that they'd happened upon an oppressive Saudi Arabian outpost. (Damn the inadequate sat-nav on those spaceships!)

To modern mentalities, of course, the 16-year age gap between Robin and Miley was meagre, while the latter was actually doing no less than the average extroverted young woman might be seen indulging in at a nightclub. The only difference was that, as a multimillion-selling pop star with paparazzi lenses fixed firmly on her, her moments of hedonism were invariably played out in public.

Regardless, the accusations prevailed, along with the ceaseless question, "What would the *parents* say?!" Indeed, Miley's father, Billy Ray, was watching at the sidelines, consumed with sadness – although not for the reasons the decency police might have thought.

In fact, this uncomfortable scenario was all too familiar for him – he'd experienced exactly the same criticism decades earlier himself when he'd become an overnight sensation with his 1992 track 'Achy Breaky Heart'. For him too, there'd been an undeniable element of salacious sex appeal in his performances. Enthralled fans would scream hysterically and throw their bras at the stage as he shook his hips and derriere in time to the music. Rumours even ran rife that he'd previously been a Chippendales erotic dancer. While his signature dance move wasn't quite a twerk, it was certainly sexually provocative, and soon became synonymous with his name.

Just as Miley's dance moves would inspire national twerking championships in her honour around the world, Billy Ray's own wiggle had achieved the same heights. However the fact that the general public regarded him as a sex symbol hadn't made his journey much easier to navigate – if anything it had blocked his road to progress. He'd struggled to be taken seriously when breaking into the music business – in fact one record executive would admit that when he first attended her office, desperate for a window into the industry, she'd thought he'd have been better suited to modelling than music – and all before she'd heard a single note. "My initial reaction to this gorgeous man," Kari Reeves would confess, "was that he should have been a model for International Male instead of an aspiring country musician."

When he finally made it in music, the backlash soon began. To traditionalists, gyration and screaming groupies wasn't a scene with which they wanted country music to be associated – they felt it gave the genre a bad name. Billy Ray's detractors jeered that it was all about sex appeal over substance and that he was a talentless no-hoper shamelessly capitalising on his only asset – his good looks. Without those handsome features, the masses had cruelly speculated, he wouldn't have stood a chance.

Whether it was jealousy or zealous over-judgment that drove the criticism, it was nonetheless deeply painful – and now that history was repeating itself, with Miley being condemned as a slutty, shock value-orientated gimmick, familiarity didn't make their claims any less wounding.

Little could the Miley bashers have guessed that her father had been watching not in horrified disapproval but rather in resigned recognition – and that he hadn't just empathised but also understood.

This showbiz story takes us back decades to Miley's roots and to the rural Kentucky upbringing of her own father – whose against-the-odds fame would shape her own future destiny.

Chapter 1

BILLY Ray Cyrus took his first breath in Flatwoods, Kentucky, where he lived out his formative years. To cynics, the area was something of a cultural wasteland whose residents suffocated in sheer despair – and that was the muted definition. As an example, the only other Flatwoods resident of note had been Dheak Gill, a man who'd gained notoriety via the dubious fame of downing 23 bull testicles in a record-breaking 23 minutes and 13 seconds for the annual Iron Stomach competition. The region wasn't exactly known for producing high flyers.

Billy Ray would proudly announce later that the jobs in which the ancestral Cyruses had toiled – on the rural area's railroads, coal mines, farms and steel mills – had been "the cornerstones of the industries that built and fed America" – and yet for all the inflated grandeur of that statement, the reality was that the Cyruses were desperately poor. Jobs were few and far between – in fact, having one at all was regarded as an uncommon blessing – and those that did exist returned a painfully meagre wage. While they might have paid highly in terms of honour and respectability, that was a slim consolation when struggling to feed tearful children with empty bellies.

Kentucky already had one of the highest child poverty rates of the nation, while country performer Loretta Lynn's recollections of her own upbringing in the state in the seventies song 'Coal Miner's Daughter' reflected the harsh reality. Just like Loretta, Billy Ray had been one of eight children and had seen his mother read the Bible by coal-oil light and scrub at a cheap, abrasive washboard until her fingers bled.

His father, Ron, had endured equally humble beginnings. At the time of Billy Ray's birth, he'd been a lowly rigger at Armco Steelworks and his first day of employment, back in 1955, had seen him sink even lower, chipping and sanding concrete bricks for the plant. The toxicity of this early lifestyle would ultimately have tragic consequences, seeing him die at the age of 70 from terminal cancer believed to have been caused by asbestos inhalation in the workplace.

Meanwhile Billy Ray's grandfather Eldon – or "Pawpa", as he called him in those early days – had been a devoutly religious Pentecostal preacher. While it might have earned him religious kudos, there was little recompense in the way of wealth. Pop songstress Katy Perry was the daughter of a preacher too and she'd recalled an upbringing so spartan she hadn't even been able to afford dental care. By the time she finally made it to the dentist's chair as a teenager, she'd been forced to have 13 thoroughly "rotten" teeth filled.

For Eldon, life was equally tough and they were forced to feed themselves via donations to the congregation pot. However, like many Southern families, their faith in God was intense and genuine – and Eldon would preach in the traditional Pentecostal style about talking in tongues, receiving messages from spirits and opening oneself to divine healing.

To demonstrate the devoutly religious nature of the family, Ron's eldest sister – 17 years his senior – had been named Mary Magdalene. Yet their unfettered faith hadn't made life on the poverty line any easier. To make matters worse, the region's reputation for "Southern hospitality" was – according to both Billy Ray and Ron – sorely overestimated.

The occasional country singing prodigy aside, at that time Kentucky's main achievements were farming and fried chicken. Yet it seemed the Cyruses were destined for greater things. Billy Ray's mother, Ruth, was a keen piano player with both a brain for business and an exuberant showbiz style personality which saw her classmates admiringly vote her in one school year as "Most Likely To Succeed and Run a Hollywood Studio". Although fame wouldn't manifest itself for another generation yet, their hunches would prove uncannily correct.

Meanwhile Ron – who would rise dramatically to become a highly respected Democratic politician – was heavily involved in a band with Eldon, known as the Crownsmen Quartet. They would regularly put on performances at the steelworks or in local bars, while young Billy Ray would watch in awe, soaking up the musical styles.

Thus on Saturday, Billy Ray would find himself at his maternal grand-father's house, falteringly playing the fiddle while his mother was the pianist and his father chimed in on guitar. They'd play bluegrass, country and Southern Gospel standards from 'Amazing Grace' and 'Rolling In My Sweet Baby's Arms' to '(Won't You Come Home) Bill Bailey'. They'd rest only to sleep because then, the following morning, they'd relocate to his paternal grandfather's church where he'd be summoned to the stage and "forced" to sing 'Swing Low, Sweet Chariot' with the Crownsmen Quartet.

Just a toddler and already self-conscious about his looks, to Billy Ray exhibitionism didn't come naturally. "I was so bashful," he would later confess to the *LA Times* of those early memories. "I was horrified. I was real ugly. My ears stuck out so far, my eyes were so big and I had a butch haircut. I always had a little dirt on me too."

It was ironic that, decades later, this painfully shy and self-conscious, self-styled 'ugly duckling' would become an international heart-throb, prompting mass female hysteria on a scale often compared with Elvis or the Beatles. Back then, however, music was a momentary – and not always welcome – escape from the dark cloud that hung over him at home.

Furious arguments would break out between Ruth and Ron Cyrus on an almost daily basis while a helpless Billy Ray could only look on in terror, begging them to stop – and not even places of worship were safe. The fighting between his parents rose to fever pitch until, at the tender age of four, he witnessed an enraged, jealousy-fuelled assault by his mother on a love rival outside – of all places – his grandfather's church. As it turned out, monogamy hadn't been Ron's strong point and, when Ruth had seen him leave the building with another woman, her fiery temper had got the better of her. "It all got ugly there in the church parking lot," Billy Ray would later recall. "My mom jumped on, fought some woman, beat her." He added, "I seen my mom pull one woman out of my dad's convertible by the hair of the head and stomp her ass in the ditch!"

Family life was volatile to say the least and it was to no one's surprise when Ron and Ruth announced their divorce. Little Billy Ray was just five years old. When Ruth had ominously announced, "Your father and I are going to have a big fight tonight," he might cynically have wondered what was new. However the clue that this one might be particularly vicious was that this time she locked him in an upstairs bedroom with his brother Kevin. Poor as they were, this so-called bedroom was in reality just an oversized wardrobe modelled into a sanctuary for him and Kevin (affectionately named Kebo), courtesy of a few Jimi Hendrix posters on the walls. Once inside, the tiny structure echoed and almost rocked with the sounds of confrontation. Glass plates smashed to the ground, fists collided with walls and furniture was overturned – all to the soundtrack of blood-curdling angry screams.

Eventually Billy Ray would break out of the bedroom and wedge himself between the two warring parents, putting a momentary halt to the battle. After an eerie silence, his father coldly announced he was leaving. "I wrapped my arms around his chest," Billy Ray would later recall, "and my legs around his waist, clinging like a little monkey." Yet having already uttered the last words he would speak as a resident of the house, Ron would simply step silently over the broken furniture and leave without a backward glance.

The aftermath of the divorce was equally harrowing, not least because they lived in a conservative sixties area of America where Southern values and religious faith were paramount and where divorce was not just taboo but almost unheard of. Puerile gossip followed that the family had been disgraced in the eyes of God and could no longer be counted as Christians.

Then there were the financial implications of separation – Ruth was forced to sell her beloved piano and work all hours as a cleaner just to make ends meet, while philandering Ron's meagre wages were mainly spent on the needs of his new wife, Joannie.

A troubled Billy Ray was belittled and taunted by the other children in school, not just because the alien concept of divorce didn't sit well with their Southern beliefs, but because his mother was now so poor, they were the only family in the neighbourhood without a home telephone. He would come to dread standing in front of his class at the start of each school term to recite his address and number, only to be serenaded by titters as he confessed in shame that he still made calls on a makeshift out-house payphone.

And if he was self-conscious about his protruding ears then, he would soon become even more so. One morning, a group of older boys rounded on him in the school hallway, jeering and pulling their ears outwards in mock exaggeration. Billy Ray turned and fled, before finally running home and collapsing in the arms of his mother. That night he made an impassioned prayer: "Dear God, I know I'm ugly, but when I grow up, just make people think I'm funny. Amen." The plea would become a night-time ritual for years to come.

From that day forth, he was a regular target for bullying because, in this small close-knit community, he stood out as different. Music could have provided an escape for him, as it did for his elder brother, but due to his left-handedness he found strumming on his father's guitar near impossible. The old wives' tale that being left-handed was a sign of affiliation with the Devil – long since dismissed as nonsense in more modern locales – still prevailed in much of God-fearing Kentucky and disapproving elders strongly encouraged him to overcome his instinct and learn to use the other hand.

Unsurprisingly, this felt clumsy and unnatural to him. Defeated by music, he instead began to spend his days in the woods, first crying, contemplating and praying and then, as his mother remarried and the black cloud of his parents' divorce began to move away, he progressed to rowdy games. Childhood friend Gregg Davidson recalled, "In those days, children could still play freely in the open woods like Huckleberry Finn and Billy romped through the trees with rapturous abandon, playing hide and seek or cowboys and Indians with his brother [and] building forts and waging mock attacks on the 'enemy'."

In middle school, he also became a roving reporter for the 25-cents-per-issue school magazine. Although he was still prohibitively shy when it came to asking girls out on dates, he took a special interest in each issue's 'Cute Couples' section, where he would mischievously and fictitiously pair himself with the most beautiful girls in school.

Then in 1975 – the same year that his father broke free of his humble background to be successfully elected as a politician – 14-year-old Billy Ray entered a rebellious stage, becoming a self-described "wild juvenile delinquent hoodlum". The phase was characterised by shoplifting, drug-taking, vandalism, streaking through the streets of Kentucky and, worst of all, an ill-advised penchant for matches. "My papa was a Pentecostal preacher and my dad in the government," he would recall later to CNN. "Yet at the same time, on any given night, if I could get the police to chase me, that was a successful night."

While Ron scaled prestigious heights, becoming a member of the

Federal Reserve Board and a respected Democrat politician – it seemed Billy Ray was craving attention of his own, and acting up was proving a reliable way to get it. His stabilising influence turned out to be sport – not only did it distract him from creating mayhem and boost his "confidence and focus", but it also brought to the surface "the warrior in me".

That said, he was far from committed. "Indecisiveness was my major," he would later groan. "Every year, when I'd fill out the little card stating my major, I'd check off 'undecided'. That's how I knew I was heading in the wrong direction."

Nonetheless, he half-heartedly modelled himself on Johnny Bench – arguably one of the greatest catchers in baseball history – and resolved to follow in his idol's footsteps by becoming a member of the Cincinnati Reds. He felt a glow of pride when he was awarded a local baseball scholarship at Georgetown College, a prestigious Christian-themed liberal arts establishment affiliated with Britain's Oxford University – but his satisfaction was short-lived. As much as he loved sport, his heart wasn't in professional competition and, shyly swatting away promises that he could be a star, the reluctant baseball prodigy spent the start of his junior year trying to find a purpose that resonated with him.

It wasn't long before the voices began in the back of his head – strong, powerful, insistent and impossible to ignore. "Buy a guitar and form a band and you'll fulfil your purpose," they asserted. "Just trade in your catcher's mitt and buy a guitar."

To say he was dumbfounded was an understatement – he adored music but was no musician and his early attempts to master his father's instruments had been disastrous. "As a teenager," Gregg reasoned, "he didn't realise you had to re-string it if you were a leftie."

He was bashful too, shying away from crowds, but he listened to the inner voice. His more competitively driven classmates, on the other hand, thought he'd lost his mind to a foolish fantasy. Meanwhile his first girl-friend – who was quite enamoured with the idea of a WAG-lifestyle – almost dumped him over it. Yet whether the voices were messages from God, or merely his intuition, Billy Ray was convinced they were real.

He duly returned his catcher's mitt, gave up his scholarship after just five weeks – ignoring pleas from his tutors that he was professional-league material and squandering the chance of a lifetime – and bought a left-handed guitar. As he would later recall, "I just knew inside my soul it was the right thing to do."

That very night, he wrote his first song, and by the following morning he'd recruited his brother Kebo to join his band – one that until that moment had existed only in his imagination. Things began to move surreally fast – yesterday's baseball champion was now setting a goal to be "the next Elvis Presley" – and all within 10 months.

That was the time limit he'd set for success and he'd resolved that Sly Dog – named after a volatile one-eyed mutt he'd owned at the time – would become a resident house band at a bar or club before his 20th birthday. Sure enough, in August 1981 – just a week before the deadline expired – he earned a daily slot at the Ohio club Changes. The next three years passed in a blur of pot-smoking and persistent groupies until, one fateful day in 1984, the entire club – and all Billy Ray's equipment in it – burnt to the ground. He was devastated – it was a reality check that snapped him out of his pleasure-filled oblivion fast.

For Billy Ray, unknown outside of Ohio, an enormous challenge lay ahead. Then he noticed a miniature two-inch-by-two-inch Bible he'd hidden inside a guitar amp for good luck was the only thing that had survived the wreckage. To him it was a sign – a God-sent symbol of resilience proving that, as long as his faith survived and he never gave up, he would succeed.

The words of Eldon Cyrus – his now deceased preacher grandfather – flooded back into his head reminding him that "with every adversity lies the seed to something better". Believing he had to be proactive about where to plant that seed, Billy Ray upped sticks and relocated to LA. The move was partly a reaction to Nashville and Kentucky record executives repeatedly slamming the door in his face for being "too rock'n'roll" – he hoped that in the original city of showbiz, he'd stand a better chance of fitting the mould. Yet the moment he arrived, he was rejected for exactly the opposite reason – being "too country". He could have been forgiven for wondering whether he truly belonged anywhere.

Having formerly reaped the benefits of being a big fish in a small pond, his hustle was now about to become more arduous than ever. He was soon reduced to living in his car and working in a poorly paid retail role in a store called Baby Toy Town – so embarrassingly kitsch that it seemed the kiss of death for any aspiring rocker. "I guess desperate stores do desperate things," he would later chuckle of the mismatch. "They hired a hillbilly from Kentucky and I was terrible. I didn't know nothing about baby beds and baby strollers!"

Not to mention that it was hardly the coolest place for a musician to be hanging out – the arrangement would prove cringe-inducing. Just when the indignity of earning a living discussing nappies, prams and toddlers' toys became almost too much to bear, he was saved by a customer who – impressed by his charisma – offered him a job on the spot at her husband's car dealership.

Hapless Billy Ray knew even less about cars than he did about infants – in fact he didn't even know how to perform basic maintenance on his own – and at first his new role seemed to be yet another disaster in the making. As a newcomer, he also lacked the persuasive, polished and pushy sales pitch that was hard-wired into Californian culture and his hesitation led to a two month stint without making a single sale.

The owner, who had ranted that hiring Billy Ray had been "the biggest mistake of his life" was all set to make him redundant when, in the latter's eyes, God performed another miracle. The very next day he netted his first customer and his winning streak continued until, within weeks, he had become the highest performing salesperson in the company. He went from a penniless no-hoper to a high flyer, earning $20,000 per month in commission. He even began dating a *Playboy* centrefold – with a beautiful Californian blonde on his arm, perhaps the looks he'd agonised over since childhood weren't as bad as he'd thought.

Yet little by little, homesickness took over – not to mention his longing to get back to the stage where he felt he'd be better appreciated. "I was a musician," he explained simply. "I didn't belong out in LA selling Oldsmobiles [cars] . . . I was going back to my roots."

By the time he hit his twenty-fifth birthday, he was back at Changes – now resurrected after the fire – and his shows had become wilder. Injected with a lot of Californian confidence, he would rip off his shirt and belt out Billy Idol's 'Rebel Yell'. This was his scene – and what was more, he'd traded in the centrefold model back in LA for a local tobacco sales rep, Cindy, to prove it. Perhaps she was a little less glamorous, but she was a Southern belle after his own heart.

Three months later, he found himself marrying her Las Vegas style, in a little white chapel in Tennessee's Smoky Mountains. The six hour drive down the highway had originally been in aid of submitting his demo tape to record companies but, by now thoroughly sick of rejection, Billy Ray made a spur of the moment deliberate wrong turning and ended up drink driving his way to marriage instead.

Yet the hasty coupling was one of inebriated frivolity – as crazy as the drunken drive down the highway to exchange vows. Billy Ray himself would confess that their marriage was more of a party than a partnership – and the cracks quickly began to show. When two jealous would-be groupies set Cindy's hair on fire – consumed with rage that the man of their dreams was hers – it was deemed too dangerous for her to watch her husband at the club any more. While psychotic arsonist groupies didn't pose much of a threat, others did – and without Cindy around to supervise him, his eye began to wander.

It was a constant battle to resist. "We had way too many women coming at us from all angles," he would recall, "and too much sex, drugs and rock'n'roll." To complicate matters further, Billy Ray's model for married life – inherited from his volatile parents – was a chaotic blend of bar-room brawls and broken dishes, not to mention serial philandering. Soon, the fights with Cindy over his infidelity brought the couple almost to breaking point.

History had repeated itself – and the relationship was also straining under the weight of Billy Ray's career woes. In 1987, he was forced to sack Kebo from Sly Dog due to conflict he'd had with other members and shortly afterwards, the band as they knew it fell apart altogether. Forced to go it alone, he suffered producers who tried to extort thousands of dollars from him on the dubious promise of securing him a number one single. He regularly plucked up the courage to make the 12-hour round trip to Nashville too, only to be met with a string of rejections.

Just when it seemed as though he'd exhausted every possibility in the industry, an unexpected door opened for him in the form of legendary Grand Ole Opry star Del Reeves's daughter Kari. As well as managing her father's record company, Kari also freelanced regularly for a national country music magazine, and Billy Ray had blagged his way into an interview with her, billing himself as the next big country star.

It was a phrase Kari had heard all too often before – in fact, he was the sixth interviewee that week who allegedly met that description – and at first, her reaction bordered on jaded indifference. However, Billy Ray was different – within minutes, she'd pledged to help him become a star and almost as quickly (unbeknown to Cindy) the pair had embroiled themselves in a passionate affair.

To the cynic, neither's motives were entirely pure. Billy Ray himself had confessed, "As the daughter of a certified country music legend, she had access to the inside. I was both intrigued and intoxicated." This, after all, was a man who'd been "hammering away at the doors on Music Row with nothing to show [for it] but black and blue knuckles", so meeting Kari had been like a breath of fresh air. The tantalising promise of success by mere association with her was surely almost as seductive as her sex appeal. Was his frequently professed love for her fake, calculated and tactical? Was it a show of desperate gratitude? Or were they, as he insisted, genuinely "soul-mates"?

Then there were Kari's motives to consider. As much as she may have appreciated his songs, she would later recall, "My initial reaction to this gorgeous man was that he should have been a model for International Male rather than an aspiring country musician." Was this a matter of mere sexual attraction – had she been dangling the carrot of her father's ability to transform aspiring stars into real ones, capitalising on its currency to lure in the man she craved?

The pair's respective motives lay firmly in blurred lines territory, but whether it was sex or the hope of success that tempted Billy Ray away from his wife, thoughts of Cindy ended up getting left behind. This was no one night stand akin to his liaisons with groupies – it was a full-blown affair complete with the exchange of love notes, lyrics and poetry. Kari had even adapted the lyrics of the Frankie Miller track 'Gladly Go Blind', supplementing them with 'Gladly Go Blind (If I Don't Get You Signed)'. Humiliatingly for Cindy, nothing was out of bounds in the pursuit of their affair – not even the Cyrus marital bed.

Yet if it had been a tactic on Billy Ray's part, it had worked. Kari, despite seeming to be more mesmerised by his classic good looks than his music, successfully arranged for her father to see him in concert. Whatever her motives, this could change his life. Sure enough, an impressed Del

Reeves handed him a production agreement and introduced him to veteran Jack McFadden, who would go on to become his manager full-time.

He was on his way – but there were consequences to his rash affair, and one morning he came home to find every possession he owned strewn across the front lawn. The shame was palpable – his smartly suited next door neighbour had stared incredulously over the hedge on his way to work at the sight of Billy Ray in his sharply contrasting, sweat-stained, eau-de-marijuana-tinted outfit from the night before, fishing all of his worldly possessions out of the gutter.

The silver lining was that the episode prompted him to pen the heartfelt 'Where'm I Gonna Live?', which would later be part of a debut album that would earn him millions. He gave Cindy a co-writers' credit "because she was kind enough to set my stuff out in the yard one morning at about 4.30 a.m. in the pouring rain", and even managed to crawl his way back into the marital home after serenading her with it. He'd made amends – for now – but it wasn't to last, and his divorce would be finalised by 1991.

Not, of course, that lady-loving Billy Ray could stay out of trouble for long. The same month he filed for divorce from Cindy, he discovered he'd impregnated a South Carolina cocktail waitress by the name of Kristin Luckey. So much, Kari would rage later, for his promise that they would be together – in fact, after his divorce, she saw less of him than ever.

Within a few weeks of learning that he'd be a father, he'd moved on to a new affair with a woman much closer to home – Leticia Finley of Ashland, Kentucky – known to her friends as Tish. Regrettably, however, this was one woman who didn't have many friends – due in no small part to her intimidatingly good looks. Presumably, it was hard for the average homely Kentucky farmhand to be hanging out with a companion who looked as though she'd stepped fresh from the pages of a Louis Vuitton advert, without feeling a little inadequate.

Women wanted to be her, while men simply wanted to be with her. Boasting waist-length blonde hair, a generously curvy bosom and large wide-set eyes, she had most of Ashland, and beyond, eating out of the palm of her hand.

Tish had been a model since age four, when she'd paraded in the children's collections from her mother's dress shop and she'd since progressed to winning a string of local beauty pageants such as "Miss Tristate Beauty". Magazines would comment admiringly on her "ash blonde hair and sparkling blue eyes", before predicting her future as a glamorous runway favourite. Back then, prior to the nineties advent of "heroin chic", models were slim instead of thin and much less Amazonian than the present day – and 5′ 5″ Tish, a dwarf by today's fashion standards, met the prototype perfectly.

Yet she would fall prey to the classic curse endured by beautiful women, with words such as "slut" and "whore" bandied about gratuitously – not a single former classmate approached by this book's author had a positive word to say about her. Perpetuating the stereotype that beauty meant being a brainless bimbo, they raged that she was vacuous and empty-headed – a "dumb slutty cheerleader" with no other aspiration in life than to become a groupie.

Tish had fuelled the fire by defiantly maintaining her position as a regular on the music circuit and, by age 14, she'd given birth to a local drummer's baby. The gossip mongers returned with a vengeance, spreading rumours around town that she was a "rock'n'roll groupie".

What the naysayers omitted from these rather damning reports was that Tish was a child of privilege herself. Her wealthy family owned several Wendy's fast food joints and convenience stores, not to mention her mother's fashion boutique – and the men she dated sometimes had less money to spend than she did.

That said, the vision of a beautiful and glamorous pin-up model on the arm of a rock star was the biggest cliché around – and physically there was no doubt that Tish fit the bill. By the time she and Billy Ray crossed paths at country club the Ragtime Joint in 1991, she was 23 and already had two children – Brandi and Neal – by two different fathers. Both lived with her mother while, according to the locals, she lived the party lifestyle – first with a succession of roadies from whom she blagged backstage passes and then the musicians themselves.

Yet whatever prior entanglements she may have had, nothing could have compared to the baggage of Billy Ray. With the ink barely dry on his divorce papers, he'd already made Kristin pregnant – and what was more, he was still enjoying the occasional dalliance with Kari, who lived in hope the two of them would soon be getting married.

With both Tish and Billy Ray in high demand – and neither squeaky clean – it looked as though their relationship was doomed to be just another sordid fling. On the contrary, however, Billy Ray – who prided himself on his intuition and on receiving Pentecostal messages from God – had the premonition that this relationship was something special.

"I have no coincidences, ever," he'd later insist. "I don't even believe in coincidence. Everything in my life has happened for a reason."

If, by his logic, the silver lining of his last relationship had been a ticket to fame, the reason for this one was Miley, his baby girl – someone who, in his eyes, was clearly destined to take over the world before she'd so much as left the womb.

Chapter 3

TRUE to character, and in a taste of things to come, young Miley Cyrus was indeed a miniature celebrity before she'd so much as left the womb. There could scarcely be a more rock'n'roll entrance to the world, after all, than a high profile national gossip column rolling out the red carpet for your arrival.

By that time Billy Ray was hot property – he'd been finally signed to Mercury Records courtesy of the leg-up he'd received from Kari's father and, the same month that Tish conceived, his debut single, 'Achy Breaky Heart', had begun to storm the charts. The hysteria surrounding him was so intense that the tiny foetus in Tish's belly already had a status akin to America's first ever royal baby.

The headlines screamed that a mysterious woman of Kentucky origin was pregnant, complete with a quote from manager Jack McFadden to confirm, "Billy Ray knows the young lady and if it is proven to be his child, I know he'll stand up to his obligations."

Clearly the outing of the news was less than romantic, with newspapers inferring between the lines that Tish was a gold-digger who'd manipulatively tricked the nation's latest golden boy into starting a family. Nonetheless, the fanfare around the baby's arrival was characteristic of exactly how much of the mark she would make on the world in the years to follow.

Despite the circumstances, Billy Ray instinctively felt that the birth was meant to be. The premonition was as insistent and forceful as the one that had urged him, against all logic, to abandon his baseball scholarship and step into the unknown by buying a guitar. "She was named Destiny Hope before she was born," he would later tell the Christian faith website Beliefnet, "because I was positive that there was a voice telling me that it was her destiny to bring hope to the world."

Destiny Hope, soon to become Miley, was born on November 23,

1992 – just seven months after the arrival of Billy Ray's first child, son Christopher Cody. The timing was a stark reminder to all concerned that he had been involved with multiple women at the same time. This time, he'd pledged to be by Tish's side, but – due to complications – she was induced in hospital three weeks early while he was on tour, trapped helplessly on a plane. This was just the beginning of the unwelcome tension that his touring schedule would bring to the family.

A sickly Destiny had to be fed continuous oxygen in an incubator and it was over a week before mother and daughter were given the green light to go home. However, once she'd been nursed back to health, an exuberant Miley could barely stop grinning. As Billy Ray would later recall, "No newborn that I knew of had ever seemed so happy to have arrived in this world!"

The persistent rumours that Tish was a gold-digger – driven both by jealous women and newspapers with an eye for a story – continued to blight the relationship but, chaotic as things were, Billy Ray had fallen in love with both members of his new family.

By the time of his daughter's birth, Billy Ray was also riding high on the wave of his debut single and album, which – in a matter of weeks – had carried him from penniless obscurity to worldwide fame. The first stroke of luck had come via 'Achy Breaky Heart'. Originally titled 'Don't Tell My Heart', it had been released by fellow country group the Marcy Brothers the previous year, but had flopped miserably, failing even to chart.

Then Billy Ray reinvented the song and injected a new ingredient – sex appeal. He used its beat to parade his rippling muscles and showcase what would quickly become a trademark hip shake and bum wiggle. His label sent a promo video for the song – which, bizarrely, featured both Tish and ex-wife, Cindi, simultaneously – to dozens of nightclubs across the country, and a line-dance craze was born.

Billy Ray knew all too well that the interest was due in no small part to the sexuality he exuded, but he was initially nonplussed. "I consider myself a serious artist," he affirmed to celebrity gossip magazine *People*, "but if the outside of Billy Ray Cyrus makes it happen, I hope they're getting every bit they want!"

They certainly were – and Billy Ray watched, open-mouthed, as the song proceeded to break record after record. After its April 14 release, 'Achy Breaky Heart' became the first single to achieve triple platinum sales since records began. It sold over a million copies before his label had even printed an album cover. (Needless to say, when it did, it featured a close-up view of the main attraction.) It also became the first country single to go platinum since Kenny Rogers and Dolly Parton's 1983 effort 'Islands In the Stream'.

It was ironic that the rock'n'roll tinged rebellion and refusal to play it safe that had initially earmarked him as unsuitable for country crowds and had seen the Nashville labels advise him to try his luck in LA was actually driving his fame. It was exactly that flavour which had sent a country track into the mainstream – for the first time in almost a decade.

Meanwhile, courtesy of his May 19 album, *Some Gave All*, the accolades just kept coming. The CD was the best seller of 1992, spending 17 consecutive weeks at number one on the *Billboard* chart, and it went nine times platinum, ultimately selling over 20 million copies. First it boasted the status of best-selling debut album for a country artist and then it became the best-selling album of all time and across all genres for a male solo artist. As the *LA Times* would joke, "The last time anyone named Cyrus conquered so quickly, it was the sixth century BC and the result was the Persian Empire." He even intimidated Madonna, derailing her plans to release a cover of Nancy Sinatra's 'These Boots Are Made For Walkin'', when his own version hit the airwaves.

Of course he was most famed for making his brand of raunchy line-dancing an international trend. Just as Miley would make the twerk famous, bringing it out of Caribbean backstreets and into worldwide popular culture, her father before her had given birth to the Billy Ray hip wiggle.

Yet just as Miley would be hounded by jealousy and judgment, years earlier Billy Ray had experienced exactly the same accusations from his own critics. Onstage, of course, it was a different world – he was adored. As Gregg, now a roadie who bussed him from city to city, would recall of the shows, "[It] was a spectacle [unseen] since the early career of Elvis Presley – a packed house of adoring females that seemingly lost all grip on their senses over Billy Ray, amorously tossing clothing and underclothing onstage in a primal and feverish nature reminiscent of some beastly mating ritual, all the while screaming in sheer ecstasy." The hysterical screams were almost deafening, while "hair-pulling marathons and fist fights" were conducted among the groupies. Billy Ray, the ugly duckling from Flatwoods, was officially a sex symbol.

Yet outside the sweaty, adrenalin-induced heat of the arenas, it was a cold, cold world – and the vultures were waiting to swoop for his blood. It seemed a lady-magnet status wasn't the only thing he'd shared in common with Elvis, as sex appeal began to sharply overshadow the songs, and he received what the *Chicago Tribune* would describe as "perhaps the most savage media onslaught endured by a performer since Elvis brought rock'n' roll to America's living rooms."

It began with patronising barbs that it was his "rugged good looks and sculpted body" that had propelled him to stardom rather than his talent, with the *LA Times* adding, "It doesn't hurt that Cyrus wears his stubble as handsomely as Mel Gibson, or that the 'Achy Breaky' video showcases him shimmying and swivelling his weightlifter's six-foot, 185-pound physique to sexy effect."

However what had begun gently swiftly degenerated to outright hostility. On December 11, 1992, *Entertainment Weekly* gave his live show a D-grade, sneering, "The summer of '92 will be remembered as the time when a hip-thrusting song and the fling of a trashy ponytail propelled a fourth-rate talent into the national spotlight." It added, "Billy Ray Cyrus may be country's most potent groin teaser, but he's so spectacularly ungifted and delusional about his contribution that it's almost cruel to fuel his dreams." The *LA Times* review was scarcely more flattering, condemning his onstage banter as "far and above the biggest bunch of egotistical drool ever heard".

Even Billy Ray's manager, Jack McFadden, thought his most distinguishing assets were "his butt and his ponytail". By now some regarded him as the equivalent of a promotions model – like a lingerie-clad glamour girl draping herself provocatively over the bonnet of a car at a roadshow, he had become the face and body of a product critics sneered at as lifeless. When he defended his fans, "I believe eight million people realise there's much more to this book than the cover," *People* magazine joked back, "Fair enough – but a lot of them wouldn't mind running a finger down the pages."

The journalistic puns suggested he wasn't being taken seriously – and those puns were perpetuated by the public. The stereotype was that visually appealing stars were flaunting their physical assets because they had little else to offer, that they were using their bodies to disguise or compensate for a lack of talent. Of course, it wasn't outside the realm of possibility that someone could be both gifted *and* attractive at the same time, but, perhaps due to jealousy or intimidation, his detractors refused to accept the notion. In his case, it was believed that he was merely a man-whore, that he was incapable of using two heads at once and that the predominant one lay in his trousers. Perhaps it might serve as a cheap ego boost to soothe their own inadequacies if critics insisted the cruel jokes were true and that a performer couldn't sport both brains and beauty at once, but it was frustrating for Billy Ray, who longed to be viewed as a credible artist – not just for his saucy stage routine, but for his voice, songwriting and musicianship.

Somewhat understandably, he was defiant. Why should he be forced to rein in his onstage antics for fear of being labelled a talentless no-hoper hiding behind the magnetism of his hips? He continued to swivel them, ripping off his shirt and throwing it into hysterical female crowds before cheering them on and urging them, in a style that betrayed his country roots, to "party 'til the cows come home!"

He continued to dance and the critics continued to criticise. Another day, another dollar – or, in Billy Ray's case, a whole lot more of them. Tabloids modelled him into a gimmicky novelty act good only as the subject of celebrity gossip – the American equivalent, perhaps, of Jedward. They printed stories claiming he'd once been a male stripper in his LA days, working at Chippendales, which he wrote off as "an absolute lie". "I wouldn't even dance at the high-school dance!" he would exclaim whenever the subject came up. "I was always too embarrassed."

The media also diced with danger when they labelled him a former wife beater and told of a fictitious affair with Dolly Parton – a woman who, at that time, he'd never met. Yet the silver lining occurred when they bonded over their shared distaste of fictional media scandal and became close friends – Dolly was even officially declared Miley's godmother.

In his public life, the boundaries blurred between truth and lies and the ambiguous smoke screen that separated artist from fans thickened. Yet the most wounding blows by far came from within the Nashville music industry. Travis Tritt had griped that Billy Ray had set a dangerous precedent where superficial appearance was valued over skill, insisting "what we're going to have to do to be popular in country music [in future] is get into an ass-wiggling contest". Another Nashville insider merely shook his head disapprovingly at a show, commenting of his gyration, "You just can't tell me that's country."

Yet the early nineties was a time for redefining the mould of the country artist. To entertain a stereotype, it had formerly been the preserve of the conservative Southern man with traditional values – someone who kept a Bible under his pillow and referred to it on a daily basis, yet believed feminism was a new brand of lady-shave. Stars and fans alike had often seemed to meet that description – and Billy Ray's overtly sexual stage act was alienating both male listeners and hardcore committed Christians, who saw his "immodest" displays as an "abomination".

That said, a more diverse, new breed of country was developing, featuring less fixed views – in 1992, Garth Brooks' track, 'We Shall Be Free', saw him advocate the right to homosexuality and atheism, the exact opposite of what Nashville had previously represented. (A decade later, the industry would evolve even further when a door opened for Taylor Swift in the formerly male-dominated industry – despite veterans' protests that no one was interested in listening to the songs of a teenage girl, she went on to become, statistically, the most successful country star of her time.)

The slow but steady evolution had partially been the reason that Billy Ray had succeeded. Favouring high-top trainers over cowboy boots and sporting an incongruous ponytail, he was the antithesis of traditional, and – egged on by his legion of female cheerleaders – he was redefining the genre.

Unfortunately, that hadn't been enough to save him. By February 1993, he was sitting inches from Michael Jackson at that year's annual Grammy Awards in LA. He'd been nominated for five awards – and he left with none. On the aeroplane on the way home, his eyes were directed to a newspaper, the front cover of which read, in no uncertain terms, "CYRUS BIG LOSER". It stung – and that was only the beginning. Headlines emblazoned across every tabloid began to report that he was a "has been" and that he couldn't live up to the fanfare surrounding his first album. Even his record label begrudgingly admitted, "People are asking, 'Is he a one-hit wonder, or a legitimate star?'"

As if to prove critics correct when they jeered their predictions of a sophomore slump, his second album – ambitiously titled *It Won't Be The Last* – fell far short of expectations. While it had reached platinum status – a princely accolade for most new artists – in comparison to his former heights, it was nothing short of inadequate. The label was clear that multi-platinum was required – that he had to justify the vast sums it had spent in good faith on his marketing. The higher a star climbed, the further he had to fall – and the pressures at the top were enormous.

Some might say what Billy Ray was experiencing was the typical American way – worshipping artists and placing them on an impossibly high pedestal before breaking them down and laughing at them on their journey back to Earth. The public was equally fickle – tastes changed, trends moved on. Yet he couldn't shake the feeling that serious artists were meant to stand the test of time, while only those without substance became the buzzword of a painfully brief moment before crumbling and fading away. What did his career path say about him?

In a bid to be taken more seriously, he'd even insisted his record company reverse its decision to use his face on the second album cover – but seemingly to no avail. What was more, before the end of the year, he was set to come to metaphorical blows with his label yet again when, against their wishes, he resolved to marry Destiny's mother, Tish.

After an impromptu love-making session in the woods, she'd fallen pregnant again and, tired of playing second fiddle to his exhausting tour schedule, had given him an ultimatum – "Marry me, or else."

His record label, on the other hand, had only just stopped short of expressly forbidding marriage – purely because his contract didn't allow the company that privilege. To tie the knot would shatter the fantasies of the army of female fans he'd worked so hard to build up, and he risked that they'd move on to another – unattached, and therefore in their eyes more accessible – target. Given the huge role that sex appeal had played in his rise to fame, to be seen playing the loving family man had to be career suicide. And yet family had taken on a meaning to him that he valued more than anything – even that painstakingly sought-after career.

"I remember looking across the room and seeing Tish playing with

Miley," he would later recall, "[and] I loved her and wanted to be with her forever." Yet with Tish threatening to take their daughter back to Kentucky if he continued to dither over marriage, he knew he wouldn't have the luxury of that option much longer. "It was that simple," a family friend confirmed to the author. "Make a proper commitment or lose the kids forever."

Tish took control of the wedding plans – and for a conflicted and uncertain Billy Ray, it was simpler to switch to passivity mode and silently let her. She'd decided the vows should be uttered in their living room – fittingly, their house had a two-storey cathedral-style ceiling and could almost have passed for a church.

She'd planned the no-frills nuptials down to the very last detail, even buying comical glasses and a moustache from a fancy dress costume shop and awkwardly fashioning them into a disguise. The plan was that Billy Ray – with his trademark ponytail tucked inconspicuously into his shirt – would sneak into the courthouse, undetected in the disguise, and pick up their marriage licence.

Even on the morning of the wedding, however – December 28, 1993 – he was still battling with the conflict between heart and head. He'd risen early and walked to the highest peak on his 32 acres of land – the place where he always went in times of trouble, to pray, contemplate and philosophise. "I crawled into my Apache nest, a little shelter I'd built out of roots and sticks and mud," he later recalled, "and I lit a fire and tried to imagine what the future looked like."

He was starting to have second thoughts about marriage, when his mind flickered back to a tender moment he'd shared with Miley. He'd been disheartened over his Grammy losses and media humiliation – and not even a letter of encouragement from much-idolised country veteran Johnny Cash could cheer him up. As he sat, crestfallen and alone on a corner of his land, little Miley – barely a year old, but already uncommonly articulate – had falteringly trotted over to him with a broad grin and informed him earnestly, "Daddy, if you put your ear to the ground, you can hear the grass growing. Don't you want to hear that again?"

He did. Not that he quite knew what she was talking about, but hearing her shrill, cherubic little voice alone would suffice. With a surge of understanding, he realised God had given him his answer – and he almost ran down the hill, back home to marry Tish.

That day, the peaceful media-intrusion-free wedding the pair wanted became a reality – and Tish, still clad in a dress over the top of a catsuit – joined him afterwards for an astonishingly low-key slap-up chicken sandwich in Burger King. For all his millions, a day free from hype, glamour and material things was almost a tonic.

That day set the tone for things to come, too. He'd been scheduled to take part in a long Europe-wide tour starting in January 1994, during which he would meet the Queen of England. Yet now the prospect of a simple country life with his family tugged on his heartstrings far more persuasively than the prospect of the bragging rights he'd earn after spending an evening entertaining the Queen.

In spite of his initial excitement at meeting her and Princess Diana – a woman he regarded as "so beautiful and graceful" – he approached the dawn of his tour with increasing fear and dread. "Something about being gone for such a long time didn't feel right," he recounted in memory of that time. "Instead of wanting to go on tour, I could feel myself being drawn in another direction, and I knew why. I had a chance to have the one thing I had always wanted, the one thing I never had – a home where the mom and dad live together with their children in happiness and love. Now I had toys, homes, cars, trucks, horses and land. I had everything that money could buy. But money didn't buy family. Not a happy, loving family – and here it was right in front of me."

After a few days of soul searching, Billy Ray made a move that had his label bosses wringing their hands in despair – he cancelled his entire European tour. The turning point for him had been imagining the look of joy on Miley's face when she realised her father was there to stay.

"It didn't take long before I said to myself, 'You know what? I'm going to trade the Queen for the King and the King is Almighty God,'" he recalled. "'I'm going to be a good husband and a good daddy. I'm going to do what my family needs.'"

Miley had instantly become the apple of her father's eye and his adoration was reciprocated – whenever she was around him, she would grin broadly from ear to ear, earning her the nickname 'Smiley Miley'. Cradling her in his arms and exchanging nonsense talk, Billy Ray devised the rhyme "Smiley Miley, puddin' piley, kissed the boys and made them

Miley." Of course, it was an adaptation of the well-known children's nursery rhyme that read 'Georgie Porgie, pudding and pie, kissed the girls and made them cry.' Hardly one of his best songwriting efforts, the remake was unlikely to win him a Grammy – but Miley loved it. Already his biggest fan, she would break into a grin of gurgling laughter every time he recited it. Within weeks, her nickname had stuck.

To this day, Billy Ray credits Miley with saving him from something bordering on clinical depression. His life had been full of material possessions and yet, in other ways, he'd felt empty and poor. The good-time girls who'd clamoured around him had offered and expected a mere quick fix of lust, while – as clichéd as it sounded – what had been sorely lacking from his life was authentic love. Even after grossing $40 million in a single year, happiness had been elusive. Yet Miley was just the antidote to his pressured life of fame and, reminding him of exactly why he'd named her Destiny Hope, and then Smiley Miley, she'd lifted him out of his fog of depression. In her eyes, he found the love he had been seeking and he discovered the – by his account, unparalleled – joy of being a father.

The joy doubled by May 9, 1994, when son Braison Chance was born – named in a tongue-in-cheek style in honour of the brazen risks Billy Ray had taken in his life. It seemed Miley, along with her new brother, had tamed him where every other woman had failed – now fully ensconced in family life, he was treating music almost as a side project.

His third album, *Storm In The Heartland*, was released that autumn to an even more lacklustre response than his second, barely scraping gold status. What was more, it was almost totally ignored by country radio. However, by that point, Billy Ray genuinely didn't care. Now even his pared-down touring schedule was centred around his new family. When infatuated groupies tossed their bras on the stage, he resisted their advances, instead sneaking them home to model into hammocks for Miley's dolls. If it wasn't already apparent, this little girl's childhood had been far from conventional.

To highlight this yet further, she had her first experience in the entertainment industry at just 22 months old. It was October 8, 1994, and she was watching her father onstage at a Memphis venue known as the Pyramid. The concert was a star-studded tribute to the life of Elvis Presley, and big names such as Faith Hill and Tony Bennett were performing. Yet

31

an unexpected guest joined the bill in the form of Miley. Barely able to contain her breathless excitement, she suddenly broke free of her nanny and sprinted towards the stage, waving her arms animatedly in time with the music. "I kicked and ran and I went up there and grabbed the microphone and started singing," she recalled mischievously of her desperation to emulate her father. She ended up being passed around like a parcel by a group of adoring vocalists and musicians during the tune 'Amazing Grace', whose faces all betrayed the fact many thought she was the cutest infant they'd ever seen.

Some predicted even more – some thought she had star potential. Noting admiringly how unfazed she was by large crowds, Billy Ray would reminisce, "She was born to perform. She came out onstage with some of the biggest stars in the world – the last guy to hold her at the end of the song was Tony Bennett and, as the song ended, he said, 'You've got a special little girl here.'"

Not even yet two, she had already learnt how to steal the show. Revelling in all the attention, Miley tried her hardest to make it a regular event. "It was so much fun," she recalled fondly, "that I would escape whenever I could to try and grab the microphone."

Of course, with a famous father around, there were plenty of opportunities. After a few increasingly proficient renditions of classic songs like 'Hound Dog', a proud Billy Ray elected to take his daughter out on national TV to perform to the world. "Hey Miley, look in the camera – do your eyes!" he would urge, egging her on to flutter her eyelashes, Betty Boop style – not, of course, that she needed much encouragement. "Now this is very dangerous," a female on the set joked. "You're teaching her to flirt at a very young age. You're going to be in big trouble when she's 12 or 13!" Little did anyone know just how true that prediction would turn out to be.

Yet for the most part, young Miley spent her preschool years protected from the public eye. In a bid to escape paparazzi and guarantee his family's privacy, Billy Ray had purchased a country mansion with a vast, secluded, 212-acre stretch of unspoilt land. The location – Thompson's Station, just 25 miles from Nashville – embraced both his country roots and his need to be close to Music City. Plus, having earned a gross profit of more than $40 million in one year alone, he could afford to be extravagant. A separate plot of land was even allocated to Tish's mother, who played a committed role in raising her daughter's four children – now all together under one roof. "Having a large family he was devoted to was a way to resolve his feelings of not having had that in his own childhood," a family friend revealed to the author. "He really didn't want to let history repeat itself and this new home spelt out the moment he would step back from showbiz culture for a while and focus on being the father he'd never had at home."

During this hiatus, it quickly became apparent to Billy Ray – and everyone around him – just how much little Miley stood apart from her siblings. A miniature version of her flamboyant father, it seemed that showbiz was in her blood – and she used any excuse to turn everyday life into a performance. Plus, much to the embarrassment of her parents, she would turn their personal lives into a soap opera for the entertainment of anyone who came visiting.

Anything she overheard – from cheerful conversations to petty rows – was theatrically acted out, with Miley taking on the character of each person in turn to sing out their point of view. "She had an uncanny ability to remember and recite entire conversations after they'd happened," continued a family friend, "which was astonishing for a preschool kid. This one time, in front of all these big-shot country musician friends of Billy's, Miley jumped out of nowhere and started re-enacting everything that had happened in the house that day. There'd been a fight about Billy's work commitments and so she was singing, 'Tish, you know I gotta do this!' and then Tish's response of 'No, you don't! For once, why don't you put your family first?'"

Contrary to the rumours that she was a gold-digger, Tish was actually deeply ambivalent about Billy Ray's fame – she'd fallen for him before he'd hit the big time and success on such a large scale, with all its attendant responsibilities, was hardly what she had signed up for. Although Billy Ray had obligingly scaled back his work schedule to play the role of family man, his situation still remained a source of tension between them – not least because, in Tish's eyes, there were "fawning women around everywhere". Meanwhile, thanks to Miley's impromptu musical news broadcasts, the private elements of these conversations became public knowledge.

Unsurprisingly, her parents were both relieved when she channelled her love of performance into musicals and movies instead. She would learn numbers such as Nat King Cole's 'L.O.V.E.' from *The Parent Trap*, 'Tomorrow' from *Annie* and even a jazzy Eva Cassidy-inspired version of 'Over The Rainbow' from *The Wizard Of Oz* – and would rehearse them religiously.

Miley constantly craved attention – and went to extraordinary lengths to guarantee she got it. She would imprison unsuspecting friends and family members in a glass shower in the bathroom, ramming the door closed before breaking into song while her captive audience peered out like wide-eyed goldfish in a bowl.

She might have been in rural Tennessee but in Miley's mind, her bathroom was equivalent to a sold-out stage in downtown Las Vegas. Often, she looked the part too – like a magpie, she sought out anything glitzy to wrap around herself, favouring sequins, glitter and crystals on her clothes. Ironically, in the years to come, she would end up a self-confessed tomboy, but in those early years, rummaging through her glamorous mother's wardrobe and trying on her make-up and oversized shoes was one of Miley's favourite ways to pass the time.

Indeed, she had time on her hands all too regularly. Spending her days on remote and self-contained grounds with no immediate neighbours to play with and no nearby preschool facility, she relied almost exclusively on her siblings for company. The isolated surroundings also meant there was little need for clothes – and the young Miley became something of a "semi-nudist". Billy Ray, on the other hand, positively revelled in the isolation – a refreshing change from the critics' acid tongues and the harsh glare of the spotlight. With a wave of nostalgia, he found the open spaces transported him back to his own childhood, roaming the woods as a place to play and pray. Consequently he wasted no time in introducing Miley to the great outdoors – and she learnt to love it, later recalling fondly, "I spent most of my childhood outside with my dad."

That said, she and her accident-prone father weren't immune from mishaps. One morning, when his daughter was just two, Billy Ray scooped her up and invited her to go for a ride through the terrain on his quad bike. "Her eyes lit up as I strapped her into a baby-toter on my back and zoomed across the large flat fields and up the hill into the woods," he would later recall. "Every time I stopped to check on her, she was all smiles, Smiley Miley. She loved to go fast."

It might have seemed that there was no traffic in this private corner of the woods — the occasional privately commissioned tractor aside — but as he sped around, foot firmly on the accelerator while his daughter gurgled happily at the thrill, he hadn't bargained on a patch of fallen trees damaged in a recent storm. "In that instant, I had to make a quick decision," he recalled. "Duck or stop. I ducked and made it — but I forgot I had a baby on my back."

Hearing a sickening thud, he realised with horror that his daughter's head had just collided full-force with a heavy branch. He raced home — watching this time for fallen trees, although too little, too late — as blood poured from a gash in her head. Fearing concussion, he was relieved to find that — true to form — Smiley Miley was laughing and giggling again within minutes of Tish dressing her wound. However, he would recall, "I still remember this with a shudder as the day I almost took her head off."

Miley wasn't about to let him forget it either, later quipping satirically, "I can only imagine what I might have achieved if Dad hadn't given me minor brain damage!" What was more, it wasn't an isolated incident, either. On another night, keen for his children to witness a forecast meteorite shower light up the sky, he'd driven Miley and Braison to their favourite spot — a tiny clearing atop a hill surrounded by forest. They'd been roasting marshmallows and chatting around the open fire when — suddenly, without warning, and seemingly faster than she'd scaled the stage at the Elvis Presley tribute — Miley dashed off into the darkness. "She got about four feet in the pitch black, before tripping over a tree stump," Billy Ray would wince in memory of it. "She flew an equal distance in the air and landed against the bumper of my truck. Oh, man. A baseball-size bump appeared on her forehead. Blood spurted everywhere."

This time a mere dab of a damp cloth wasn't about to heal Miley's wound and the family found themselves queuing at the local hospital's emergency room. Tish was horrified — although not in the least bit surprised. "Whose idea was it to play in the woods close to midnight?" she asked accusingly, already knowing the answer. "I got five kids and one overgrown, terminal teenager!"

Of course, Billy Ray had been raised in an era and location when the abundant government health and safety warnings of the 21st century hadn't existed, when children played outside liberally without a care. This, combined with a risk-taking personality, had influenced the way he would raise Miley. "Not one picture of me on a horse or a quad-bike has me wearing a helmet!" she later recalled of her childhood. "Dad always says he could've given some of those celebrity mums a run for their money in the unsafe parenting department. It never occurred to him to put us kids in helmets – or to wear one himself!"

Miley's gentle scolding revealed a dynamic where the father of the household had been almost more rebellious than the children. His willingness to live for the moment and embrace the outdoors with childlike joy meant he could easily bond with Miley – and what seemed to make their relationship closer and more intense than the average rapport between parent and child was that there were fewer boundaries between them. Just like the average preteen, he felt invincible and immune to danger. This had given outings with him a sense of fun, a tantalising hint of danger – when he was at one with the great outdoors, nothing else mattered.

While Tish's heart took up a near permanent residence in her mouth, she scarcely stood between father and daughter and their pursuit of fun – and the pair continued to recklessly ride, trek and sprint their way through the woods.

Billy Ray's feisty, devil-may-care attitude might have left her safety hanging precariously in the balance – never more prominently so than when she was climbing or swinging through the trees like Tarzan or riding shotgun and helmet-free on her father's motorbikes, but – besides inspiring her younger brother's name – this attitude would instil within her a confidence and fearlessness that would later stand her in good stead for a future in performance.

Steve Peterman, producer and talent scout for the hit TV series *Hannah Montana*, offered an example that illustrated that Cyrus instinct perfectly. "Miley was out at the farm, at a barn on the property," he recalled, "standing on some landing. Billy said, 'Be careful, honey,' and she put her hands on her hips and said, 'I'm not afraid of anything!'" "And that," he added incredulously, "was at two and a half!"

There certainly seemed to be a genetic basis to that ethos because, although her half-brother Neal was terrified of horses and would refuse point blank to ride on one, Miley could barely be prised off them. While later she would recall discomfort at "putting horses to work" in such a way, at that time she very much enjoyed it.

When she and her father weren't riding together through the estate's vast trails, they were trucking or biking at breakneck speed to her paternal grandfather's log cabin, where they'd often spend the night. Mischievous Ron was equally unorthodox, making up a bedroom for Miley but arranging a bear-skin rug to be placed with the head of the animal pointing upright, causing her to scream first in fear and then in laughter. No matter how many times she experienced the routine, she would always react exactly the same way.

The three would also attend an annual celebration called Mule Day, which took place in the nearby town of Columbia. Formerly a traders' market to buy and sell animals, it was a comical Tennessee tradition that now centred around mules as the "pets of the equine industry". Each week-long event would kick off with a ceremonial Wagon Train Parade, in which carriages pulled by mules would transport people on a route that covered much of rural Tennessee. The event was a chance for farm folk to show off, with mule teams competing for a championship title recognising which could pull the most weight. They'd pull sleds full of logs – often weighing close to 3,000 pounds – and would perform in show-jumping contests and races.

Meanwhile there'd be lumberjack competitions for the humans, demonstrating their sawing, chipping, log-rolling and climbing skills – seeing contestants scale 60ft cedar poles. This part was all about physical agility and endurance, demonstrating that timid Southern folk were far from afraid to get their hands dirty. They were accustomed to the countryside and confident about navigating its challenges.

While the risks Billy Ray had taken with little Miley strapped to his back would have seemed irresponsible to urbanites, to him it was simply a more extreme version of the traditional Tennessee spirit. Any less than careering around on dirt bikes, regularly getting knees scraped, was tantamount to patronising the children and wrapping them in cotton wool.

Her surrounds gradually turned Miley into a tomboy, and in fact, after a little time spent living on the farm, even her mother – originally from a larger town than Billy Ray and a committed glamour puss – would tone it down and slowly replace her glitzy wardrobe with casualwear. She too would often join the others for Mule Day and together they'd visit on-site flea markets and craft fairs. There was gospel singing, bluegrass concerts and a host of traditional Appalachian food on offer, from funnel cakes and home-made pies to roasted corn – anything that celebrated their heritage. For Billy Ray, part Native American himself, this was more important than anything.

There was even an on-site beauty pageant – although fortunately this was the preserve of the women of the county and not the animals. Miley, however, was adamant that the mules *were* beautiful and, humouring her eccentricity, her grandfather presented her with a donkey. "He drove it all the way down from Kentucky in a horse trailer," she later reminisced. "He told me the donkey – I named him Eeyore – was half-zebra and that was why it had stripes on its ankles. [Eventually] I had my 'Hey, wait a minute . . .' moment and realised that *all* donkeys have white ankles!"

From the event, which would see Miley return home each year clutching miniature mule figurines and T-shirts emblazoned with their faces, to receiving her very own donkey, Miley's love of wildlife was well nurtured.

She would spot horses, deer, rabbits, eagles, hawks, quails and even flocks of wild turkeys roaming on her father's ample estate – and she soon grew to feel an affinity for animals and a desire to protect them.

This manifested itself one particularly memorable day on a trip to a petting zoo at California's Topanga Canyon. She'd spotted a huddle of baby chickens which were being fattened up to be slaughtered and fed to the zoo's resident snakes – and had promptly burst into tears. Desperate to keep a lid on his daughter's distress, Billy Ray stepped in to rescue them, but the zoo-keepers refused his offer to buy them. Instead, the family defiantly stole a pair and smuggled them back to their hotel, where they took up residence in the bath-tub. An enraptured Miley spent the remainder of the trip feeding and cooing over them.

The magnitude of their problem only became clear when it was time to check in at the airport for the flight home. Thinking quickly, Billy Ray convinced security staff that they were extremely volatile, nervous and rare African cockatoos who could not be exposed to light, meaning that the covering of their cage must remain intact. In the era prior to the 9/11 terrorist attacks, checks were more relaxed, and security staff simply shrugged, exchanging bemused glances with one another, and waved the family through.

Back home, Miley continued her idyllic existence, riding horses, chasing butterflies and enjoying the freedom of the open air. Her father would soon buy even more of the surrounding fields, extending the estate to an impressive 500 acres. He would also give Miley – who'd learnt to ride by the age of two – seven horses. Her attitude to her beloved pets was evidence of how much she adored nature – while some girls were occupied with styling their own hair, she was spending summer afternoons at the stables, braiding her horses' manes. By now, she personified American country living.

Chapter 3

THUS far, Miley had spent most of her childhood hidden away, ensconced on her vast farm like a princess in a gilded cage, with only her extended family for company. It wasn't until she began to grow up that she would discover, for better and worse, the true nature of her resident corner of Tennessee. Aged five, she started her studies at Heritage Elementary School, located just south of one of the region's main towns, Franklin.

Some 25 miles outside of Nashville, with vast horse farms dotted around its perimeter, it was small-town America personified. Nearby neighbours included country music sensations Dolly Parton, Faith Hill and Tim McGraw, whose purchasing power had elevated Williamson County to the wealthiest region in the USA. However, for the most part, its residents were ordinary folk – with the exception that they were staunchly conservative and, almost universally, deeply religious. "Imagine the religious fervour in Kentucky or Nashville and multiply that by one or two thousand and you've got Franklin," one resident advised the author. Meanwhile country singer Billy Cerveny told a local website, "You can't swing a dead cat and not hit a church – it's very evangelical." So much so, in fact, that in 2010, it was voted to the top spot of America's 100 Most Conservative Friendly Towns. Was Franklin ready for Miley Cyrus?

While the entire Cyrus family were devout Christians, they could scarcely call themselves conventional ones. Billy Ray, with his former penchant for pelvic thrusts and groupie love, was undeniably the black sheep of the religious world, while Miley's less than domesticated personality – developed through years of farm living – could barely be suppressed. This unkempt, gap-toothed girl with her cheeky grin and windswept hair stood out a mile – and would soon make a name for herself. She was a big bundle of untamed, boisterous energy that everyone from her teachers to even Miley herself found impossible to control. If it wasn't her tendency to hyperactively spin around in circles and sprint madly around the class-room like a headless chicken, it was her mouth – and the endless stream of mischief that poured from it – that was getting her into trouble. "There was no way I could sit still and focus for hours on end," she would later admit. "People didn't know exactly how to handle me. It's not that I was trying to be disrespectful but I. Could. Not. Be. Quiet!"

Once, when a tutor barked out that, if she uttered one more word, she'd get a detention, she playfully leaned over to the girl sitting next to her and whispered in mock conspiracy, "One more word!"

To say that Miley was naughty was an understatement. Unsurprisingly, she did get a detention – that week and the next. While her classmates were still water, she was a very strong, fizzy alcoholic beverage that came with a flame.

Meanwhile, although other parents were straight-edged, Billy Ray would pick her up from school on his Harley Davidson motorbike. Had she been a few years older, boasting a Harley as her own personal limo might well have earned her serious bragging rights, but back then, as a preteen, her peers couldn't make sense of it. In their tiny, sheltered town, they hadn't seen anything like it before.

Plus, thanks to the permanence his affectionate nickname for her had taken on, a feisty Miley would refuse to answer to the moniker on her birth certificate. When pressed by her teachers, she would simply insist earnestly – and firmly – "I'm Miley." Bemused staff eventually sent the Cyruses a letter, asking quizzically, "Destiny Hope will only sign her name as Miley. Is that what you call her? If so, is that OK?" That moment marked the unofficial death of the name Destiny Hope – and, although he'd given it to her, Billy Ray was totally relaxed about it.

Casually and unconventionally, he did little to foster his daughter's academic performance and was open about how much he despised maths. He retrospectively admitted to CNN, "I love being outside building big fires up on top of the hill, sitting out looking at the stars and roasting marshmallows and wieners. I was good at those types of things with my kids – I was never so good at sitting them down and telling them to do their algebra." He added, "I've never been good – non-existent, really – with discipline [either]. I've never been able to spank 'em or command that kind of fatherly figure with my kids."

41

As part of his unorthodox approach to education, he didn't believe in pressuring children to succeed, instead emphasising that it was more important to be happy, remain true to oneself and follow one's individual dreams. Consequently, while Miley stood out when it came to all things artistic and creative – by age seven, she would already be a talented poet and lyricist with a love of producing artwork – she lagged behind when it came to maths, languages and science.

While some might have disapproved of Billy Ray's attitude to school as much as they frowned upon his lackadaisical track record with safety, he was a multimillionaire with a huge farm and riches of which the average white-collar worker could only hopelessly dream – against this backdrop of opulence, what did a little allergy to mathematical equations matter?

And while Miley's speech would be littered with Southern slang and copious grammatical errors, Billy Ray was loyally and defiantly proud of his daughter's local style of lingo, believing it represented what being a true Southern girl was all about. On the rare occasion that he did get serious, he also held controversial views on how best to help his children learn, forcing Miley to write with her right hand from day one, despite her strong instincts to do just the opposite.

Remembering his own painful struggles as a child – including his inability to master his father's guitar – he was adamant that his beloved Miley would not follow him in becoming a left-hander. In his words, left-handed people were afflicted with a curse that meant they had to "learn the world backwards". He was convinced that if she learnt to oppose her hard-wired instincts from an early age, then she would conquer them and become a competent right-hander despite not being born that way. However it was something of a losing battle, akin in logic to gay religious zealots attempting to 'unlearn' their homosexuality. In fact, Miley would later joke that anyone who struggled to decipher her faltering hand-writing should "blame my dad"!

As discipline wasn't her father's strong point, she was forever brimming with uncontainable mischievous exuberance – and that, combined with her free-spirited nature and her intimidating excellence in music and drama, meant that Miley wasn't exactly a perfect fit in the social network of Franklin. The closest local children got to performance was causing a scene over who would take ownership of the TV remote control. All of this meant that Miley struggled to join in with the community and make new friends – and even when she did, her distance from the hub of the town made it a little prohibitive for them to regularly visit her.

This meant that Miley spent much of her spare time playing alone on the grounds of the farm. "Chickens are pretty darn fun to watch," she would comment later on one of her favourite childhood pastimes. "They walk around bobbing their wonky heads. Seriously, there's nothing more relaxing than to kick back and watch chickens be chickens . . . you can kind of make them into pets! My chicken, Lucy, will sit in your lap and let you pet her for hours on end. . . ."

Tish was understandably concerned that Miley's only friends were of the farmyard variety. She'd been a social butterfly in her younger years and she couldn't help feeling that – in the friendships department, at least – her otherwise lively child was borderline reclusive. To help, she began thinking about what she herself had enjoyed doing as a six-year-old and that prompted her to enrol Miley in cheerleading classes. Her daughter, on the other hand, was less than keen – and extremely vocal about her reluctance. "The first day I was supposed to go to practice, I was not happy," she later recalled. "I begged, 'PLEASE don't make me go! What's wrong with hiring horses and chickens and little brothers as my only friends? They won't let me down.'"

Miley was almost reduced to tears in her desperation to stay at home, but her mother was adamant that she'd enjoy it – and sure enough, within weeks, she was nothing short of addicted. She made a new best friend, Lesley Patterson, and the pair bonded over their shared love of showing off. In a town Miley described as "la-di-da" and "humdrum", she'd finally met her match. They would religiously rehearse dance routines and practise gymnastics, with Miley perfecting handstands and back flips by the age of seven. Soon, she looked forward to practice more than any other event of the week.

Part of her pleasure may have had its roots in the fact that Tish was the true antithesis of the archetypal pushy stage mother. Instead of pressuring her to play to win and make sure she was the fastest, most beautiful and most athletic – or else – she would produce a gleaming trophy after every competition with Miley's name embossed on it – regardless of whether she won or lost. The implicit message was that what mattered most wasn't winning, but trying her best, and she would teach her daughter that she was a winner purely by virtue of participating.

Ironically, after that first tearful practice session, it was Miley who made herself feel obligated to win – and she became her own harshest critic. She threw herself wholeheartedly into "intense, incredibly hardcore competitions", thriving on the adrenalin and the desire to out-perform her rivals.

There were times when she took this to extremes. Even when a stomach bug left her barely able to stand, let alone cheer, she insisted that nothing would stop her from competing. The show was in Gatlinburg, Tennessee, almost a five-hour drive from their home, but Miley dragged herself – shivering violently and occasionally retching – into the car and ordered her gobsmacked mother to drive. She then collapsed, sprawling herself over the entire length of the back seat, and sank into exhausted sleep, rising only to vomit into a dustbin – she couldn't stomach so much as a sip of water without retching, over and over again. Unlike Fatboy Slim's dance anthem 'Eat, Sleep, Rave, Repeat', this routine more closely resembled 'Sleep, Drink, Retch, Repeat' – and Miley was miserable.

When they finally arrived at their hotel in Gatlinsburg – more realistically a tiny motel on the motorway with mouldy carpets and no TV – the best the remote immediate area could offer – her coach was horrified, insisting there was no way she could perform. Yet a formidably determined Miley declated, "If I push myself, I know I can do it!" and, ignoring the protests of mother, coach and co-cheerleaders alike, she sprinted out to compete. Plus, in the ultimate rock'n'roll exit, she vomited into a dustbin on her way offstage, but she'd done it. She'd demonstrated exactly the tenacity and steely determination that would one day make her a star.

One family friend believed Miley's desire to succeed at all costs was motivated by her father, revealing to the author, "Billy Ray was a big believer in visualising things. He believed that mind and spirit were stronger than body and that as long as you had faith in God and could see what you wanted, you could make it happen in the end."

His belief was not an uncommon one. In the past, legends have been told of nuns who, wishing to maintain total purity for their relationship with God, had willed themselves with the power of thought to stop menstruating. Then there was the placebo effect, a phenomenon where those who are unwell believe themselves to be cured after receiving medication – even when that medication is merely an empty sugar pill. It is believed that a positive thinker's brain floods with endorphins that conquer discomfort and pain, while phrases such as "Laughter is the best medicine" also suggest that the power of positive thought can help to overcome the body's every limitation. No doubt this was what was happening to Miley as she willed herself to move. It mimicked the moment she'd stood defiantly, tiny hand on hip, to let her father know she wasn't afraid of anything.

Her love of cheerleading continued to grow and it also provided a distraction and escape from the tension at home. While Billy Ray and Tish remained very much in love, unorthodox couples suffered from unorthodox problems and the Cyruses were no exception – 1998 would prove one of the toughest years of their marriage.

The first test of faith for the family came when a bitter court battle ensued over Miley's half-brother Neal. He'd returned home from a visit to his biological father one evening, crying hysterically and near inconsolable, and begged for Tish to promise he'd never have to see him again.

A deeply sensitive boy, with none of the boisterous confidence of his siblings, Neal experienced extreme separation anxiety at the thought of being parted from his grandmother – the woman who'd been his sole carer back in the days when Miley was a baby. Tish – feeling Billy Ray needed supervision to protect him from the perils of overly persuasive groupies – had often grabbed Miley and babysat both her daughter and husband on the road.

Yet while Miley had happily woken in a new city each morning, Neal, who'd stayed at home, had become terrified of change. This extended to a phobia of having his hair cut – something his father insisted on doing almost every visit. There was also distress surrounding his name – his father refused to refer to him by his preferred nickname, Trace, and continued to use his birth name, which he despised.

While these might have seemed like minor trivialities to the average child, Trace – as he was now called – would become hysterical. Both his grandmother and an independent psychiatrist were forced to testify as to his desperation to avoid seeing his father, who prior to that time had been legally entitled to regular visitation. Deciding that it would be detrimental to the relationship between parent and child to force contact, the court ultimately ruled that the decision was Trace's, and an appeal by his father was overthrown.

The legal battle – centring around a pleading and tearful child – had been heartbreaking for all involved, and yet the worst was yet to come. Locals back in Kentucky began gloating about "trouble in paradise" and revelling in rumours that one of America's most envied couples had a demonstrably dysfunctional family.

Miley's beloved paternal grandfather found himself in the dock too, accused of embezzlement of hundreds of thousands of dollars of public funds. Until his retirement in 1996, Ron had been the executive secretary treasurer for the Kentucky AFL-CIO, a key organisation which represented 90,000 members across 51 unions. The role carried enormous responsibility, handing him sole authority to write state cheques. Therefore when it emerged that not only was there a gaping deficit of almost $300,000 of state funds, but that multiple cheques had been improperly written on the state office account to book-keeper Donna Bayliss, the finger of blame was pointed at Ron.

He'd originally aroused suspicion by claiming he couldn't afford to pay area councils the fees due to them. Then Gary Best, the secretary treasurer for the United Food and Commercial Workers Union, pulled the plug, informing the national office that Ron had repeatedly withheld financial records. "He was just not giving me the records I was entitled to as an executive board member – he just would not comply," he went on record to say, implying that his secrecy had been no accident. "Ron Cyrus found every reason in the world not to give me those records. I later found out there hadn't been any audits in 10 years."

This was another breach of policy, as twice-yearly audits were a legal requirement. Now Ron stood accused of mishandling the state's pension plan – and his actions were becoming increasingly difficult to defend. When the news got out, rumours spread that he had been siphoning off large quantities of public money to Donna Bayliss, because she was either a part-time prostitute to him, or a high-maintenance lover. Ron hadn't exactly been renowned for monogamy in his time and the fact that he was a married family man at the time of the investigation only added to the scandal.

Donna was never able to give her side of the story as, in the wake of the sordid gossip, crippled by shame, she'd hanged herself before the case went to court. Meanwhile Ron was suspended – never to return – and control of the organisation was handed to the national office, marking the first time emergency monitoring had needed to be placed on a state federation in a quarter of a century. The plot thickened when, before any evidence could be collected, a mysterious fire broke out in the office records area, which authorities had treated as arson and burglary.

Painfully, Billy Ray's last memory of the AFL-CIO – just four years earlier – had been of gatecrashing its offices with a triumphant grin to show his father two new trophies. They'd symbolised 'Achy Breaky Heart' becoming the first single in musical history to achieve multi-platinum sales in Australia. As it turned out, he'd interrupted a congratulatory toast by the entire board to his father, with admiring glances all around the table focused firmly on him.

Needless to say, however, the atmosphere surrounding the court case couldn't have been more different. Tish and Billy Ray had tried to be upfront with Miley before she heard the gossip elsewhere, but at her young age the most she could comprehend was that the man she called 'Pappy' was in serious trouble.

As so much of the potential evidence had gone up in flames, Ron was eventually released without charge, but nonetheless, the scandal left a near indelible mark on his reputation. To a God-fearing, church-going traditional Southern family, displaying moral righteousness – especially honesty – meant everything. Could they survive this blow to the now unmistakeable Cyrus name?

In an extension of the agony, Billy Ray's fourth album, *Shot Full Of Love* – released the same year – became his lowest performing yet. Its first single, 'Under The Hood', which he'd comically described as a "groovy barn burner", failed to even surface in the charts at all.

In hard times, he reminded himself of the message in one of his album tracks, 'Busy Man'. Describing the moment Miley's arrival changed his perspective on life, it told of his former self – someone so consumed by chart statistics and radio play and so busy chasing fame that he'd started to neglect his family. Writing the song had served as a wake-up call for him to realise those things in his life that were truly important.

Not for the first time, Billy Ray resolved to prioritise his children, although – according to one family friend – this marked a time when he became almost unhealthily clingy. "He'd been through so much – these were serious traumas," she told the author. "He clung to those kids. He wanted to devote himself to them to the point that he barely wanted them to leave the house. Brandi was interested in learning how to show horses, Braison was a fan of sports and then there was little Miley with her cheer-leading, but Billy Ray would beg her sometimes not to go. He'd say she didn't need that in her life and that family was the most important thing. He'd suffocate her."

As a young girl talking her first steps into the outside world, however, Miley was unstoppable. Meanwhile, concerned that his son was sliding back into depression, Ron urged him to attempt to re-salvage his career. Until that time, he'd been a slave to showbiz, anxiously monitoring chart positions, throwing himself at the mercy of fickle radio hosts (whose day-to-day decisions to add or remove him from playlists could make or break his career) and feeling that – after just a few years of fame – he was already a contemptible has-been. Yet what if there was another way?

Ron began encouraging him to emulate Dolly Parton and become a multifaceted performer. Instead of putting all his eggs into one basket, he could branch out into acting, gain another string to his bow and be known for more than just his voice. Yet was it really that easy? Thanks to his status as a household name, he managed easily enough to find an agent, but prior to that, his sole acting experience had been very small slots on TV shows such as *The Nanny* and *Diagnosis Murder*. What was more, the first serious film in which he landed a part, *Radical Jack*, would prove even more disastrous than his last album – so much so that when Billy Ray penned his memoirs years later, he failed to give it so much as a brief mention.

The film portrayed him as an undercover government agent out to expose – and thus wreak havoc on – a small-town arms dealer who brought about the savage death of his wife. As an independent film, it received little media attention, but that didn't spare Billy Ray – for whom *Radical Jack* was an onscreen secret agent code name – much embarrassment. In fact, viewers took to the internet in their droves to complain that the plot wasn't nearly as promising as it sounded. "It's an adequate straight-to-video flick with atrocious dialogue and cheesy action," was one typical gripe.

Admittedly many of the film's alleged flaws had been out of Billy Ray's hands, such as complaints about the quality of the writing. "A character has been kicked and beaten and was nearly killed," one reviewer recounted, dripping with sarcasm. "He's being nursed back to health by an attractive woman, one thing leads to another and suddenly she's on top of him, kissing his chest. 'I . . . I can't,' he says. 'Why?' she asks, and he goes off on some long tale about his tragic past. A more clever screenplay would have had him reply, 'Because I have a few miles of bandages around my broken ribs and you're sitting on my chest!'"

Yet some jibes were extremely personal, with one disgruntled viewer exclaiming, "Billy Ray Cyrus took the bold action of making an action movie almost totally devoid of action."

Set against this backdrop, his role in a guest edition of *The Love Boat*, as a depressed country singer reduced to entertaining a cruise ship's passengers, might have seemed more like a mocking caricature than an authentic acting gig. His detractors would no doubt pointedly remark that, with this persona, he didn't even need to fake it. And yet it seemed that even this latest humiliation came with a silver lining. It had been his last day on set when, by chance – or was it fate? – he picked up a trade magazine he'd seen on the table and began flicking idly through it. When he discovered that legendary film director David Lynch was casting for a new project called *Mulholland Drive*, his ears pricked up instantly. This was a man he idolised – he'd been a huge fan of former films such as *Elephant Man* and *Blue Velvet*. Yet he was realistic – this was a far cry from the bit parts and small, low-budget independent films with which he had been involved thus far – and he knew that if he was cast in a cult art-house movie, then it would be nothing short of a miracle.

Yet fortune was on his side – Lynch had admitted to casting Naomi Watts purely on the strength of a half-hour interview, without even having seen a moment of her footage onscreen. It wasn't awards or an extensive back catalogue he was interested in – he was looking for fresh blood. To that end, Billy Ray gained an interview the same day he expressed his interest and was cast as Gene almost as quickly.

Yet, to his distaste, he felt that elements of the neo-noir psychological thriller compromised his Christianity. "The script was so dark," he recalled, "I expected David to show up dressed in black, wearing a cape and burning candles."

That may have been a slight exaggeration, but there wasn't much love and light. His first scene saw him confronted by a furious husband whose wife was Gene's more than willing bed partner. The husband reacted by pouring pink paint into her jewellery box, after which there was a brutal fight scene, culminating in Billy Ray throwing the wronged man out of his own house.

Denouncing the plot as "incredibly dark", Billy Ray contemplated whether he wanted to end his flirtation with the silver screen there and then. "I feared I might have tampered with a force I didn't want in my life," he would explain. "It was bad language, sex, violence, all the things that Hollywood has to offer, and after I left Hollywood on the flight back, I felt like I'd done a deal with the devil."

His reaction might have seemed surprising, if only because, by his own admission, his own parents had been adulterous, violent and profane themselves. While the fight scenes in *Mulholland Drive* were far from savoury, they seemed to be on equal ground with the time his mother, Ruth, punched a woman to the ground, threw her in a ditch and rained down blows on her head beside a church. Understandably, however, that wasn't an atmosphere he aspired to court in his own life, and by the end of an emotionally draining production schedule he'd resolved to quit the acting business once and for all.

However, it was in fate's hands and the despised film would ultimately prove to the catalyst for a string of events that would lead to Miley becoming an international superstar. "If it wasn't for *Mulholland Drive*," he later announced, "Miley would never have been [TV star] *Hannah Montana*."

It began in 1999, when he was praying on the flight home to Nashville. Realising he was at a crossroads, he reached out to God with the words, "If you want me to be an actor, then show me what you want me to do." It was last-chance saloon for his acting career – but sure enough, two days later, he felt his prayers of desperation had been answered. There was a brand new script waiting on his doorstep.

Billy Ray devoured it. Tentatively titled *Doc*, the "values-heavy drama" centred around a doctor from Montana living in New York and depicted him bringing his conservative thinking to a fast-paced and morally bankrupt big city. The character was the complete antithesis of his former roles and he identified with his strong moral compass – it could be just what was needed to persuade him to continue acting.

That said, Tish had recently become pregnant with their final child, while the series called for him to leave his family behind and relocate to Toronto. The decision was complicated yet further when, not for the first time, Tish went into labour early.

The youngest member of the Cyrus clan, Noah Lindsey, entered the world on January 8, 2000 – and in spite of bizarrely claiming that her inconveniently timed birth had disrupted his viewing of a legendary football match, Billy Ray fell in love with her instantly. Yet, seduced by producers' promises to create a "strong, moral male role model" to be screened on national TV, he agreed to go back on the road again – this time flying the entire family out with him. He even managed to secure a cameo for them, with Tish playing an infatuated nurse with a crush, ogling him in the staff corridor. While no one was offered a speaking role, the humble part of "silent extra" would be little Miley's first introduction to the world of acting.

The pilot episode received the green light from the TV channel PAX and, by June 2001, Billy Ray had moved out to Toronto solo for an intensive four months of work shooting the first series. Ironically the role he'd been playing – that of a small-town country boy struggling to adapt to the very different way of life of the big city – mirrored his real-life experiences at that time. In Toronto, he was renting a condo in a 24-storey urban apartment block with windows that didn't open – a far cry from his spacious 500-acre farm. Not only did Billy Ray feel stifled by his new situation, but he sorely missed his family – suffice to say he wasn't an urbanite.

However, as filming coincided with school holidays, Miley was able to visit him regularly. On one occasion, the filming called for some outdoor shots in New York and the entire production moved on location to the city. While there, Billy Ray took his family to Broadway to watch *Mamma Mia* – a theatrical production complete with renditions of classic Abba songs – and this was the moment that piqued Miley's interest in the stage.

Flinging her arms around his neck, breathless with excitement, she exclaimed loudly mid-show, "Daddy! That's what I want to do!" In that moment, it seemed as though the entire theatre turned accusingly to look for the naughty child who'd disrupted the performance. This wasn't the first – or the last – time young Miley would steal the show.

Meanwhile, back home in Tennessee, her craving for attention had reached dramatic proportions. Now that she'd had a taste of the big city and knew her goal was to have her name in lights at the theatre, the every-day farm life she'd once loved had suddenly become intolerably dull and boring – and she began acting up.

It didn't help that she was now living apart from her father – the more lenient parent – and was struggling to cope with Tish's harsh, unforgiving and disciplinarian mothering style. Old-fashioned in her attitude to pun-ishment, she didn't hesitate to drag her daughter into the bathroom and force a bar of soap into her mouth so that she could gargle with the foul-tasting suds – often for something as low-key as a few profanities. "I think I called my sister a bitch for the first time [and] I was *done*," Miley recalled in horror. "I was locked in my room, my mouth washed out with soap, everything. I was like, 'Mom, she is. That's what she is. She's a bitch!' I was in so much trouble."

Tish went to extremes to keep her children's language clean – and unlike Billy Ray, she didn't even permit cartoons. "She was weird with TV," Miley explained. "My dad would always let us watch *The Simpsons* [and, when he got back from tour] we would stay up all night watching *Cartoon Network* with my dad [but my mother] hated it. She just thought everything, even *Tom & Jerry*, was too violent!" She also vetoed TV adver-tisements, apparently believing that consumer culture encouraged greed and sent children further away from God.

"Even though Miley had a charmed life and had only ever known a world where her parents were wealthy, Tish didn't want her lusting after lots of secular products and getting misled by them," confirmed one family acquaintance to the author. "She thought that was unChristian. There was a Bible proverb she'd always read to her that a camel was more likely to pass through the eye of a needle than a greedy person was to get to Heaven. She took it very seriously."

Now forbidden from watching almost all forms of TV – with the exception of carefully monitored Christian programming – Miley's mind hungered for stimulation. Yet the tiny window that offered her a viewpoint into the secular outside world was rapidly narrowing and when Tish – desperate to control her sometimes outrageous behaviour – decided to transfer Miley to an evangelical faith school, the gap closed completely. All schools in Tennessee had religious undertones to their ethos, but the New Song Academy in Franklin surpassed all of them. Each day began with an hour of dedicated Bible study, while the school totally shunned mainstream textbooks in favour of titles from an independent Christian publisher. Some completely rewrote the curriculum as a Western child would know it, claiming that science was a man-made evil intended to "subdue the Earth".

Education the evangelical way was controversial – especially as its teachings often contradicted established scientific facts. For example, the carbon dating of fossils has repeatedly indicated that the world is billions of years old, but the textbooks at Miley's school disputed that, insisting that – as written in the Bible – the world is merely 10,000 years old. Evolutionary theory – widely accepted as credible outside of evangelicalism – has also been dismissed.

One publisher which supplied books to the school, known as A Beka, claimed to "present the universe as the direct creation of God and refute the man-made idea of evolution, giving a solid foundation in all areas of science, firmly anchored in Scriptural truth". It added, "While secular science textbooks present modern science as the opposite of faith, the A Beka book science texts teach that modern science is the product of Western man's return to the Scriptures after the Protestant Reformation, leading to his desire to understand and subdue the Earth, which he saw as the orderly, law-abiding creation of the God of the Bible."

Maths was another subject that saw New Song Academy sharply divided from the mainstream. The school taught that "the dawn of maths is a creation of God, not of man" – a claim which was equally controversial. For instance, in the 1600s, when ground-breaking mathematician Galileo Galilei revealed the results of one of his experiments – the now well-known fact that the Earth revolves around the sun – much of the religious world reacted with fury. After all, his assertion was in direct contradiction with the Bible. Psalm 104.5 reads, "[God] set the Earth on its foundation and it can never be moved", while Ecclesiastes 1.5 reads, "The sun rises and the sun sets and hurries back to where it rises."

Incandescent with rage, pastors called for Galileo – whom they viewed as nothing short of blasphemous – to be subdued. At one sermon in Italy, it was announced that geometry was "of the devil" and that all mathematicians should be "banished as the authors of all heresies". Consequently, he was tried before the Roman Inquisition and was ordered to "abjure, curse and detest" his work, before being held under house arrest for the rest of his life.

At a time when religious law ruled, all of his published experiments were banned and he died a captive. It took more than 300 years to arrive, but Pope John Paul II eventually issued a public apology. Yet although the Bible's claims demonstrably differed so vastly from mathematical fact, Miley's teachers offered a purely Biblical education. They insisted that "even when using a secular text, students are taught that truth is absolute and comes from the Bible" – a claim easily proved to be incorrect.

This was the reason that many secular onlookers – atheists and Christians alike – regarded evangelicalism as a sinister cult that brainwashed its followers into false beliefs. Yet Tish – by now a little exhausted with Miley's mischief – decided the academy was the best place to tame her tempestuous ways and teach her how to grow into a wholesome and God-fearing young woman.

The school certainly promised to immerse her in religion, stating, "We believe that our most important relationship is with God – our courses reflect a Christ-centred approach [and] every one of our faculty have a committed relationship with Jesus Christ."

Yet the academy's strict guidelines had the opposite effect, merely fuelling Miley's desire for rebellion. While it vowed, "Truth can only be understood by living a life submitting to the Lordship of Jesus Christ", that wasn't quite the mission statement Miley had in mind when she interrupted a fourth-grade class full of nine- and ten-year-olds to give them detailed instructions on how to French kiss.

Most of the teachers and parents had gone to great lengths to preach chastity until marriage and even light kissing was frowned upon, particularly for those who'd barely reached double figures.

It went without saying that Miley's public service announcement earned her a black mark against her record – and that was just the beginning. "At one point, Miley lifted her skirt at chapel and mooned her friends at assembly," a former classmate told the author. "We heard the staff say more than once that she was the most badly behaved student they'd seen in their entire career of teaching – they admitted they had no chance of controlling her."

Of course, that didn't stop them trying – and they had permanent expressions of shock on their faces as they strived unsuccessfully to coax her into toeing the line. The final straw was when she hijacked an elderly teacher's motorised mobility scooter and embarked on a high-speed rampage around the school with it. Just a year after she'd started studies there, she was expelled for good.

The timing, however, was perfect – the moment of shame was the catalyst for Tish to move the entire family out to Toronto. Not only would they be reunited with Billy Ray, but the city environment would be Miley's chance to pursue her dream of acting.

Prior to her blink-and-you'll-miss-it career in *Doc*, her only experience had been an acting camp back home, called Kids On Stage. The venue, the Boiler Room, was a perfect demonstration of just how rural Tennessee could be – despite its central location next to a shopping mall, the tiny building's spartan backdrop gave the impression of a miniature church that had landed in a field.

This diminutive amateur dramatics society was the cream of the crop as far as Nashville's acting opportunities were concerned and yet – in spite of the small talent pool – Miley had never scored a lead role. She had usually been relegated to bit parts, such as that of a near totally silent elderly woman, which she achieved by coughing in a quavering fashion and donning a wig full of curly grey hair. Such roles carried more comedic value than genuine kudos and Miley was relieved that moving to Toronto might give her a fresh start.

However one thing she looked set to sacrifice was cheerleading. Toronto lacked a cheerleading culture and the nearest squad she could find was an hour's drive from the city, in the town of Burlington. Not only that, but Miley – who was a couple of months behind her 10th birthday – was instantly dismissed as much too young.

Turning on the charm, Tish begged the organisers to reconsider, emphasising that she'd been a regular since she was six. Her persistence paid off – they relented. "When I went out to the gym, they loved how teeny tiny I was," Miley would joke later. "It was really easily to throw me all over the place. I got in!"

The squad's rule to usually accept only seventh graders and above meant that the youngest of Miley's peers were two years her senior but, being outgoing, she still made friends easily. Instead, the biggest culture shock was the weather. They'd arrived just in time to welcome the coldest winter the already chilly city had seen in 15 years – and nearly every Sunday, they'd be forced to make the two-hour round trip to cheerleading in a blizzard. Tish, whose driving experience had been confined to the Deep South before meeting Billy Ray, had never encountered an icy road before, so adapting was a challenge.

She had also decided that, in view of Miley's chaotic track record at school, she didn't want to risk another expulsion – and she duly made arrangements for her to be home-schooled. The flexibility of this decision meant she was free to drop by on the set of *Doc* from time to time in between studies and, before long, warming to this tenacious, free-spirited little girl, the producers offered her a small speaking part.

She'd play the role of Kiley, a child at the mercy of her abusive alcoholic mother, and would appear in two episodes over the series. In an eerie snapshot of things to come, one scene called for Miley to frown mournfully as she auditioned for the school play, while her peers ridiculed her thick Tennessee accent. Miley herself would be no stranger to bullying as she grew up and she would wryly remark of playing the victim, "Little did I know how much I'd need the experience!"

Yet after shooting her scenes for *Doc*, Miley's acting career ground to a halt. An astute and independently minded child, she was acutely aware that her opportunity to appear in the series had come about purely because of her father. In fact, despite her tender age, she was already highly sensitive about the issue. Her relationship to Billy Ray meant that she held the perpetual status of the daughter of a star, rather than being acknowledged as a separate person. Starting life with a blank slate to fill was a luxury she couldn't afford as her father's shadow was already projected onto it and she knew she'd be prejudged by his achievements. To this end, when she'd been living in Nashville, she'd done everything she could to avoid being eclipsed by his celebrity status, even going to the lengths of concealing her true identity. "I wouldn't tell people who my dad was," she later confessed, "because I wanted to have friends who really loved me for me. To those who knew, I was always Billy Ray Cyrus' daughter – never Miley."

With that in mind, she set about taking acting lessons, desperate to prove she could stand alone and be a success in her own right. "She was quite determined, diligent and persistent," Billy Ray later recalled. "She found the best coaches, worked on her chops, went to auditions and did all the different things to reach her goal."

And yet that goal was elusive. Despite intensive lessons with acclaimed tutor Dean Armstrong and regular visits to the USA's unofficial showbiz capital, LA, for auditions, all roads had led to failure. Even little Noah had a more successful back catalogue – she'd racked up more appearances in *Doc* than Miley had and had even played a key role in a video for her father's gospel track 'The Face Of God', which featured her swinging on a makeshift rope swing suspended from the branch of a tree.

Miley was already a little resentful of the newer arrival at the best of times – so much so that she'd vandalised her own home in protest at the attention Noah was getting. "My brother and I were kind of jealous of the new baby," she recounted, "[and] we went down and broke a window. And my dad was like, 'You vandalised! And not only did you vandalise, but you vandalised your own home! How dumb are you?' We hid in our treehouse for a few hours but then we needed snacks and had to go home." Yet the feeling of being pushed aside didn't end quite so quickly. There was no greater humiliation for a nine-year-old than to know that her baby sister, eight years her junior, was already more successful than she was.

However, doubtless a large factor in Miley's subsequent success was that the impetus to succeed came not from pushy showbiz parents, but from within – and there were few children more determined. After all, this was a girl who'd dragged herself, shivering and vomiting, to a cheerleading event at the opposite end of the state.

Eventually her tenacity paid off – and when she was least expecting it. On a brief trip back home, Miley was intrigued to discover that a family friend, Wendi Foy Green, was taking her children to audition for a TV advert promoting a company called Banquet Foods. The advert, to be recorded in Nashville, would feature the country signer Lee Ann

Womack. When it emerged that Wendi's children were a little too young for the role, Miley got the chance she'd be waiting for – and she didn't disappoint. She was hired on the spot.

While she convincingly swooned over the food, it was safe to say she was utilising her emerging acting skills because, in between takes, she was surreptitiously spitting out entire handfuls of beans underneath the table. Her explanation? "I'm a picky eater."

Becoming the poster child of a cheap food company was hardly the glittering start she'd hoped for, but it did bring her to the attention of an agent, who swiftly signed her up. With a trusted and well-connected talent scout taking care of her interests, she no longer had to fight so hard to be noticed – and she was soon offered her first film.

With legendary director Tim Burton on board, *Big Fish* promised to be a hit from the beginning. Burton produced *The Nightmare Before Christmas* and directed *Edward Scissorhands*, *Planet Of The Apes* and two *Batman* movies, one of which, *Batman Returns*, had boasted a gross profit of more than $282 million. Everything Burton touched seemed to turn to gold – and Miley, of course, was hoping she'd be no exception.

Yet on receiving the news of her big break, she was stunned to learn that she had just two days to travel to the set in Alabama. Her mother, however, was unfazed, perceiving that anything had to be better than the icy temperatures of Toronto – and instead of booking a seat on a plane, she opted to leave straightaway, braving a 20-hour drive. "Mum must have been pretty desperate to go somewhere warm," Miley later recalled, "because the minute she hung up [the phone], she started throwing all of our clothes into the car. Dad said, 'You can't drive to Alabama! You're in Toronto!', but Mum was too busy fantasising about sunny Alabama. Without pausing, she said, 'Oh yes, we can. We're crossing the border tonight.'"

After a mind-numbingly long drive, followed by a stay at "the worst fleabag of a hotel in history", with armed police swarming outside, it was time for a bleary-eyed Miley to venture on set and get acquainted with the plot.

The star of the show, Edward Bloom, is a metaphorical 'big fish' who has made a name for himself in life by entertaining people with far-fetched stories about his past. As he lies terminally ill on his deathbed, he retells some of them in an attempt to bond with his grieving son, and his animated imagination conjures up a world of werewolves, witches and giants. In one fantastical plot, after being conscripted by the army against his will, he parachutes into a show for North Korean troops and enlists the help of a pair of bejewelled Siamese twin showgirls to help him flee the city. After the military declares him dead, he goes on to orchestrate a bank robbery.

Another ludicrous story, in which Miley makes her brief appearance, sees Edward brave a "cold, wet insect-ridden swamp", where a wicked witch ominously shows him a depiction of death in her glass eye. Her character is eight-year-old Ruthie, "a goody-two-shoes Southern girl dressed in little Mary Janes, telling the boys not to curse". In the dark, shadowy scene, she joins a group of children running through the woods brandishing flashlights before taking on a wide-eyed look of fear and imploring Edward to beware the sinister-looking witch.

The reality was far less glamorous than appearing in a Tim Burton movie might have sounded – shooting in the dead of night was colder than she'd anticipated or packed for, and there were weeds up to Miley's waist. However, there was one plus – unlike many of the others, she didn't need to fake a broad Southern accent.

The film featured three UK actors (Albert Finney as the older Edward who appears on his deathbed, Ewan McGregor as the younger version living out his adventures and Helena Bonham Carter as the wicked witch), plus the French actress Marion Cotillard, who played the wife of William Bloom. All had to immerse themselves in a new accent. Contrastingly, Miley had been contemplating elocution training to rid herself of her Nashville twang, fearing it would limit her and damage her chances of success, so a film that allowed her to speak unselfconsciously was very welcome.

After shooting her scene, Miley spent some time in Nashville with her family and, in honour of her experiences, begged country star Ed King to teach her the chord progression of his track 'Sweet Home Alabama'. Realising that a true performance artist often excelled in more than one field, Miley had become keen on music too; each time her father invited one of his musician friends over, she'd join the party. When Waylon Jennings came to the house, she begged him to show her the chords to his classic tune 'Good Hearted Woman'. "Waylon couldn't have been happier to show her," Billy Ray would recall. "He took her guitar and played the song right there as Miley watched, her face as close to the guitar as she could get. She was like a sponge!"

She also sang along fearlessly with Carl Perkins to his track 'Blue Suede Shoes'. Yet most fun of all for Miley at that time was memorising the lyrics to Billy Ray's songs and performing impromptu duets with him – something that only strengthened their father-daughter bond. Yet the one thing that stood between them was his reluctance to give his blessing for her to join the entertainment industry.

He had experienced the lurid kiss and tells and paparazzi run-ins, humiliating tabloid rumours and – worst of all of these factors combined – the angst of rejection. The constant highs and lows made for a life that lacked balance and stability, something Miley was about to experience first-hand. She was elated when, on its release in December 2003, *Big Fish* became a box office hit – it was screened in 2,406 theatres and earned almost $14 million in its first weekend. Yet her big dream of appearing in the next big Tim Burton hit – this time in the lead role – were crushed. There were brief flashes of hope, such as an appearance on the Rhonda Vincent video 'If Heartaches Have Wings' and a co-hosting slot with her father on Colgate-sponsored contest *The Country Showdown*, but most of her subsequent auditions ended in failure.

She tried out for *The Adventures Of Sharkboy And Lavagirl* but lost out to Taylor Lautner, failed to get a callback for the TV series *The Closer* and was desperate to take part in Nickelodeon's *Zoey 101*, but was pipped to the post by Britney Spears' sister Jamie Lynn. That said, she didn't hold any grudges about the latter disappointment. By her own admission one of Britney's biggest fans, she'd later tell the singer that her songs "represent my whole childhood".

However, the string of rejections was beginning to weigh heavily on Miley's psyche. At one audition for a film starring one of her most admired actresses, Shirley MacLaine, the bored-looking casting directors made phone calls throughout and completely ignored her. With a supportive, attentive and doting father behind her to praise her efforts, Miley was unaccustomed to such icy indifference and she left the building in floods of tears. "I'd see those little tears come down her face," Billy Ray recalled, "and I'd hold her and say, 'Enjoy being a kid. There is too much heartache to mess up your childhood.'"

He added, "I tried to discourage Miley from pursuing the entertainment business because it's a double-edged sword. For everything that makes you happy, there's something equally heartbreaking. I told her, 'You don't want to be a part of this business. There are things you can do that are less abusive.'"

The message, told by someone who'd been there, couldn't have been much clearer than that, and yet Miley was adamant. Her father, who'd seen too much of the dark side of fame to cheer her on, was happy to move back to Tennessee when *Doc* completed its final series, looking forward to "watching the grass grow and being at one with my Heavenly Father and my Mother Earth".

Yet Miley felt differently – and it seemed that trying to stop Miley – trying to protect her from the pain – might be like trying to fight the tide. As Billy Ray acknowledged, "From the day she could talk, she said she was going to be onstage."

Chapter 4

MILEY was by now so determined that – aged 11 and on the brink of starting middle school back in Nashville – she switched the first two weeks of term for a trip to LA for an intensive stint of auditions. She made that decision with a heavy heart – this was the time of year when friendships were formed and cliques took shape, and yet in LA it was the annual TV show pilot season, something no aspiring actress could afford to miss.

She'd already been absent from school for the previous two years – first for her disastrous spell at New Song Academy and then for home-schooling in Toronto – and she knew that, against the backdrop of a gang of fickle pre-teens, she was risking social exclusion. She flew to LA with her parents' reluctant blessing, but when the trip didn't yield a single call-back, she wondered if she'd become the school outcast for nothing.

Yet one show turned out to be advertising a little later than usual – a new Disney Channel series called *Hannah Montana* – and Miley was invited to audition. The plot featured a seemingly ordinary schoolgirl, Chloe Stewart, who by night leads a secret double life as a pop star. She disguises her true identity to blend in at school by donning a blonde wig onstage – and more often than not, a glittery rhinestone jacket – when she rocks out as the nation's hottest new star, Hannah Montana.

However, much to the indignation of her father, Miley had been invited to audition for the part of Chloe's best friend, Lily. "Have they heard her sing?" he would exclaim incredulously to his wife after just a few minutes of reading the script. "She's trying out for the wrong part."

While this might have been interpreted as mere parental bias – paternal pride – it turned out that Disney felt the same. After receiving Miley's first audition tape – which featured her belting out a spirited version of Joan Jett's 'I Love Rock 'N' Roll' – the response was almost instant. Weeks later, they were soliciting another tape, but this time for the part of Chloe.

Shrieking seemingly loud enough to frighten all of the animals on her farm, Miley set about recording a second tape – but this time Disney reacted almost as fast by doling out an instant rejection. The following day, the email apologetically informed her that Chloe was intended to be 15 years old. Not only was Miley four years too young, but – at less than 5ft tall – she was more petite than most of the peers in her own age group, too. She had to face facts – becoming Hannah Montana was an impossibility.

Yet ironically she already had something in common with her fictional character that transcended superficial height stats – they both led double lives. Miley was all too familiar with school bullies jealous of the family's celebrity status, who would taunt, "Your dad's a one-hit wonder. He'll never amount to anything and neither will you."

Doubtless the girls who targeted her were merely green with envy, but that didn't make school much easier and before long, she'd learnt to disguise her identity when meeting new people. She neither wanted to live in Billy Ray's shadow nor become a punch-bag for others to act out their insecurities.

Meanwhile, although Chloe's classmates thought she was an ordinary girl, she still experienced bullying in the script. As a victim of unkind jibes herself, Miley wouldn't have had to dig too deep to project that persona. The sum total of her acting experience might have been a couple of lines in *Big Fish* and a small part in *Doc* won purely thanks to her father but, in many ways, she had the experience that mattered most of all – not least that of living in a superstar family for real. Nonetheless, as Disney execs would later claim, she appeared closer to nine than 15 and, without a more mature look, all of her other assets counted for nothing.

As if Miley wasn't devastated enough, she'd predicted correctly that missing the start of school would reduce her to an outcast. A group she'd thought of as her friends turned against her and embarked on a campaign she would later jokingly refer to as 'Operation Make Miley Miserable'. At the time, she didn't see the funny side. They stole her books, ripped her homework assignments to shreds before she could hand them in, spread malicious gossip about her, mocked her hair and clothes and threatened her with physical violence. Of course the aspect that Miley feared the most was not the physical blows, but the emotional ones – the gradual undermining of her confidence, the humiliation of daily ridicule.

To an adult such as Miley's mother – who'd taken on her fair share of bullies in her time on account of her unusual beauty – it was merely petty turf war, and she'd simply reassure her daughter with a knowing roll of the eyes that, "Girls will be girls." However these particular ones had upped the ante – never missing an opportunity to unleash their venom, they made the cast of *Mean Girls* look like interns for Mother Teresa in comparison.

They were cunning too, with one pretending to befriend Miley, telling her she "wanted the fight to be over" purely to coax her true feelings about her former friends out of her. When she'd extracted a confession – that, unsurprisingly, she thought the bullies were "being mean" – she ran back to the others, crowing. This was just more ammunition to use against her. "She'd been faking it," Miley groaned later. "Looking back, I think maybe she was the one who should have been an actress."

As rumours circulated that she was a judgmental snob for criticising her peers as "mean", she was at her wits' end. Like Chloe Stewart, she had painstakingly ensured that the reason for her trips to LA remained a secret, but that didn't save her from her peers' acid tongues. On one occasion, they even stole the school caretaker's key to the toilets, dragged her inside and locked the door. "I was trapped," she recalled later. "I banged on the door until my fists hurt but nobody came. In that moment, I was friendless, lonely and miserable."

Yet the worst anguish by far for a cheerleading fanatic like Miley was when the bullies' intervention cost her a place on the squad. They'd complained to the principal – falsely – that she'd cheated by memorising the dance moves in advance of the auditions, and as a result, she was banned from trying out at all. Nothing she could say would convince school authorities of her innocence.

While such calculated cruelty rarely occurred randomly and should perhaps have been seen as a compliment, as it suggested they felt threatened by her – the girl who could competently perform a back-hand flip with her eyes closed – that was little consolation for Miley at the time. Until the next pilot season, her entire life revolved around the classroom and, without a single friendship, happiness was frustratingly elusive.

She eventually secured herself a place on a cheerleading squad independent of her school, which meant, in Miley's words, that her life was

Yet to reach double figures, a barely recognisable young Miley, all chubby cheeks and innocent smile, resembles a miniature catalogue model whose image is miles away from that of the boundary-pushing pop star she would later become.

Barely two years old, Miley poses proudly with her country rocker father Billy Ray at a 1994 Elvis Presley tribute concert in Memphis, Tennessee. Moments earlier she'd gatecrashed the stage for her first ever public performance. SCOTT WEINER/RETNA LTD./CORBIS

Miley enjoys the early perks of stardom as she attends the plush Stars of Disney Channel bash in New York in February 2006.
CHRIS DANIELS /RETNA LTD./CORBIS

Miley with Billy Ray, who serves as both her real life and onscreen father simultaneously as part of her TV show *Hannah Montana*.
CHRIS DANIELS /RETNA/CORBIS

Entering her teenage years, Miley projects the wholesome image that secured her fame, posing in Pasadena, California as part of her summer 2006 press tour, with ever-present mother Tish by her side.
LISA O'CONNOR/ZUMA/CORBIS

Miley and her parents behind the scenes at a free concert to promote the June 2007 release of her *Hannah Montana: Pop Star Profile* DVD. Also with her are supportive half-siblings Trace and Brandi. GREGG DEGUIRE/WIREIMAGE

Miley takes to the stage to belt out a tune at the HP Pavilion in San Jose, California, as part of her summer 2006 concert tour.
TIM MOSENFELDER/CORBIS

Clad in her near-obligatory uniform of rhinestone belt, cowboy boots and white jeans, Miley channels her inner diva, blowing a kiss backstage at the June 2007 New York Licensing Show. RICHIE BUXO/SPLASH NEWS/CORBIS

Miley balances in the arms of her backing dancers during a November 2007 show in Oakland, California, a routine that the same year would see her accidentally topple to the floor. JAY BLAKESBERG/RETNA LTD./CORBIS

Miley shows yet another side to her chameleon-like personality, hanging out of her glitzy pink costume into a simple grey dress to perform a duet with her father. JAY BLAKESBERG/RETNA/CORBIS

A star-struck Miley alongside her idol Beyoncé as the pair sing together at the 2008 Fashion Rocks concert, both representing the cause Stand Up To Cancer. LUCAS JACKSON/REUTERS/CORBIS

Miley performs at the Idol Gives Back charity concert on April 6, 2008, held at Hollywood's Kodak Theater.
MARIO ANZUONI/REUTERS/CORBIS

now "only hell between 8 a.m. and 3 p.m.". The rest of the time, she threw herself with absolute commitment into the squad.

Then, to her amazement, she received a phone call about *Hannah Montana*. "We looked all over the country and all over the world to try and find the girl to play this part," Emmy award-winning executive producer Steve Peterman recalled, "and there was one girl we kept coming back to. We saw the tape of this skinny little stick of a girl from Tennessee, with this amazing face and these incredible eyes. She was green and inexperienced . . . but there was something about her face – you couldn't take your eyes off her. There was a wonderful transparency – a sense of a young girl desperately wanting to be something."

And while Miley's insatiable energy and animated million–miles–a–minute penchant for chatter had caused disapproving teachers to recommend she be assessed for ADHD, these qualities were exactly the ones Disney was looking for in its new star. Surely, the company reasoned, it was worth giving her a second try. After all, young girls on the brink of puberty went through some enormous growth spurts – didn't they?

Not in Miley's case. When she flew to LA to audition for them in person, it was noted with disappointment that she was just as small and slight as ever. There was no way she could pass as a teenager. "They're gonna see how old I can really look," Miley had reasoned, "so I'll dress up and wear mama's shoes and make-up . . . and I just looked like a little girl playing dress-up. I don't know that I would have hired me at that point."

Duly, Miley was sent home – but she refused to give up that easily. After picking herself up and lobotomising her pride, she offered to try a second time – this time promising she'd pick up the bill for travel by herself. "We got a call from an agent who said, 'Miley will fly herself out to audition again,'" recalled Disney Channel President Gary Marsh incredulously. "Let me tell you, we've done a lot of auditions over the years and no one has ever made that offer before. I said, 'We have to see this girl again.'"

Two weeks later – missing cheerleading practice for a second time running – Miley flew out again. By now, the competition had narrowed from 1,000 girls in the running to around 50, all of whom were congregating in the waiting room.

As Miley would vividly recall later, the room had the sterile scent of a dental surgery – a factor which, purely by association, hardly helped to take the edge off her nerves. As she moved closer to the other actresses, an overwhelming, sickly stench of perfume took over – and the many combined fragrances served to make her head ache from chemical inhalation. Her eyes scanned the room at the dozens of intimidatingly beautiful, immaculately turned out girls – and that was just the parents.

Her heart sank. However, this was a teen show, not a slot on Babe Station, and producers were seeking more than superficial surface beauty. They sought someone likeable, relatable and multifaceted – a girl equally capable of playing both a glamorous superstar and an unremarkable girl next door; someone who looked so normal and approachable that the average TV viewer could plausibly fantasise about making the same transformation themselves. A girl who served as an inspiration, not someone so achingly and inaccessibly beautiful that it made others lose all hope of measuring up. As Billy Ray would later comment, his daughter was "beautiful, but not a beauty" – and that made all the difference.

Meanwhile, her inexperience, which had initially been regarded as a turn-off by perfection-seeking producers, could also ultimately work in her favour, as it made her transformation appear all the more authentic. The role called for her to take on the persona of an ordinary girl, plucked from obscurity to become a star, not a seasoned professional who already was one – and in this regard too, Miley excelled.

However, the acid test was whether she could sing. Gary Marsh had been adamant that he would "not go forward [with the show] until we can find an actress who can carry a sitcom as well as she can carry a tune". No one concerned was willing to commit to the financial risk of launching a multi-million dollar nationwide TV show without the right girl with precisely the right qualities to front it and, as auditions continued fruitlessly, the future of the show hung precariously in the balance.

They'd searched the world for a girl who could fit the glass slipper and, had Miley not already been so wealthy, it could have been a modern-day *Cinderella* story. The moment she sang in person, according to Marsh, was the moment when "it crystallised that she was the 'it' girl". Her presence in the audition room was far more commanding than that of the tape – and they began to wonder if they'd acted a little too hastily in underestimating her.

"We asked her if she would mind singing for us and she basically said,

'You can bring the whole building. I'll sing for everybody,'" Peterman would marvel. "This little girl opened up her mouth and this amazing voice came out of her that was from somebody twice as big and several years older. And then we realised that Miley Cyrus was the daughter of Billy Ray Cyrus and those genes are very apparent. So we took a deep breath. We said to ourselves, 'We can go with someone with more experience, but if we were lucky – if Miley was able to bring out what we saw – we would have something very special.' Because we looked at her with her Tennessee twang and those eyes, that face – there's nobody on TV like this girl."

Their enthusiasm was almost beginning to match Miley's, who'd insisted, "I would have hung wallpaper while wearing a tutu if I thought it would prove that I was meant to play Hannah." However, there was no such thing as a quick decision in showbiz, as Miley was gradually starting to find out – and yet again, she was sent home without a word.

In crisis, the decision makers called a conference. Their biggest concern was still her age, which saw them muse, "This is going to be an enormous weight on somebody's shoulders." Yet even that wasn't an insurmountable obstacle – and talk began about lowering Chloe's age so that Miley, if she was chosen, could more realistically portray her character. Moreover, there'd be less chance of her getting into trouble outside the show. One insider exclusively revealed to the author, "Disney came round to seeing a younger girl as a good thing because it meant she was controllable for a lot longer. They knew from other child stars that an innocent Disney image has a shelf life because all kids eventually grow up. Around that time, Britney [Spears] was starting to go off the rails and Christina [Aguilera] had already gone, but as Miley was so young she could be that pure, wholesome kids' role model for much longer – there'd be less risk of her damaging their reputation."

In Disney's world, being wholesome was not so much morally desirable as a marketable financial commodity – one that would encourage the conservative parents of middle America to put their hands in their purses. In a world of increasingly sexualised imagery, channels like Disney were relied upon to provide an atmosphere that was the antithesis of that. Yet Britney and Christina, both of whom cut their teeth on Disney's *The New Mickey Mouse Club*, would go on to discover the pleasure of hedonism – and while it might have made the stars seem edgy, it had been a costly embarrassment to the channel's reputation.

Britney's case was an unusual one – by wearing a school uniform aged 16 for the video to her first single, 'Hit Me Baby One More Time', she'd managed both to conform to the eyebrow-raising, morally questionable fantasies of older men and meet the expectations of strait-laced parents and naïve children simultaneously. She was a chaste role model and a lusted-after sex symbol, both at the same time – a rare combination that was not easy to juggle, but which had secured her widespread popularity. Although she had been one of the purity ring brigade, fluttering her eyelashes, while insisting she was a good Southern girl who didn't believe in sex before marriage, she soon broke out of the oppressive mould and began to move at lightning speed in the opposite direction. Some might have seen the public's reaction as a little unfair – she'd arguably been used as a sex symbol for profit for years and yet the outrage only began when she started to enjoy and finally take control of her own sexuality.

While it was wryly acknowledged that many child stars were destined to end up in the headlines accused of "meltdown", as the insider commented, there was a consensus that Miley's virginal image could be preserved for several years longer. Ironically, one of the main reasons that Disney hadn't hired her might actually now become a major factor in her success.

Yet Miley, who was still struggling with school bullies, was less than impressed with Disney's third invitation to fly back to LA. Days before she heard the news, she'd received a note threatening her with unspeakable violence if she showed up for lunch the following day at school. She'd ignored the warning, reasoning, "If I hid from the girls today, they'd just get me tomorrow" – but her heart was pounding. "It was like an after-school special about the runty girl who gets beat up," Miley wryly recalled. "But instead of having a happy ending with an uplifting message about overcoming adversity, this plot would end up with me living out the rest of my days as a 12-year-old hermit, friendless and alone."

She continued, "As soon as I sat down at my empty table in the Loserville area of the lunch room, three girls strutted up and started towering over me. My stomach churned. I clutched my grilled cheese sandwich like it was the hand of my best friend. It pretty much was my best friend those days. I was done for."

Without the intervention of a teacher who walked into the room after a tip-off from her concerned parents, she felt sure it would have escalated to violence. Either way, she felt continually unsafe and was not in the best of moods when it came to yet another teasing callback for *Hannah Montana*. "What were they doing, cutting one girl at a time, *American Idol* style?" she would remark sourly. "I just felt tired of it all . . . I didn't want to go back."

To complicate matters, her cheerleading squad would automatically disqualify her if she missed three practice sessions, meaning she was already on her last warning. One more trip to LA during term-time and she would have sacrificed her place – potentially for nothing. Eventually after a tip-off that she was a serious contender, she chose the audition and, sure enough, this time there were only two other girls in the waiting room. One was Taylor Momsen, of subsequent *Gossip Girl* fame, and the other was an unidentified 16-year-old – both of whom an intimidated Miley recalled as "about a foot taller than me".

Yet keen to take the pressure off and make it a trip to remember, even if the auditions were a lost cause, Tish – who by this point definitely did not have high hopes – had organised a stay at the Universal Studios theme park to coincide. That was where they were when the next callback arrived. She was still dressed in her audition outfit – a tiny white Abercrombie and Fitch mini skirt – and seconds after accidentally spilling an entire can of Dr Pepper down the front of it, she received a phone call summoning her back to the studio. It turned out that they wanted to test her chemistry with a girl who was trying out for the part of Lily. Although Miley never saw her prospective onscreen best friend again, she fared better and, within weeks, Disney called to tell her that – finally – she had the part.

The next step was to cast her onscreen father, Robbie – a successful country star who'd given up his own career to nurture his daughter's. The obvious choice, of course, was Billy Ray. However, there were contrasting stories about how he landed the part. According to him, he'd been invited to audition before Miley had been cast, but in Disney's version of events, he'd called the studio after she landed the role to ask to be considered. Gary Marsh had confessed that his thought process was, "Well, he's the dad – we can't really say no!"

It was an ironic situation because while Miley had agonised, "I was worried that if he got the part, people would think that he'd been cast first and I'd been hired because of him," if the latter account was correct, Disney had initially had absolutely no intention of giving him the role. Claiming that the production team had planned to humour him in the interest of courtesy, co-executive producer Michael Poryes would admit, "We were saying, 'We'll have him come in. We'll be polite. We'll let him audition and we'll shake his hand and he'll go away.'"

Outside the realm of everyone's expectations was the concept that Billy Ray would "absolutely nail" the role. Miley had taken the lead that morning, egging her father on to duet with her on a track he'd recently written, titled 'I Want My Mullet Back'. As they belted it out in matching Tennessee accents, producers' mouths hung open – not only did they harmonise perfectly, but they were demonstrating there and then the organic, natural chemistry of an authentic father and daughter team. He was hired.

"He approached the role with such effortlessness that we said, 'Not only is this her dad – you can't create that – but he is a rock'n'roller. He is the part," Steve Peterson mused. "On top of that, the gravy and the bonus was that Miley had a relationship to him that you can't duplicate. There was a teasingness, a warmth, a comfort and a security that these two had onstage that we said you could work for years with people and pray to get that kind of relationship."

He added, "Miley acted in a way with her father that she couldn't act with anyone else – over and over again in the filming of the show. Some of our favourite moments are things that happen simultaneously between father and daughter that we could never write . . . everything fell very quickly into place." It was a case of life imitating art – and neither party needed to act.

Miley's relationship with her onscreen brother, Jackson (played by Jason Earles), however, was a little different. One of his trademarks was a penchant for snitching – each time the pair got caught doing something forbidden, he would plot to absolve himself of all responsibility, rehearsing speeches such as, "It was nothing to do with me – I just followed Miley out here and tried to stop her. I'm just as disappointed as you are, dad!"

In contrast, Miley and her real-life biological brother, Braison, kept each other's secrets loyally. She would reveal later, "When Brazz trusts me with something, nothing could make me break that trust – someone could put a knife to me and I would not tell."

Fortunately in real life, Jason and Miley had grown to adore each other. He'd originally been intimidated at the idea of playing a spare part in a family that was already real, relating, "I was really nervous [because Miley and Billy Ray] have got all this history with each other and I am going to be the outsider. But they are classic Southern hospitality. It took me all of two days to feel accepted."

The tight relationship between Miley and her onscreen best friend, Lily (Emily Osment), however, called for her to bring her best acting skills to the fore. The pair saw each other as competition and struggled not to let their insecurities destroy the prospect of an authentic relationship. Miley felt intimidated by her blonde hair, beautiful smile and host of acting experience and she also felt that she and Emily, who hailed from LA, had very little in common. At times the tension would degenerate into down-right hostility, with each dramatically rolling her eyes if the other made a minor mistake with her lines during filming. Miley did feel guilty about her inability to bond with Emily – particularly as she knew all too well herself how it felt to be openly disliked – but one small consolation was that the professional pair hid all traces of their mutual dislike on the tape.

However, there was a far bigger issue at hand than in-fighting – despite all their hard work, filming a successful pilot offered no guarantee that it would ever hit TV screens. It was down to Disney to approve it first. When the show finally got the green light, the producers then dropped a bombshell – they expected the family to relocate to LA within a week. Barely skipping a beat, Miley's mother went online to buy "the smallest house she could find" to ease their transition. "Just like that – as if it were a T-shirt from a catalogue," Miley marvelled later. "Mum is so 21st century!"

It was also safe to say that very few beginner actresses would be in a position to buy a house in LA and move there in a matter of days for her first real role – but then the Cyruses were no ordinary family. Although everything was falling into place, Billy Ray was plagued by feelings of foreboding. One part of him was keen for his daughter to shine – after all, she was too vibrant and full of life to lock inside a gilded cage forever – but another felt an urge to pull her back and protect her from the perils of fame before it was too late.

As a safety net, the family had taken part in a joint baptism performed by their local pastor at the People's Church in Franklin – but Billy Ray felt even that wouldn't be enough. It hardly helped to ease his anxiety that the first thing he saw on the road as they arrived in LA was a sign that spelt out, "ADOPT A HIGHWAY: ATHEISTS UNITED". It was a clear and unambiguous attack on organised religion and defiant refusal to live by the Bible's rules. And while the average Californian might see the declaration as liberating, for a God-fearing man from Kentucky, anything that questioned religious teaching was nothing short of frightening. When he first saw it, he reached out and grasped his daughter's hand protectively until the knuckles turned white – as much for her reassurance as for his own. "The sign could easily have said, 'You will now be attacked by Satan!" Billy Ray would later tell *GQ*. "Entering this industry, you are now on the highway to darkness!"

Miley took a slightly less fatalistic view, but her feelings were the same – she was in showbiz to represent God in the war of good versus evil. "Faith is the main thing," she would attest earnestly. "That's why I'm here in Hollywood – to be like a light, a testimony to say God can take someone from Nashville and make me this, but it's His will that made this happen."

She was also insistent that she wouldn't go off the rails à la Britney Spears and Lindsay Lohan, believing that her faith would save her from meltdown. "[Family and friends] would never let something like that happen," she declared. "Before I came out [to LA], my parents were like, 'You know, there's no way that you can turn into any of that – and also, just me as a person, I would never let that happen.' I see things that are going on that are such bad things to put into girls' – guys' too, but mainly girls' – heads. I still go to church on a Sunday with my family and really just want to learn, because I don't want to blend in with everyone. I just want to give a good image and a good message to girls . . . you could look at other people, things that they're doing, and you say to yourself, 'I don't want to make that mistake.'"

So it seemed – for now, at least – that Miley was devoted to taking the path of a virtuous role model. Already all too familiar with the perils and pitfalls of showbiz, Miley's parents had collaborated on finding the right representation to help her achieve that. She signed on the dotted line with Mitchell Gossett – Billy Ray's own long-time agent and the man credited with "discovering" Miley. Meanwhile her musical manager would be Jason Morey of the Morey Management Group, a decision that was made on the recommendation of Dolly Parton, who'd praised their unusually "good morals" – a rarity in the business.

So it seemed that Miley was all set. However, first of all, there was a little work to do on her image. The stark contrast between her back-to-basics country existence on the farm and the high octane, perfectly polished glamour of LA couldn't have been more apparent than in the moment she arrived for the first day of filming. The look on Gary Marsh's face when he saw her was one of incredulous, abject horror – and his words were scarcely likely to ease her feelings. "What *happened* to you?"

In the short week that she'd been back in Tennessee, her bleach-ravaged hair had been dyed an ill-advised shade of blonde, she'd had two teeth extracted, leaving enormous, cavernous gaps – and she was now wearing a set of less than fashionable braces. Even worse, thanks to the windy drive down, her hair was windswept and full of static. She was given an emergency image overhaul, which included braces that – for aesthetic reasons – were fixed on the inside of her teeth, and even two dentures to disguise the gaps. Finally her locks were dyed back to their natural shade of brown.

The overtly critical eyes that were cast over Miley were a little hurtful, but thankfully she'd already been prepped for that ego-shattering reality. "My dad always told me that casting agents are like artists picturing their painting in their mind," she would recall later. "[Don't] take it too seriously [if they reject you]."

The worst part of the transformation, however, was being fitted for the 'Hannah' wig. Firstly it involved sitting still for a long period – something hyperactive Miley, who at school had regularly been chastised for squirming in her seat, struggled with at the best of times. It was also uncomfortable, requiring her head to be wrapped tightly in a shower-cap-style head covering, before being swathed in thick Sellotape until it formed a hard mound on the top of her head. This allowed the fitters to take accurate measurements of the size and shape of her head – something that, due to her age and consequent rapid growth spurts – had to be repeated more than once over the years, as the show progressed.

Suffice to say that this wasn't Miley's favourite part of becoming a star. However the wig – along with a pair of dark sunglasses to disguise her face – was a crucial part of her disguise. It was the only thing that afforded her anonymity offstage and the freedom to live a normal life. Hannah was bold, blonde and brash, while Chloe, in her guise of an ordinary school girl, wore casual clothes and her own natural, medium-brown hair. Ludicrously, no one in her life suspected a thing!

Noticing how blurred the lines were between fantasy and reality on the show, the producers adapted the roles before filming began to more closely resemble Miley's real life. For example, as Billy Ray kept mistakenly referring to Chloe as Miley, she became Miley in the script as well. This spared everyone on set some confusion, as up to that point there'd been four names – Chloe, Hannah and Miley, not to mention the Destiny Hope that was still on the latter's birth certificate. Then the name Robbie was altered to Robbie Ray in homage to Billy Ray, while her on-screen grandmother was named Ruthie in honour of her real-life paternal grandmother.

With these technicalities ironed out, filming could finally begin. The first episode featured Miley desperately trying to keep her identity secret from her best friend – and failing miserably. Fearing that she'd attract fake hangers-on or that her classmates might prefer the glamorous Hannah to who she is in real life, she resolves the identity crisis by keeping schtum and tries her best to masquerade as an ordinary girl. This way Miley – who boasts in the series' theme tune that she has "the best of both worlds" – can maintain the life of a rock star and a conventional school girl simultaneously. However, it's far from easy – Lily has a habit of calling round unannounced, which necessitates split-second costume changes while, when her friend invites her to a Hannah Montana concert, she has to devise every excuse she can think of not to go. Increasingly ludicrous explanations include a need to spend "quality time" with her brother, when Lily knows all too well there's no love lost between them. Meanwhile a more blunt approach – "I just can't go, OK?!" threatens to hurt her feelings.

Yet short of hiring a robot-style walking and talking body double to accompany Lily to the show, she knows that being in two places at once is an impossibility. Her refusal doesn't dissuade her friend from going, either.

When Lily uses a rope ladder to sneak into her dressing room through an open window on the night of the show, Miley panics, grabs a pie from her rider and plunges it into her face, passing it off to an understandably freaked-out Lily as a new and far-flung facial moisturising technique.

Just when it looks as though she may have got away with the deception, an eagle-eyed Lily – who is unsuspectingly almost hyperventilating over meeting her 'idol' for the first time, not realising she speaks to her every day – spots a charm bracelet on her wrist. Admiringly commenting that she had one exactly the same that she gave to her best friend – the only difference being that hers is engraved with the letters of her name – she turns it over to discover that this *is* the bracelet she gave to Miley. Wiping the pie from her friend's eyes, she realises the truth.

Miley feels compelled to make it up to Lily, who is hurt by the lies, by parting with another secret that she's never shared with another friend – her monumental closet. Behind the doors of her modest, meagre wardrobe lies a vast room, filled with clothes and shoes – a veritable treasure trove of glitzy fashion items. However, this isn't enough for Lily – hungry for glory by association, her first instinct is to shout from the rooftops that she's close with a star. Miley then has to persuade her not to spill the beans. Honesty isn't always easy – in one scene, Billy Ray, who'd been encouraging Miley to be open with her friend all along, comments to Lily that things would be "a lot better around here" now that she knows the truth – only to see the door unceremoniously slammed in his face.

Subsequent episodes, however, reveal that being Hannah has its pros – for example, when she discovers illicitly that her father is dating a new woman. With her mother's death still raw in her memories, Miley is devastated by the news, but feels unable to confront her father, as it would mean revealing she'd spotted the new couple at a movie premiere – one she'd been forbidden to see. She has to keep it a secret that she didn't stay at home all weekend to revise for exams as she'd promised – so, on discovering that the mystery woman works as a real estate agent, she hatches a plot to vet her by turning up as Hannah.

The realtor is initially thrilled at the prospect of selling a house to a glamorous young celebrity – until Hannah starts asking invasive questions about her relationship status, of course, even enquiring who the man is in the photo on her desk. Billy Ray chooses that moment to walk in with a bunch of flowers for his new beau, prompting Miley to barricade herself in the staff cupboard behind her. When the woman name-drops that she's just had Hannah Montana in her office, but that she seems deranged and is hiding in a cupboard, throwing in a casual and unsuspecting "I blame the parents", Billy Ray's face is priceless.

While the episode is light-hearted and full of laughs, it also touches upon a serious issue – the challenges of bereavement and the difficulty – whether parents are separated by something as dramatic as death, or merely divorce – of adapting to one of them dating afresh.

The topic meant more to Miley than it first appeared because, while filming was underway in the city of angels, her beloved 'Pappy' – paternal grandfather Ron – was on his deathbed in a different state. His inhalation of deadly asbestos from toiling in the steelworks decades earlier had finally caught up with him and he'd succumbed to terminal cancer. Worst of all, due to her pressured filming schedule, she couldn't take time off to be with him. Miley, who by now had turned 13, struggled immensely with guilt at not being able to do more, repeatedly reliving in her mind the times he'd called and she hadn't spoken to him.

The grief inspired her – along with two other writers, included Wendi Foy Green, who'd taken her to the audition for the Banquet Foods commercial – to pen a song about the distance between them. 'I Miss You' was premiered on that episode of *Hannah Montana* and every word that she sang in memory of her deceased mother on the show was in reality about him. It was yet another case of art emulating life – and it now looked as though Hannah had not a double, but a triple life.

When Miley allowed herself to dwell on her grandfather's condition, she was consumed with guilt over her absence, but the adrenalin rush of filming gave her a much-needed redirection of focus – especially when celebrity guests were involved. In just the sixth episode, Hannah was about to perform for the Queen of England – which in real life Billy Ray had passed up the opportunity to do and that, years later, Miley would genuinely do – when Emmy award-winning actress Vicki Lawrence steps in as Ruthie, Miley's grandmother.

Keen to give Jackson extra attention to compensate for the fact that he's often overshadowed by Hannah, she focuses on his upcoming volleyball tournament, turning both events into direct competition. Vicki – who'd had a number one hit in the seventies, 'The Night The Lights Went Out In Georgia' – ended up in a dance contest with the Queen.

Other guest stars included Ashley Tisdale of *High School Musical* fame and Miley's godmother Dolly Parton, who masqueraded as 'Aunt Dolly'. She appeared clad in her usual trademark denim crop top except that this time, to fit in better with the younger audience, she'd covered her ample cleavage.

The show threw up new surprises and challenges each day – and it didn't shy away from the dark side of celebrity either, featuring with surprising candour those moments which were less salubrious. In one episode, Miley is invited to sponsor a perfume and, despite finding the scent nauseating, she agrees to be its ambassador purely for the perks, which include a free courtesy car. It was a moral dilemma most stars might not admit to experiencing, although for some unnamed celebrities, the scenario seemed more than theoretical.

As well as playfully depicting the fictional Hannah as a shameless sell-out, the show also tackled a couple of other subtly controversial plotlines, too. For example, in the very first episode, a flamboyant and patently homosexual man pays the teenage Jackson $20 to dress up in women's clothing – and Miley's glittery stage costumes, no less. To some, it carried sinister undertones of paedophilia – albeit purely by implication – redeemed when Billy Ray reveals he asked him to pay Jackson to play dress-up, knowing how desperate he is for money, to embarrass him. When Miley walks in on her shamefaced brother sporting a sequined vest top and skirt, he exclaims, "I'm not getting paid nearly enough for this!" only for her to retort, "Neither am I!"

Yet in spite of its subtle pushing of the boundaries, *Hannah Montana* remained a tween and teen show at heart – innocent, frivolous and fun. The only truly dark moment for Miley emerged during the filming of episode 12, titled 'Back On The Road Again'.

It started out as light-hearted as ever, with a kindly Miley realising that her father put his own musical career on hold to focus on hers and repaying his loyalty by deciding to get him back out on tour again, doing what he loves best. As a surprise, she and Jackson turn up at one of his shows to join in with a rendition of 'I Want My Mullet Back' – all three donning comical mullet wigs for the occasion.

Yet with one phone call in the penultimate scene, all that changed and the tears of laughter that had been streaming down their faces between takes quickly threatened to turn into tears of sorrow. The call confirmed the news they'd been dreading – that on that day, February 28, 2006 – Miley's 'Pappy' had lost his battle with cancer and passed away.

Understanding producers urged the family to take the week off to grieve – and sure enough, on hearing the news, it was all Miley could do not to sprint from the room bawling. However, she flexed her acting muscles instead, gave her father a high five and echoed one of Ron's trademark phrases – "The show must go on!"

Everyone in the room was incredulous. Aside from a few moments when father and daughter had sat by the stage together in a shared "fog of sadness", Miley hadn't allowed herself to succumb to grief. Another phrase she'd learnt from her grandfather was that "strength is a choice", something that could be summoned when needed. "Come on people!" she barked, like a sergeant major. "We've got a show to do!" And to her credit, she unflinchingly carried it to its conclusion.

As soon as their work was done, she and her father went back to Kentucky for the funeral. Desperate to salvage what he knew was to be a sombre occasion – in a humorous style of which he knew his father would approve – Billy Ray even donned his mullet wig for the service. His aim was to raise a smile – and it worked. The focus was on celebrating his life, not mourning his death – although that was a lesson that would be a little harder for Miley to swallow than the others.

She struggled to accept that he'd never heard her sing 'I Miss You' for him – although he'd heard a snippet of an early taped version, which was barely a consolation – and while he'd vowed to hang on to life until *Hannah Montana* had hit the airwaves, he'd taken his last breath a month before that occasion.

Miley's mind went into a process of endless self-flagellation, berating and blaming herself for all the things she didn't do – until eventually a dream saved her. "It was Pappy," she recalled, "wanting me to move on. He said, 'I can't leave with you holding on so tightly. You can't let my death stop your life.' When I woke up, his voice was so alive in my head, it was as if he'd just said goodbye and walked out the door. Out of habit, I went to the phone to listen to his voicemail. It was gone. Deleted. Floating away out into the ether – as though Pappy was telling me to let go."

She felt with absolute conviction that her grandfather had reached out to her from beyond the grave – and from that moment things began to improve. Yet in the same month of his death, before the dream took place, Miley would have to focus her strength on getting through one of the most nerve-racking moments of her career yet – a Hannah Montana concert.

The show, held at the Alex Theater in Glendale, California – a stone's throw from Disney's studios – was billed as an event for "a group of 700 unsuspecting tweens who were invited with a promise of a concert and a chance to be on TV". Its main purpose was to pique the interest of media buyers in order to sell advertising space, but it was an equally big test for Miley as it was the moment of truth as to whether she could hold the attention of a real-life audience. The nerve-racking part was that she wasn't performing to pre-existing fans who'd already been won over – not one of those 700 people knew who she was. Imagining every member of the crowd to be casting critical, scornful and judgmental eyes over her, Miley would repeatedly seek reassurance after each song, "scurrying off-stage like a little mouse to ask my mum and the producers if I was doing OK".

However, as she worked through the songs that would eventually appear on the show, it occurred to her that there was a level of excitement no one had anticipated – one akin to Beatlemania, with girls hysterically whooping, screaming and punching the air. "It was crazy because I was expecting dead silence," she mused. "They had no idea who Hannah Montana was."

Although a cynic might interpret that the attention-seeking tweens were merely showing off for the camera, as Miley loved to do, it nonetheless did seem that something special was unfolding – a premature love affair between prospective fans and their new idol. Reviewers began to rave about the "pint-sized pop star" with an adult-sounding voice who would be hitting TV screens soon. The highlight was her live rendition of 'Pumpin' Up The Party', which – depicting an innocent teen sleepover – saw Miley take to the stage in pink polka-dotted pyjamas and bed slippers, before embarking on a boisterous pillow fight with her backing dancers. First impressions would see her glowingly compared to Ashlee Simpson and Avril Lavigne.

Of course, not all of her pre-fame experiences would run quite so smoothly. For instance, Miley and her mother subsequently attended the premiere of *Chicken Little*, only to be completely ignored. "I walked down the red carpet, towards all the flashing cameras and photographers yelling stars' names," she would recall. "'Zach! Joan! Steve!' When I strolled by, the cameras were lowered. There was silence. They had no idea who I was. So much for my red carpet fantasy!"

If the snubs on the red carpet had been humiliating, then the reception at the after-show party would prove downright traumatising. The room was full of celebrities and their managers, all of whom seemed to know each other and were mingling fast at crowded tables as they feasted on food from the buffet. Miley's heart sank when she realised there was nowhere for her to sit. For a brief moment, the collective snub was as demoralising as being shunned in the school cafeteria and demoted to the losers' table all over again. She'd arrived inflated with pride after the hype she'd generated as Hannah – and had come back down to earth with a bang. She was anonymous now, but the best of both worlds it was not, she thought bitterly as she settled down to eat on the floor.

"We were the biggest losers in history," she recalled. "It was pretty humbling."

Chapter 5

THAT turned out to be the last moment of public solitude Miley would ever experience. On March 24, 2006, the first episode of *Hannah Montana* premiered to an audience of 5.4 million viewers – and Miley Mania had officially hit the nation.

While the vast marketing budget of a large corporation like Disney almost guaranteed a hit, the public reaction took the series' status far beyond that – and it became the most watched show in the 23-year history of the Disney Channel. It would push its way up the league table to become the top-rated cable TV show and the second most popular show – with the sole exception of talent contest *American Idol* – of all time. A jubilant Gary Marsh told the media that the response had not just been unprecedented, but "beyond Disney's wildest expectations" – and that was just the beginning.

Almost instantly, normal life as she knew it was over – Miley couldn't even creep into her local grocery store incognito, without an army of hyperventilating fans in hot pursuit. The psychology behind the show's success was simple: Miley was at times an unpopular underdog who battled bullying, shyness and unrequited love – and yet in spite of having so many flaws that her audience of average American girls could identify with and relate to, she had also become a superstar. The reasoning was that if someone like Miley Stewart could have that potential within her, then so could they. Underneath the sheen of glitz and glamour was someone just like them – and this was precisely the reason for the series' appeal. Miley was one of the pin-ups they idolised, and yet she was normal and accessible at the same time.

At first, of course, she may have been a little too accessible. Totally unprepared for fame, Tish had hastily purchased the smallest, cheapest house she could find for their relocation to LA – and without Hollywood fortress-style gates to barricade strangers out, their modest home soon bordered on a tourist attraction. Their doorbell rang constantly – some-times with fans who would breathlessly beg to speak to 'Hannah' and other times courtesy of pranksters who would ring and then run away. On one occasion, a pre-teen girl arrived, crying hysterically, before collapsing and fainting when she saw Miley's face. The continuous attention would prove intrusive and at times frightening, so before long the family was forced to make an emergency move to a more isolated part of the city – high in the Hollywood Hills.

This did little to quell the frenzy. Although luxury brands like Chanel, Gucci and Prada would send her armfuls of clothes – each usually boasting a four-figure price tag – simple pleasures like going to the mall to browse through the rails herself became a point blank impossibility. On one shop-ping trip with her mother, the crowd surge became so intense that the store had to be forcibly evacuated, with security closing the entrance doors to prevent any further attention. Miley recalled that managers of shops "hated" her because of the disruption caused by her presence. A wild stampede, with apparel getting knocked to the ground left, right and centre, wasn't conducive to attracting buyers and when a store was taken over, packed to the rafters with screaming celebrity spotters, it deterred genuine shoppers from coming in. Miley's saving grace was the rapid growth of online retail because soon almost all the little luxuries that most teenagers took for granted were non-negotiably out of bounds.

Socialising was a struggle too as she could not attend school – so much for the best of both worlds. She instead received a private tutor from the Options For Youth home-schooling service, who worked with her on the set of the show. Proms and social events passed her by because, due to not belonging to a school, she rarely knew anyone who could accompany her. On one occasion, she did attend a dance, only to wearily resign herself to the knowledge that the overawed students forming a line to get her auto-graph had obliterated any chance of normality.

Even her relatives no longer treated her the same way, with then six-year-old Noah sheepishly informing her that she'd entered a competi-tion to win backstage passes for one of her shows. "You *live* with me! Miley retorted incredulously, before hastily adding, "Don't even think about swiping anything from my room to sell on eBay!"

This was how much life had changed – barely a month since the debut episode of *Hannah Montana*, it had statistically become the most popular tween show in existence. Now, in another case of art imitating life, the closest she'd ever come to normality was acting it out via the script in her show. The life of an ordinary girl was something she would have to visualise from the outside and portray despite never truly experiencing it.

Yet living an alternate reality was a sacrifice that Miley was willing to make. "Sometimes people are like, 'Oh, I wish I could go out [without being recognised], but all of my life I've wanted this so much," she would reason. "Now that it's here, it's a part of this lifestyle [and] really not a bad thing . . . it's worth it to see all these young kids looking up to you."

Of course with a country rocker as a father, even a typical family day out was far from conventional, on one occasion even culminating in a trip to a tattoo parlour. "One Sunday we were in church and Miley drew a little heart on my hand," Billy Ray recalled. "It was so sweet, but I grew sad thinking how fleeting that bond we had might be as she grew up."

In a bid to quell his insecurity, he proposed a father-daughter bonding day where Miley could be free to "do whatever you want". With a wicked grin, her instant response to the reckless invitation was to take him to get the cartoon-like heart permanently etched onto his skin. "We found a tattoo parlour in Pasadena," he recalled, "and I had her little heart on my hand for life. When that was finished, she led me to a hair salon on Ventura Boulevard called Whackos and gave the lady there instructions on how to style my big old head of hair. I left there with the craziest rock'n' roll highlights and a lasting memory of the two of us giggling till we were gasping for breath."

Well aware of the disapproving tuts about irresponsibility he'd attract from fellow parents, alongside jibes that he should be a father, not a friend, he added, "I'm far from being a perfect father – but we spent time together that day. We lived and we laughed, and that was my goal."

Miley would soon publicly praise Billy Ray for being her "best friend" – and in the meantime, the show went on. April would see the release of the *Disneymania 4* CD, featuring 15 tracks from the hottest teen and tween stars of the moment, and Miley had contributed a cover of 'Zip A Dee Doo Dah' from *Song Of The South*. Meanwhile she'd truly cement her status as a Disney icon in June when she put on a performance at Disney World in Orlando, Florida. The show prompted an almost two-month run of her signature song, 'Best Of Both Worlds' – the *Hannah Montana* theme tune – at number one on the Radio Disney chart. (By August 21, it would be knocked off the top spot, but rather than by a rival, it was by another of her own songs – this time 'I Got Nerve'.)

Yet as Miley's star was rising, Billy Ray's seemed to be in decline – and he was starting to resemble his onscreen persona more and more by the day. Like Robbie Ray, who had put his own career on the back burner to devote his energy to kindling his daughter's, it seemed that his presence on *Hannah Montana* was diverting his attention from promoting his own new album, *I Wanna Be Your Joe*. Two singles would be released from the CD, with both failing to chart, and even a duet with Miley on the track 'Stand' failed to make a strong enough impact on sales.

This created an untraditional dynamic in his relationship with his daughter, where she had become the main breadwinner for the family. As he'd never had the heart to enforce draconian discipline on her, the boundaries between the roles of parent and child had been shaky from the start – and it now seemed, with the complication of her growing success, that they'd been ripped down altogether.

According to insiders, Miley's ego was inflating even faster than her bank account – and she used the power imbalance between them as ammunition with which to ridicule her father. "Miley used to come into my hair salon to get her extensions done," one insider exclusively revealed to the author, "and she was always taunting him. She reminded him that she was paying his wages. I remember her as quite a bratty and unpleasant teenager, who he seemed to have almost no control over. She used to insult him and tell him he was nothing without her. One thing was for sure – she always made sure she got her own way."

She also claimed that Billy Ray, although embarrassed by her words, treated it as harmless banter because he was so besotted with her, and did little to stop it.

Even if that depiction was accurate, Miley's life was at least not as twisted as that of child star Macaulay Culkin, whose parents had dwindled away portions of his fortune on a bitter court battle over who would gain custody of him. It could have been much worse. That said, Billy Ray himself would acknowledge that maintaining a smooth relationship with Miley took some work. Each morning on the way to the studio, frustrated by what she described as his "random chatter" and "random music", she would simply turn up the volume on her iPod and drown him out. Billy Ray turned a blind eye to her manners – or lack of them – because in his words, now that they were both living and working together, he'd have to remain sensitive to the need to "give her space".

Any conflict between them looked as though it had been resolved when they took to the stage that year for various public appearances as a duo, however. They would sing the national anthem at Game Four of the Cardinals vs The Tigers World Series and would even co-present a trophy to Carrie Underwood for Female Vocalist of the Year at the 2006 Country Music Awards. The same night they'd engage in the same playful banter that had made *Hannah Montana* a hit. Miley would urge Billy Ray to take off his sunglasses, to which he simply retorted, "I don't tell you what to wear." "That's right," she witheringly responded, making reference to one of the famous hairstyles of his career. "Remember the mullet?!" Regardless of the rumours that blighted them, Billy Ray and Miley were a comedic team – and audiences loved them.

That year – aged barely 13 and a half – Miley would also fall in love for the first time. She met the boy she would refer to as her "Prince Charming" at a charity event for the Elizabeth Glaser Paediatric AIDS Foundation at which both were performing on June 11, 2006. The foundation had been formed in honour of actor Paul Michael Glaser's wife, who'd contracted AIDS after a contaminated blood transfusion she'd received during complications in childbirth. Miley was one of several artists performing at the event in a bid to raise funds and awareness, as was her beau – Nick Jonas.

Nick made up one third of the Jonas Brothers, a trio of devout Christian musicians and actors, whose unusual commitment to their faith had been widely publicised. Their father was a pastor, while their mother, a stay-at-home housewife, had home-schooled them to an evangelical curriculum to shield them from unwholesome influences. All three wore purity rings as a signature of their commitment to abstain from sex until marriage and they also planned to shun alcohol – even in adulthood. The strict rules they lived by might well have made the average Christian appear to be a morally bankrupt worshipper of Satan by comparison, but a besotted Miley was undeterred. Claiming to have fallen in love at first

sight, she recalled telling him that she was "a hardcore Christian", only for
him to respond, predictably, "That's what we call ourselves in my family."

When he'd gingerly extended a hand of greeting to her at that first
meeting, she'd responded with a smitten "I don't do handshakes – I do
hugs!" Fortunately for her, hugging was within the remit of Nick's view
of a God-fearing lifestyle – if he'd been Amish, she wouldn't have been so
lucky.

"Instantly I wanted all [his friends] to go away, so I could just be with
him," she later recalled. There was little chance of that, although she did
manage to put their names down for a joint karaoke version of 'I Want To
Be Like You' from *The Jungle Book*. "It would have been a funny, silly
song to do together," she explained. "But when the song came on, I
couldn't find him, so I had to karaoke all by myself. Let's just say people
were laughing *at* me, not with me."

Nick soon returned, however. That evening they went to dinner
together and, although Miley reluctantly complied with Tish's request not
to come home late, due to a painfully early start the next day, that didn't
prevent her from picking up the conversation on the phone later that
night, this time chatting until 4 a.m.

Their miles-apart love affair seemed doomed at first, with Nick living a
several-hour flight away on the East Coast, but when he relocated to LA –
just a few streets from Miley's own home – they rekindled the romance.
They'd play basketball and Nintendo – something that a competitive
Miley, a tomboy at heart, revelled in – but there'd also be tender
moments, such as when he walked beside her as she rode her bike. He
would also serenade her with one of her favourite songs, 'My Girl' by the
Temptations, only to substitute the words for her name, singing, "Miley,
talkin' about Miley . . ."

However, snatching time together was hard. By September 15, she was
out on the road for her first ever concert tour. She'd be stepping out in
support of the Cheetah Girls, a musical group whose 2003 feature film of
the same name – about the ups and downs of striving to break into the
industry – had spawned a multimillion-selling soundtrack. The movie had
even boasted co-production by Whitney Houston. When their follow-up
film had appeared in 2006, its premiere had attracted over eight million
viewers and the vast range of merchandise bearing their faces was so

diverse that it even included a singing toothbrush. With this level of fame to their names, the girls were perfect touring companions to help Miley find her feet. In fact, demand was so high that 80,000 tickets were sold in less than three minutes.

However for Miley – as yet an untested live act – the low-budget reality was far less glamorous. Her costumes, which in later years would be custom-made by the most prestigious designers – were this time around all from the rack of Forever 21 – an ultra-cheap American clothing store akin to the UK's Primark.

"Hannah's a fictional singer – maybe all her fame was fictional too," Miley had explained, "so the concert creators kept it cheap." Of course this meant that there was no Swarovski crystal in these costumes – just plastic-based sequins that shed rapidly every time she moved. That said, leaving a trail of glitter behind her was a way to make a statement in itself. There was then the indignity of her not-so-grand entrance – instead of the velvet curtain that would part to reveal the Cheetah Girls onstage, Miley had to be content with a plain white bed sheet. "My dad always says that a real musician can make a great show out of anything," she would insist, undeterred, "no matter how small. I was determined to be a great musician."

The one luxury that she did allow herself – and one that her mother insisted on, even though the Cyruses were forced to pay from their own pockets for the privilege – was a bus to herself. The touring group had originally consisted of around 100 people across four buses and Miley's backing dancers were four drinking, smoking, party-loving hedonists in their 20s – an environment Tish was keen to shield her 13-year-old from. It would just be her mother and maternal grandmother and little Noah making the journeys with her, away from the craziness – and, as it turned out, that was just as well.

During the tour, a sickly Miley would repeatedly run offstage fearing she needed to vomit. The first doctor she saw dismissed her worries as a simple case of stage fright, but her intuition told her that "something felt really wrong" – and she sought a second opinion.

Following an echocardiogram – an ultrasound scan of the heart – she discovered she'd had a hole in her heart since birth, but that the condition had gone undiagnosed until the physical exertion of a tour, with its fast-paced dance routines, had brought the problem to light. She was also diagnosed with tachycardia, a condition where her heart rate often accelerated at a faster rate than her body could keep up with, causing nausea and faintness.

Miley knew instantly that her life had to change. Up until the diagnosis, she'd been borderline anorexic, sometimes surviving on just one Poptart per day – and exercising manically all the while. In an industry where image was everything, and where she was still continually hounded by rumours that she'd landed her *Hannah Montana* role purely because she was a Cyrus, she felt extra pressure to prove herself – and was determined to look the part.

To make matters worse, egged on by the expensive designers who now lined her closet for free, Miley had adopted high fashion as a hobby – a world synonymous with the word 'skinny'. She'd been leafing through monthly fashion bibles such as *Vogue* and *Harper's Bazaar*, only to be faced with models such as Kate Moss, whose motto was "Nothing tastes as good as skinny feels". In high fashion, a US size 6 (equivalent to a UK 10) – already three sizes smaller than the national average – was regarded as plus size, and body-shaming was de rigueur. The catwalk ambassadors of the brands Miley was sent in the mail, despite being adult women, typically had fleshless physiques and A–cup breasts.

This was something that resonated with Miley due to the pressures she faced to maintain a childlike figure for TV. "When *Hannah Montana* hit TV, it had been remodelled as a show for six to 14-year-olds – and there was pressure on Miley to look the part," an anonymous insider revealed to the author. "Certain people were horrified when she began to develop breasts, because it wasn't in keeping with the young Disney image. Because they wanted to disguise the signs of puberty, she would often wear clothes that hid or flattened her breasts. Losing weight was another way of staying childlike for longer, because at that time she knew her career depended on it. For quite some time, she was anorexic."

As breasts are typically made up of 75% fat and just 25% breast tissue, weight loss would effectively minimise the impact of physical development, while it would also maintain her narrow hips – another indicator of pre-pubescence. With a body type that represented the majority of her target audience and shied away from being overtly sexual, it was felt that both fans and parents would relate to her as a wholesome role model. In a child-protective culture, one that sought to ban even red lipstick from children's presenters for being too lascivious, even the slightest hint of a sexualised look was frowned upon.

Yet regardless of all these pressures, extreme dieting could no longer be a part of her lifestyle. It would put a strain on her heart, which was now so sensitive that it would even race harder in response to minuscule changes in body temperature. "When I wear a wig, I get hot, my body has to cool down and my heart goes extra fast . . . it sometimes gets so I can't breathe and can't think – I feel claustrophobic," Miley explained. "There is never a time onstage when I'm not thinking about my heart." She added, "I've always struggled with my weight, but there was no way that being skinny was worth sacrificing my health . . . I have to take care of myself or I'll get sick."

Her stance was well-timed, as life was about to become crazier than ever. On October 24, 2006, just 10 days after the Cheetah Girls tour drew to a close, the *Hannah Montana* soundtrack was released – to nationwide hysteria. Producers had felt Miley was too young to shoulder the entire album by herself – not least because she hadn't been tried and tested as a singer yet – and had consequently added tracks by artists such as Jesse McCartney and the Click Five to share the billing. However eight tracks were credited to Hannah, while a ninth – a duet with Billy Ray – was credited to Miley herself.

Designed to win kudos from parents, 'I Learned From You' was a tender platonic-love ballad between father and daughter, with Miley reluctantly acknowledging that, as much as she might hate to admit it, in their battle of wills, he is usually right. Asserting that he provided the right blend of authority and kindness to morally guide her through life, she adds that he ultimately taught her the strength to "stand on my own". Of course behind the scenes, Billy Ray had been the first to admit that he was anything but a disciplinarian, seeing himself as more of a buddy than a parent, and claiming that he'd often made mistakes – and yet if the track was intended as a strategic marketing ploy, it had been a success. It tapped into parental insecurity at the prospect of losing their children to the rites of a passage of puberty, reassuring the masses by presenting Miley as someone who hadn't grown apart from her father, but who had instead leaned on him and accepted his input on her journey to becoming a righteous adult.

Other tracks centred around female empowerment and feminism, such as 'Who Said', with lyrics that challenged, "Who said I won't be President?" While these songs insisted that every girl could choose to lead her "own parade" – statements made to appeal to feisty and ambitious children – there was an irony about them. After all, at the time she belted them out, she was under the control of the Disney Corporation, which arguably merely saw the expression of individuality as a marketable concept.

While Miley – as a walking ambassador of the Disney brand values – was singing about doing things her own way, off camera she was undergoing intensive instruction on every aspect of her public persona. This training was to mould her into Middle America's definition of a good girl and therefore what to wear, what to weigh, who to date and even, thanks to a course in PR, what to say, were not necessarily outside the remit of her management's control.

As the face of a multimillion dollar show, money, time and trust had been invested in her and for Miley to spontaneously be herself was a risk that could scarcely be afforded. Later, she herself would admit that no part of her true self was unmasked during the *Hannah Montana* years. While she recited her pre-written lines, she was merely a pretty mirror, a vessel through which to reflect someone else's very lucrative brand of virtuosity.

However at such a young age, Miley didn't yet feel irritation at being stifled – instead she was thrilled just to have the opportunity, and even more so when the soundtrack debuted at number one. It was the first soundtrack ever to do so and the first in over two decades even to reach the top spot at all, setting a new precedent for the potential of children's TV series. Selling well in excess of a quarter of a million copies in the first week alone – almost one for every 150 under-18 girls in America – it warded off established artists across multiple genres such as John Legend and My Chemical Romance. Albeit in her guise as a fictional character, Miley would soon boast the accolade of becoming the first act to have six songs debut in the *Billboard* Top 100 chart in the same week – and the album would eventually sell over 6.5 million copies worldwide.

Miley's double life gave children a sense of escape – the feeling that all they had to do to take on the fantasy persona of their choice was to don a long blonde wig and a rhinestone jacket – and Disney execs even issued public advice on how to create a Hannah Halloween costume. This advice would prove controversial as, due to a high content of the toxic metal lead, official guidelines stress that rhinestones are not recommended in costumes for children under 16, especially those with a tendency to put their hands near their mouths after handling it.

Nonetheless Miley's reign continued, with Hannah making an appearance at other milestone events that year, such as the Macy's Thanksgiving Parade. To celebrate the holiday edition of the soundtrack – released to iTunes on December 19, 2006, and including bonus tracks such as 'Rockin' Around The Christmas Tree' – she'd perform at the Disney World Christmas Day Parade that year too. Her set list included festive songs such as 'Santa Claus Is Coming To Town', while her father joined her for a rendition of 'Run Rudolph Run'.

Miley Mania was in full force and, by early 2007, Disney TV even had their sights set on world domination. In April, her plans to perform an intimate one-off show at Camden's Club Koko in the UK saw Disney Radio's switchboards jammed by a deluge of fans desperate for tickets. "We had 80,000 calls in just one day," the London spokesperson reported. "*Hannah Montana* is like the teenage equivalent of Elvis." To demonstrate that the love was reciprocated, promotional photos taken on the trip featured a grinning Miley clutching the Union Jack flag on a tourists' London City Sightseeing bus.

A show at Disneyland Paris was equally well-received – all good preparation for the show's eventual translation into 100 languages for worldwide viewing. Plus while Tish had affectionately taunted – after her daughter fled offstage, prior to her tachycardia diagnosis, claiming that she "had to hurl" – that with language like that, she would never be invited to Buckingham Palace, she did make it to the next best thing. That year, she cemented her status as American Royalty when she was invited to perform the National Anthem at the White House's Easter Egg Roll.

By Miley's account, she had grown out of stage fright by this time. Presumably the adulation of hundreds of thousands of supportive fans singing the words back to her had aided in that transformation – and she proved it by joyfully and fearlessly doing back handsprings on the South Lawn. Her stage that day would be the same balcony on which George Bush and, subsequently, Barack Obama, stood to make his speeches, while – in the same sentence as words of gratitude for the members of Congress and Presidential Cabinet – the then First Lady, Laura Bush, spared a few words for Miley, gushing, "I especially want to thank Miley Cyrus for singing the National Anthem – wasn't she terrific?"

Yet just when *Hannah Montana* looked set to become a worldwide phenomenon, her real life doppelganger teetered on the edge of a breakdown so severe that she could scarcely summon the self-confidence to leave her bed – and the episode threatened to derail the life of the show altogether.

By now, Hannah Montana's celebrity had reached fever pitch and a dizzying range of merchandise was available, from lunchboxes to loo rolls – but, ironically, Miley was feeling more and more alienated from the face that stared back at her from each product. Like most teenagers, she had been suffering outbreaks of acne and, in addition to her weight and career path, this was just another aspect of her life that she struggled to control. For most, it might merely have seemed a slightly embarrassing rite of passage – all part of the normal onset of puberty – but Miley was no ordinary girl. The teenage ardours of only half-successfully concealing rampant acne for the school prom might be bad enough, but when an audience of a couple of dozen classmates was substituted for a crowd of 20,000, who – aided by the unforgiving stage lighting – could see every crevice, every wrinkle and every pore of her skin in close-up, high-definition technicolour, the humiliation was hard to bear. "I couldn't get out of bed because my skin looked awful," Miley recalled of the day of her mini meltdown. "I didn't believe I was beautiful. Nothing could change that fact . . . I honestly believed there was nothing special about me."

The biggest source of her insecurity wasn't merely the spots themselves, but the gaping chasm between her onscreen perfection and offscreen reality. It wasn't just her alter-ego, Hannah, who looked stunning – even her character as an ordinary schoolgirl was increasingly presented as effortlessly perfect and unattainably flawless.

The irony, of course, was that the fantasy image was equally unattainable even to the person portraying it. A combination of top-of-the-range make-up artists and over-zealous Photoshop airbrushing meant that the girl Miley saw on magazine covers, merchandise and TV screens was little more than an optical illusion.

Yet it was one that she felt obliged to unfalteringly portray – and with limited success. "I'd see this perfect airbrushed version of myself," she recalled, "and then I'd look in the mirror and see reality."

With this burden on her shoulders, it was little wonder she was experiencing self-doubt – how could she live a lie when the person the fans worshipped wasn't really her – and on some days, bore very little resemblance? "You know how all those magazines are doctored, how none of the models or celebrities or stars look as good in real life as they do when they've been styled, made up and airbrushed?" she questioned. "Well, if you ever find yourself wishing you looked as good as Miley Cyrus in a photo, just remember, *Miley Cyrus* doesn't look as good as Miley Cyrus in that photo. Take it from me."

Knowing this, of course – that airbrushing was all part of the game – was not enough to quell her self-destructive urges. "I became obsessed with the way I looked," she recounted. "I'd stare at the mirror for hours, hating myself outside and in. If all eyes were on me, why did I have to look like this? It started with my skin and then it snowballed. I didn't like my looks, my body, my personality – anything about myself."

The public's appetite for humiliating celebrities and taking them down a peg or two for entertainment only served to feed Miley's self-hatred. Her father had a motto about the uglier side of fame that he would recite to his daughter – "For every action there is an equal and opposite reaction." As he had warned, she would experience the opposite of the mass adulation in the form of cruel internet taunts that deconstructed and analysed her appearance. Followers in their droves took to the web to mock and ridicule her appearance, taunting that she was ugly and worthless. All the while, Miley felt that her real self, underneath the make-up, looked a million times less pretty than the version of her they were ridiculing. She became fearful to leave the house in case the paparazzi snatched a less than flattering photo of her that betrayed reality – for example, make-up-free and drenched in sweat as she left the gym. Each comment she read fuelled the fire of self-disgust, while googling herself to find comments that validated the worthlessness she wallowed in became a masochistic obsession.

Overall, the culture of airbrushing meant a lose-lose situation between a star and her public – fellow teenagers would react with hostility towards a celebrity that they perceived to be intimidatingly perfect, ironically little knowing that she too was insecure and that their comments made her even more so. Although Miley Stewart was "just a typical schoolgirl", typical schoolgirls rarely looked as manicured, glamorous and runway ready – and onlookers, feeling they didn't measure up, would overcompensate for not feeling good enough by putting Miley down, sniping that she "isn't all that".

Each time they lashed out, it was a symptom of their own inadequacy – but 14-year-old Miley wasn't to know that. Behind the scenes, she would continue to harbour her own insecurities about the dramatic gulf between the retouched-to-perfection poster girl she saw smiling down from every loftily high billboard and the spotty, less than sanguine Miley who lay in bed consumed with self-hatred.

Some might have been under the illusion that words didn't hurt celebrities – that their wealthy, successful lives afforded them some immunity from the sting of the online gossip – but in fact for those under the microscope on a daily basis, the pain could be all the more intense.

Rightly or wrongly, physical appearance was central to Miley's career – and the foundations of her success were built almost entirely on how others perceived her. As superficial as it might seem, the average teenage girl – a product of her larger-than-life, all-American upbringing – *did* tend to judge books by their covers. Miley was enslaved by public opinion, and she saw beauty and talent as a singular package – in showbiz, she felt, one couldn't exist without the other.

Meanwhile, although her friends back in Franklin might have found cringeworthy moments easy to eventually put behind them, she had no such luxury. Embarrassing memories might be relegated to the contents of dusty old diaries in childhood bedrooms, or confined to a few unwanted Facebook photos, which could be removed or de-tagged in a single click, but for a superstar, it would be documented and destined to forever remain in her back catalogue. That was how Miley now viewed even something as trivial as acne – her situation meant that she had lost all sense of proportion.

That was why, that morning, a tearful Miley point blank refused to get out of bed. By 2 p.m., a concerned Tish threatened to call her father, who was out of the city due to work commitments, and ask him to fly home. "She wanted to get me out of my bedroom and back in the real world," Miley recalled, "but it wasn't that simple."

Even a visit to a dermatologist failed to offer any magical solution. "I figured: this is Los Angeles. LA doctors had to have all sorts of magical ways to instantly make actors look perfect," Miley observed wryly. "I thought they'd, like, airbrush me in real life with special cover-up that would last until my 20th birthday. Yeah, not so much. If you've ever had acne, you know that there's no instant solution. I walked out of that office even more depressed than I went in."

Realistically, there was little anyone could say to comfort Miley. Telling her that looks were unimportant was a hollow promise, not to mention an inaccurate one – in her industry, they meant everything. Telling her that beauty was defined by inner qualities and not superficial, instantly visible ones, was equally futile – not least because each time she left the house she was hounded by paparazzi fighting to get that all-important photo – in the words of Robbie Williams, celebrities lived their lives through a lens.

Girls like Miley – who had it all and yet felt more discontented than ever – could spend forever searching for the elusive, ambiguous and perhaps even undefinable characteristic that was beauty. Yet over time she would come to learn that a beautiful woman was merely someone who was confident and comfortable in their own skin, and that the peace that radiated as a result of self-acceptance would in itself provide a means to be beautiful.

That said, it was a slow journey for Miley – one which began with the realisation that she was "being a brat". "I couldn't see beyond my own issues," she recalled. "Stardom had changed me. I wasn't Miley any more. I was Hollywood. Something had to shift."

Consequently, she looked to her childhood, recalling how she had been raised visiting churches and hospitals with her father, donating the gifts he'd received on tour to needy children – and those flashbacks gave her a much-needed dose of perspective. Yet no wake-up call was greater than the resolution she made to do her own tour of young people's hospitals, witnessing the change *Hannah Montana* had made to their lives first-hand. On hearing her music, cancer-ravaged children who had been staring defeatedly at the wall waiting to meet death, came alive and smiled for the first time in months.

Now Miley became acutely aware of the things that truly mattered. "One little girl pulling an oxygen monitor came in to meet me," Miley recalled of her first visit to one LA hospital. "She was going through yet another round of chemotherapy. She had no hair remaining and little time to live. [Yet] when I handed her my CD, she said, 'I'm the luckiest girl in the world.' It was so hard to see. She was dying before my eyes."

The gratitude Miley saw was humbling – just one visit from her was precious to these children. Meanwhile another girl named Vanessa, who at just nine years old was terminally ill with cystic fibrosis, became a close friend, someone she would visit in hospital whenever the opportunity arose. Vanessa had even visited the set of *Hannah Montana*, although she was so sensitive that Miley had to wear a mask around her and, due to the "germ factor", she was forbidden even from using her mother's lip gloss.

Despite the gap in age and unusual circumstances surrounding their meeting, the pair quickly formed an intense bond, leading Miley to believe they'd been brought together by divine intervention to heal each other. She would dub Vanessa "the sister God forgot to give me". The day she finally lost her battle for life, Miley was so distraught that she fled the tour bus, despite being "in the middle of nowhere", lay down on the snow-covered ground and began to cry. Then her mother noted something poignant: "You knew she needed you, but it seems like you didn't realise how much you needed her."

Perhaps indeed they'd crossed each other's paths for a reason – Miley had given Vanessa the gift of happiness in what had remained of her short life, while she'd reciprocated by providing some much needed perspective and, in a world of designer brands and bitchiness, had sent her right back down to earth.

"When I met Vanessa," Miley revealed, "all the superficial obsession over my skin and the darkness I'd been feeling fell away. Seeing children suffering was a jolt. How could I think about my skin problems – and all the other self-criticism – when I had so much to be grateful for?"

Finally, to survive in the image-obsessed celebrity culture that she called home, Miley learnt an important lesson about beauty. "Beauty is the enemy," she would declare. "We try to conquer not feeling beautiful all our lives. It's a battle that can't be won. The only way to achieve beauty is to feel it from inside."

Chapter 6

"WE hear your nickname is Smiley!" one MTV reporter joked to a grinning Miley, "so we're going to see if, for a minute, we can stop you from smiling." He'd fail in his efforts that day, as bringing her face to face with a waddling, ample-bodied and semi-naked sumo wrestler live on the show only prompted her to dissolve into fits of giggles. At that point, the world knew nothing of a brave-faced, tight-lipped Miley's inner struggle to achieve and maintain the universal definition of beauty, but she would soon be met by a pain too public to turn away from, and her trademark toothy smile truly would be wiped away from her face.

In an ominous predictor of things to come, the next chapter in Miley's life began with the single 'Nobody's Perfect' – words she would soon come to use in self defence. The song was a taster to promote the double album soundtrack *Hannah Montana 2/Meet Miley Cyrus*, which – on its release on June 26, 2007 – was set to introduce the world to both sides of Miley's dual personality.

For Miley, this moment couldn't have come soon enough. The first time around, to her indignation, she'd been regarded as too young and inexperienced to carry the weight of an album on her own, and a host of other artists had been drafted in for metaphorical hand-holding duties. Originally eclipsed by her father's fame, she'd then experienced invisibility in the shadow of Hannah – a persona the public had falsely regarded as her own. She'd even received letters and packages addressed to Miley, along with a request from each fan to forward the contents to Hannah. The two characters – real and imagined – had begun to masquerade as one and the same and, as the perpetual middle child of the Cyrus family, constantly striving for attention, real-life Miley wanted a piece of the limelight for herself.

Meet Miley Cyrus was set to be the antithesis of the past, allowing her to express herself as a serious recording artist in her own right, independent of the show, and not merely the face of a fictional character whose puppet strings were pulled by agenda-fuelled record label bosses. Shunning pre-created lyrics, she'd even pulled together a series of self-written love songs chronicling the good, the bad and the twisted aspects of her relationship with Nick Jonas. It was an opportunity to rise above the shiny, candy-coated theme songs that were by now synonymous with her name and take the reins to portray to the world who she really was.

However, although the album instantly debuted at number one, selling 326,000 copies in its first week, the reality was starkly different. Despite a fashion line to her name and her face now adorning everything from T-shirts, singing dolls and alarm clocks to toothbrushes and sticker sets – and of course national TV – the only spot Miley couldn't be found in was US radio. With her Disney roots all too prominent, it seemed that, to presenters, she fell firmly into the tween entertainment category – a child to be scoffed at by anyone over the age of 12, rather than a serious musical contender. "We had the number one album of the year and nobody seemed to pay any attention in the mainstream radio world," Gary Marsh illustrated. "They didn't care."

It seemed as though the legacy of *Hannah Montana* was now both a blessing and a curse. Miley was now a novelty act, although, by all accounts, a very well paid one – by the end of the year, she'd see her name in *Forbes* magazine as one of the Top 20 Highest Earning Young Superstars, credited with $3.5 million per year to her name. Plus, fortunately, she wasn't banished from radio altogether – in fact, a duet she performed with her father, 'Ready Steady, Don't Go', would soon become a playlist favourite. Appearing on Billy Ray's 10th album, *Home At Last*, she netted him his first international chart entry since 1992.

The song, which peaked at a respectable number 37 on the US *Billboard* chart, was written when Billy Ray heard she'd landed the part of Hannah and would be moving to LA, but was as yet unsure whether he'd be joining her. It expressed his struggle to accept his daughter's growing autonomy and the conflict between his instinct to proudly support her success and help her on the way and the other, opposing, instinct to protect her from the evils of showbiz and rein her in.

When he'd spotted the 'Atheists United' sign on the LA motorway, it had sent a shiver of foreboding down his spine – a fear for his daughter's future and the corruption he suspected would lie ahead. On the surface, things had fallen into place and Miley's dreams of fame had come true, but due to his own insecurity, Billy Ray perceived the opposite – that everything, including life as he knew it, had "fallen apart". For a brief moment, he'd had the urge to turn the truck around and take Miley back to the comfortable familiarity of Tennessee. Yet to avoid suffocating his daughter, and to allow her to grow and develop unimpeded, he would have to cut the invisible umbilical cord of possessive parental love, brush his fears aside and allow Miley to make life's decisions on her own.

A real-life dilemma for many parents, the song struck a chord with listeners. It also benefited from additional exposure when its July release coincided with a *Hannah Montana* episode where the duet was performed as part of the story.

As it would soon emerge, Billy Ray had been right to be concerned about his daughter, although it would take time for the cracks to show.

By contrast, 2007 was the year that Miley Mania reached its peak – and when she announced a three-month concert tour to touch every corner of the USA and Canada, the response was unprecedented. After tickets sold out in a matter of seconds, contests were held for fans to compete for the few seats that remained – with jaw-dropping consequences.

Rugged macho men were willing to transform themselves into cross-dressers with red lipstick, blonde wigs and high heels, to win tickets for their pleading daughters, while one man stood motionlessly touching a stone statue for 11 hours to claim the prize. Meanwhile normally sensible adults camped out for days at a time. Those who weren't successful were exploited by merciless touts who resold tickets in bulk on eBay for up to 70 times the original retail price. Even standing tickets were trading hands for up to $4,000 a pair.

Joe Freeman, the vice president of Ticketmaster, stated, "Hell hath no fury like the parent of a child throwing a tantrum. People who have been in this business a long time are watching what's happening and they say there hasn't been a demand of this level or intensity since the Beatles or Elvis Presley."

Of course it had all been said before – but this time it seemed there was scarcely a limit to what the public would do to satisfy their Miley Mania. This was demonstrated in sinister circumstances when one six-year-old girl wrote an essay claiming her soldier father had lost his life during a roadside bombing in Iraq, a heartfelt story which netted her four free tickets to the New York show courtesy of a local department store – only for the story to later be exposed as false. Her remorseless mother would simply claim, "We did what we could to win."

There was a more positive side to the situation too, with another girl selling her tickets to pay for vital medical surgery that she would otherwise have been unable to afford. Overall, however, tensions ran high, with enraged followers who'd signed up for paid memberships to Miley's fan club to gain perks such as priority access to tickets claiming they'd been duped. Insisting that the money they'd invested counted for nothing, they argued that such a small percentage of people had been able to buy tickets that it was "more of a lottery than a realistic benefit of a club membership". Some would even launch lawsuits against her management. Looking on in horror, Miley would exclaim, "Wow, I really have to be good . . . this is [fans'] one chance to see the show and it's the one night I'm going to be here, so it has to be perfect."

With the priciest tickets setting back the average American household two weeks' wages, the burden of public expectation had become unbearable. Regrettably, Miley's followers had placed her on such a lofty pedestal that she was bound to fail. She was widely criticised for using a body double for a mere "one to two minutes" of each show, which her publicist explained was "in order to allow Miley to remove the Hannah wig and costume and transform into Miley for her solo set". Unsurprisingly, the double – a vocally untrained backing dancer – lip-synched for the remainder of the song, 'Got The Party', but this momentarily gave rise to speculation about whether the real Miley sang any of the concert live at all.

Even worse, about a week into the tour, she almost broke her leg. Fast-paced choreography during a rendition of 'I Got Nerve' had required "four big, strong male dancers [to] throw me in the air and catch me", but on this occasion she was thrown so forcefully that she came down faster than expected and fell right into their arms. The audience barely saved her embarrassment. "I was up and dancing again in a split second, but not before I heard the audience gasp," she shuddered. "Then a whisper went around the stadium as everyone turned to the person sitting next to them to say, 'She fell!' . . . My worst nightmare." Terrified of falling again, she begged director Kenny Ortega, who'd also developed tours for the Cheetah Girls and *High School Musical*, to drop the move from the routine, but her pleas fell on deaf ears. Eventually Tish was forced to step in to coach Miley through her fear.

Then, mid-tour, in December 2007, Miley experienced her first heartbreak, as she and Nick mutually decided to bring their relationship to an end. Neither ruled out a reconciliation, but Nick felt they'd grown apart and that it was time to move on. When two partners fall out of love, they rarely do so at the same time and Miley, who still harboured a deep attachment, was devastated. "My life felt like it had ground to a halt," she recalled, "but the rest of the world kept right on rolling. I was on tour. People were counting on me [yet] I wrote 10 pages, front and back, about why I loved my Prince Charming, how I would wait for him, why we needed to be together. When I love someone, I love them with everything in me. But when the love's not there any more, what do you do?"

As if the ending wasn't awkward enough, the Jonas Brothers were one of the support acts at each show, meaning Miley was forced to come face-to-face with her ex on a daily basis. The tour had become bittersweet for her and yet, at all costs, the show had to go on. Ultimately the three-month stint would gross an impressive $54 million, while a dollar from each ticket was donated to a cancer charity, the City of Hope National Medical Center, earning over $2 million for the cause.

Next came the 3D film version of the tour, *The Hannah Montana And Miley Cyrus: Best Of Both Worlds Concert,* which brought the gigging experience to movie theatres as well. Interspersing concert footage with backstage interviews and rehearsals, it was originally billed as a one-week only show, which quickly extended to a further week due to "exceptional demand" and, before long, it clinched the number one spot in the box office charts. Earning over $42,000 per theatre – double the expected amount – Disney then made the decision to run the film indefinitely. It quickly became the highest-selling concert film of all time, with a gross profit of $70.6 million – a feat that was only surpassed with the release of the late Michael Jackson's *This Is It*, which screened the final rehearsals of the deceased star.

The record-breaking tour had spelt immense success, but with it came immense responsibility – appropriate or otherwise. As if the pressure on Miley's shoulders wasn't already enough, it seemed she had been placed on a pure white pedestal of unwavering morals, committed chastity and devout religious beliefs – a tall order for any 15-year-old, let alone one who, in the public's eyes, was located somewhere between the Virgin Mary and Mother Teresa on the morality scale. Miley hadn't assumed the position of role model entirely by choice – rather, the public had moulded her into it – but, by implication, she was now parenting a nation's children. Like Britney before her, she was expected to be a God-fearing, moral-upholding philanthropist who, in spite of vast fame and celebrity, was never selfish or egotistical and thought only of others.

A people-pleaser at heart, Miley didn't disappoint, earnestly assuring the media of her good intentions. "I look up to and idolise all the Disney girls, [especially Hilary Duff, because she's] saying that it is OK to be a good girl," she told MTV. "Like, that's cool! [In my] 3D movie, you get to see that it's not fake, it's not just being at an interview and saying, 'Yeah, I wanna be a good girl!' It's really showing you making right decisions in the movie."

Yet years later, she would claim the exact opposite – that she believed everyone knew her carefully constructed 'good girl' persona was fake. If so, it was an ever-increasing strain to maintain the façade. Meanwhile the public's perception of Miley was so unrealistic that it had become inevitable that she'd fall from grace – and, in the spring of 2008, that was exactly what happened.

The first departure from the squeaky clean image began in April, when a hacker accessed her email account and made scantily clad photos of her public. In one, she was seen draped over the lap of one of her producer's sons, with a bare midriff on show, while another featured her mischievously flashing a hint of a bright green bra.

The pictures were playful and mildly provocative and, had she not been representing a multimillion dollar corporation that thrived on its squeaky-clean image, they might well have been dismissed as a tame prototype of the average teenager's Facebook wall. Yet with the help of slightly over-exuberant tabloid journalism, they were re-invented as 'racy', with the *LA Times* insisting the exposure would "taint her image" – possibly permanently.

Instead of rebuking the individual who'd committed an illegal act by hacking into her private emails, the media instead concentrated on Miley's alleged misconduct, obliging her to make a grovelling apology for her actions behind closed doors. Gary Marsh delivered a backhanded compliment, pointedly remarking – perhaps as a reminder to the girl herself – that although "being the most famous 15-year-old in the world is exciting", it would also be fraught with responsibility and that Miley understood "the trust kids and parents have in her". As he'd envisaged, some parents were distinctly unimpressed, with one asking plaintively, "With her career being so hot, and being on top of the world, why would she even take these pictures?"

It was evident that, had her privacy not been violated, she would not have intended the snapshots to go public, but nonetheless she dutifully delivered the apology Middle America had been waiting for. "The pictures of me on the internet were silly, inappropriate shots," she released a statement to say. "I appreciate all the support of my fans and hope they understand that along the way I am going to make mistakes and I am not perfect. I never intended for any of this to happen and I am truly sorry if I have disappointed anyone."

"Most of all," she added, "I have let myself down. I will learn from my mistakes and trust my support team. My family and my faith will guide me through my life's journey."

Yet was it too little, too late? The incident had rocked Miley's reputation and, as soon as the scandal became public, the original *Hannah Montana* soundtrack plummeted out of the Top 10 in the *Billboard* chart for the first time since its release two years previously.

The promise not to let her fans down again might have smoothed the waters temporarily. Yet just two months later, Miley was in trouble again. This time around, she'd been interviewed by *Vanity Fair*, which had recruited Annie Leibovitz – one of the world's most famous photographers, who wasn't herself if she wasn't pushing the boundaries – to capture her on camera.

Annie's extensive back catalogue included a stint as the on-tour photographer for the Rolling Stones back in the seventies, while, in the same year as Miley's birth, she'd snapped a heavily pregnant Demi Moore in the nude – a shot that would become iconic the world over. The same decade, she'd persuaded Kate Moss to strip off in a hotel bedroom while her then boyfriend Johnny Depp lay provocatively between her legs. However, perhaps her most famous image of all was one of a naked John Lennon in a fetal position, clinging to his fully clothed wife, Yoko Ono. The poignancy about this image was the timing – just five hours later, he was shot dead, making the shoot his last ever public outing.

'Boring' wasn't a word in Annie's vocabulary, but 'controversial' certainly was, making her a risky choice of creative partner for a disgraced Disney girl desperate to redeem herself. The *Vanity Fair* feature was to be her first cover shoot, and indeed first major interview, since the last set of risqué photos had emerged, so surely the last thing she'd want to do was pose for another – or was it?

Annie had formerly shot Miley's godmother, Dolly Parton, tastefully – not to mention that she'd have both her parents on set, combined with the army of two dozen paparazzi who awaited her outside. The end result had everyone's seal of approval – except, of course, for the public.

When the shoot emerged, it had featured photos of Miley and her father together, including one where she was reclining on his lap – and the pair were instantly blighted by incest allegations. While the poses were not uncommon between lovers, the body language between them was anything but sexual, signalling an overreaction on the part of the protesters. Yet the photo that ignited the most fury – along with accusations of exploitation and paedophilia – was one of Miley seemingly naked beneath a blanket, her bare back exposed and her hair tangled and tousled, as if fresh from a passionate encounter. While the face and eyes conveyed an expression of youth and innocence and did not communicate sexuality at all – and *Vanity Fair* staff were quick to point out that she'd been wearing lingerie underneath the blanket – her pose revealed a large portion of bare back, giving rise to concern that the shots had sexualised a minor. In photography terms, they would have been described as depicting "implied nudity".

In the midst of the furore that followed, the internationally renowned feminist Germaine Greer – who'd infamously claimed that Cheryl Cole could not be a feminist because she wasn't ample-bottomed enough – insisted matter-of-factly that the exploitation of children for sexual kicks was routine and unremarkable. "In western art, most of the women portrayed semi-clad or totally nude are children," she declared. "When Lucian Freud paints girl children, nobody cares."

Greer, who, oddly, counted herself as the author of a lavishly illustrated book titled *The Boy*, celebrating the "short-lived beauty" of the young male, continued, "Kate Moss has been able to earn millions only as long as she could continue to project the body image of a 13-year-old."

Needless to say, this reasoning was unlikely to exonerate Miley in the eyes of her fans. She'd gone on record at the time of the shoot to say she felt the finished product looked "pretty, really natural and really artsy", but had then fuelled the rumours of exploitation when she'd added, "[Besides] you can't say no to Annie. She gets this puppy dog look and you're like, 'OK . . .' "

Building on this in a swift bid for damage limitation, Disney released a statement claiming, "Unfortunately a situation was created to deliberately manipulate a 15-year-old in order to sell magazines."

Yet a spokesperson for *Vanity Fair* angrily countered, "Miley's parents and/or minders were on the set all day. Since the photo was taken digitally, they saw it on the shoot and everyone thought it was a beautiful and natural portrait of Miley."

Annie too would defend the image, insisting that a fine art photo had been misinterpreted to stir up publicity. "Miley and I looked at fashion photographs together and we discussed the picture in that context before we shot it," her own statement revealed. "The photograph is a simple, classic portrait shot with very little make-up and I think it is very beautiful."

Yet media sources, referencing Miley's friendship with good-girls-gone-bad Britney Spears and Lindsay Lohan, painted the episode as the start of a meltdown. Ironically, much of the negative publicity was focused not on the photographer who put her in a compromising position, but on Miley herself – in spite of the fact that she was a minor – for allowing it. The furore prompted Justin Timberlake to comment that the media deliberately targeted "wholesome" celebrities and then, through exaggeration, built revenue-boosting scandal around them. Jason Earles, Miley's on-screen brother, concurred, "Like any 15-year-old, she is not going to make the best decisions. When you get to her level of popularity, it's so easy to find little chinks in the armour and try to tear her down."

And, in a curious form of airbrushing in reverse, when chinks couldn't be found, they were often invented. For example, the US magazine *J-14* – perhaps inspired by the teen single mother scandal surrounding Britney's sister Jamie Lynn Spears – published a fictitious interview claiming that Miley had "accidentally" become pregnant. It cattily added a false admission from her that she had since gained five pounds.

The story was later retracted by the editor, who claimed an undisclosed employee of the magazine had incorrectly added it to the news page at the last minute. The world was waiting for her to crash and burn, but she found an unexpected source of support in *Hannah Montana* creator Michael Poryes. "They don't give her a break for being able to go through the aches and pains of being an adolescent," he sympathised. "Everyone has the right to go through being an adolescent. [The public] blow everything out of proportion and a little misstep becomes the biggest tragedy that ever struck mankind!"

That was certainly the reaction of Brooke Shields, the former model, actress and wife to tennis star Andre Agassi, who'd made several cameo appearances on Miley's show as her late mother. While she was a self-modelled pariah of Christian moral conduct, "Thou shalt not judge others" was clearly not a commandment in her repertoire. The star, who'd remained a virgin until age 22, explaining that there was "no way I'd ever have sex just for the pleasure of it", echoed the connotations of paedophilia and expressed concern about who was advising Miley. The biggest irony, however, was that, at the age of 12, Brooke had appeared nude on camera herself. In the 1978 film *Pretty Baby*, she'd masqueraded as a child prostitute rescued from a New Orleans brothel by a photographer who then embarked on an illegal sexual affair with her.

Regardless, the criticism had felt like a betrayal to Miley, who'd treated Brooke and her young daughter Rowan like members of her own family. By now the *Vanity Fair* website had crashed due to the sheer volume of readers logging on to see what the fuss was about and, in a desperate bid to stop the criticism coming, Miley issued her second dramatic public apology of the year. Telling *People* magazine that she felt she'd failed to live up to her purpose as a performer – "to make people happy" – she claimed, "I was so honoured and thrilled to work with Annie. I took part in a photo shoot that was supposed to be 'artistic' and now, seeing the photographs and reading the story, I feel so embarrassed."

Yet that apology wasn't enough for conservative TV presenter Bill O'Reilly, who modelled himself as a "devout Catholic traditionalist". As part of a *Fox News* bulletin he was presenting, Miley became the subject of fierce speculation over whether she'd simultaneously debased Disney and destroyed her career. "There are some estimates that say she could be a billion dollar brand," Lea Goldman, features editor of *Marie Claire*, mused on the show, "but not with this on her back . . . the tween merchandising gig is where the money's at." O'Reilly would nod in agreement, adding, "Who's picking up the bill for [tweens]? The parents are the gate-keepers. They say, 'No, this is not who I want my kids emulating.'"

While O'Reilly would regularly profess concern for Miley on his show, however, comically making public appeals to her father to safeguard her virginity, the motives for his interest were sometimes called into question – especially when his background suggested he might not be the squeaky clean Christian he portrayed himself to be. In 2004, a female *Fox News* presenter filed a lawsuit against him accusing him of "offensive touching" and sexual harassment, including unwelcome explicit conversation about vibrators, threesomes, phone sex and masturbation.

Among those who believed O'Reilly to be a hypocrite was an anonymous New Jersey parent, who dismissed the incriminating photo as much ado about nothing. "This is a tasteful shot which reveals less 15-year-old flesh than you can see as a matter of routine on any summer beach," she defended. "She isn't showing any more of her back than if she were wearing a backless dress. If people really think the picture is provocative, they should get out more, or examine what is going on in their own heads. They remind me of fundamentalists who insist on women being covered from head to foot to cover their sinfulness, when the only sinful thing is what they are thinking about the women." She would add that, after all, in South Carolina, 14 was the age of sexual consent.

So it seemed that not everyone was shaking their heads in disapproval – and, once the initial embarrassment had died down, Miley re-emerged as defiant. "Every career thing that I do can't be perfect," she reasoned to *Billboard*. "I think that just makes me even more relatable. I don't think people will look at me any differently because they're like, 'You know what, I'm going to do stupid stuff too and I'm going to make mistakes and that's fine.' It still hurts when I think about it, but you know what, it doesn't mean that you can't move on."

Not if the public had anything to do with it – but by the time rumours of a lesbian affair hit the news-stands, a weary Miley had upgraded her stance to unrepentant, contemptuous disdain. This time the incriminating visual had depicted Miley and a friend sharing a Twizzler sweet cradled between their mouths.

Surely, the media questioned, someone must have painfully betrayed her trust – after all, how else could such a risqué photo have surfaced? "It was me," she retorted, casually. "On Myspace. For me, it was like, 'That's two girls. It's not a big deal.' But they got spread around. Like, someone copied and pasted and said, 'Ohmigod, look at this, blah, blah, blah.' Everyone's like, 'Maybe she'll learn her lesson this time.' *Nope.*"

Growing from a child to an adult in public meant there were bound to be transitional changes and yet parents had become so attached to the fantasy image they'd built up as to who Miley was and what she represented that they seemed to view any deviation from this as a betrayal – both of her true self and of those who'd supported her. In reality, she was undergoing a period of immense and dizzyingly rapid development and doubtless knew as little about defining who she was as the outsiders who passed judgment on her.

However, the situation wasn't all bad. It might have flawed her relationship with parents, but tweens grow up and Miley's audience – many of whom were at the age where loud and defiant rebellion against parents wasn't just de rigueur but almost obligatory – were growing up alongside her.

Rather than her transgressions damaging her career, then, could raunchy, racy Miley actually be worth more than her good-girl twin? According to the *LA Times*, which published a piece declaring, "All Eyes Are On Miley", the lucky photographer who captured her first public kiss on camera could net up to $150,000 for the evidence – and potentially even more if her love interest happened to be famous. Meanwhile even pictures of her engaged in an activity as mundane as going to church had increased almost six-fold in value. According to Francis Navarre, owner of the X17 photo agency, the *Vanity Fair* stir had been the cause. "It used to be $300 for a shot," he explained, "and now it's $2,000 . . . we are watching her and if she goes out of town, we try to follow her." Quite simply, she now had the type of notoriety that sold newspapers.

The paparazzi, described as a "scrum of ferocious man dogs who camp outside her home", duly began to follow her with even more intensity than before. Even a simple shopping trip could attract three or four dozen camera-toting hangers-on. Yet if she could handle the attention, it could re-launch her with even more success than before. Could she have been heading for a Kate Moss style comeback? The catwalk queen had lost a few lucrative modelling contracts herself in the wake of photos that depicted her with cocaine, but within weeks she was milking the notoriety and her new rock'n'roll image – propelled further by her relationship with Pete Doherty – was worth more financially than ever before.

In the case of Miley's audience, the effect of scandal might be even more pronounced. "It's really difficult when your core audience is preteen," mused *Pollstar* editor Gary Bongiovanni, "because as those kids get older, what was beyond cool to them one moment, is something they won't even admit they were fans of three years later."

Reinventing herself as an edgy teenager, then, might be a way to rekindle her lost followers' interest. Some TV and radio hosts speculated that the scandal was a deliberate and calculated bid to move beyond the allegedly short shelf life of *Hannah Montana* and remain successful and current, while others saw the events as a natural and inevitable progression. Either way, it could not be denied that she was now providing intriguingly mixed signals. In conversation with *TV Guide,* she professed a passion for the adult-themed series *Sex And The City*, while in the same interview, she listed the Bible as the number one item she could not live without. Readers also learnt that she'd started to wear a purity ring – a symbol of her commitment to shunning premarital sex. Yet no event demonstrated her transition to adulthood better than the release of a brand new single.

At the time, Miley was still desperate to win Nick Jonas back, even posting a photo of herself online wearing a necklace that spelt out his name in large wooden blocks – and yet releasing a song titled '7 Things (I Hate About You)' probably wasn't the best place to start.

It was to be the debut single for her third album – fittingly titled *Breakout* – and it was symbolic of her further transition into an independent artist.

Now the lyrics came from her own soul, detailing authentic relationship dilemmas such as the frustration she'd felt when Nick simultaneously made her want to both laugh and cry. Although she loathed some aspects of him with a passion, she couldn't help loving him with equal fervor – and so the heartache began.

Plus, by publicly identifying him as her beau, she'd guaranteed even more stormy weather to come. Fearing it would impact on his heart-throb status if he was no longer single and equally believing, not unreasonably, that media attention was the kiss of death for a budding relationship, Nick had made a pact with Miley from the beginning to keep their romance secret.

At the time, she'd been happy to comply – after all, both of them had a mutual understanding of what it felt like to be manipulated by the industry and coerced into over-disclosure. For example, Nick and his brothers had each worn purity rings since the age of 11 – and as an anti-sex pledge was an unusual vow for a young boy to take, let alone one who had groupies at his fingertips, it had attracted an overwhelming amount of media attention. "I remember this interview with this guy whose entire agenda was to focus on the rings," Nick would recall later. "He kept pushing the subject and when we insisted that we didn't want to talk about it, he told us, 'I can write whatever I want,' which terrified us. We didn't know any better and we just wanted to make people happy. Now I know I don't have to answer any questions I don't want to. Like, why do you even care about my 15-year-old brother's sex life?!"

A lesson well learnt, he'd since decided that when anything came into his life that was precious, it needed to be preserved and protected by keeping it hidden. Miley, of course, was no exception and, due to her own run-in with the press, he'd thought she'd been on exactly the same page. Yet when the relationship started to turn sour, she'd felt the urge to vent her feelings – and thanks to the track's accompanying video, there would be absolutely no ambiguity as to who Miley was directing her anger towards.

She and director Brett Ratner had leafed through a box of souvenirs she'd stored under her bed as a sentimental reminder of Miley and Nick's time together, from dirty socks to Polaroid photos – and then she stumbled across the diabetes necklace he'd given her as a gift. The pendant –

designed to alert passers-by to the sufferer's need for medical attention should they fall unconscious due to insulin deficiency – would adorn her neck in the video. As Nick had been a vocal spokesperson for diabetes – in fact, he'd even written a track, 'A Little Bit Longer', about his experiences living with the condition – and he and Miley had regularly been spotted out together, albeit posturing as friends, the pieces of the puzzle began to fall into place.

Yet Miley would remove every remaining shred of uncertainty when she publicly named and shamed him in interviews as the man who'd broken her heart. "I'm very disappointed in Miley," Nick had retorted. "I can't see the good in her taking the relationship public. The song and her behaviour makes me really sad."

That wasn't to say he was above featuring her in songs – his own single, 'Burning Up', hit radio stations the same month as '7 Things', in June 2008, and it was partly inspired by Miley. What was more, he inflamed the tension between them by featuring his rebound girl, Selena Gomez, in the video. The Jonas Brothers album that followed soon after also referenced Miley on the guilt-ridden 'Sorry', a track about "broken hearts and last goodbyes". Finally 'Love Bug', which he'd secretly written with her prior to their break-up, was a product of the pair articulating to each other their experiences of falling in love – before they knew it, the lyrics had been written and although it now seemed things might be over for good, he'd still wanted to document the memories.

That said, he'd done so subtly – in stark contrast to Miley's own disclosures. "Our relationship has been damaged," she would admit to *Nylon* of the lingering friendship they shared, "because he wanted everything super private. When I opened up about it, he felt out of his comfort zone and it became awkward."

Before long even she was sick of discussing it and was beginning to understand the merits of privacy, confessing, "Some [interviews are] fake because people ask me questions I can't answer . . . They'll ask, 'What was your inspiration for '7 Things'?' You already know the answer, everyone knows the answer, so why do you ask me? They're trying to get me upset, or make me uncomfortable, because that makes a 'hot' interview."

That said, the publicity helped Miley to revive her flagging career and, when the album followed on July 22, it peaked at number one on the

Billboard chart. *Meet Miley Cyrus* had been a mere introduction, while *Breakout* – her first release totally unassociated with the *Hannah Montana* name – aimed to definitively "show everyone what Miley Cyrus is all about". It was overwhelming to detach herself from the safe, familiar innocence that had earned her the status of America's sweetheart – risking that, beneath the façade, fans wouldn't like who she really was – and yet a chance conversation with Cyndi Lauper at the 2008 Grammy Awards had armed her with the confidence she needed to branch out afresh. "Don't be scared of anything," she'd told Miley. "People waste their lives being scared. Lasso the moon – but don't do it because someone tells you it's the right idea."

As a symbol of appreciation for the advice, Miley recorded a cover of her idol's 1983 hit 'Girls Just Wanna Have Fun'. The album's other highlights included the title track, 'Breakout' – a song originally intended for Katy Perry's sophomore album, *One Of The Boys*, but which never made the cut. However Katy's version would be incorporated into the song as backing vocals.

Miley, who'd written on all but two of the tracks, sought to illustrate that she was not merely more grown up, but that she had new-found depth as well. "No matter how long what I'm doing here lasts," she declared, "I want to be a songwriter for the rest of my life. I love it and it's my escape. I just hope this record showcases that – more than anything – I'm a writer."

Although at first glance, tracks like 'Bottom Of The Ocean' – originally an ode to Lyric and Melody, the deceased goldfish of her childhood – might have seemed puerile and shallow, the song was actually a metaphorical way of putting the painful experiences of a failed relationship to rest. "It was about so much more than my silly fish," Miley recalled. "It's saying if there's someone you've loved, but for some reason you can't love them any more, you have to take your feelings, scoop them out and put them at the bottom of the ocean. Hide them there, carefully and respectfully, in the one place they can't ever be found. 'Bottom Of The Ocean' is a goodbye song, a love song – you'd never think it was about fish!"

Those seemingly boring goldfish had also taught a valuable, if unexpected, lesson. "Since then, any time I want to write a song, I tell myself, 'Think outside of the bowl.' It's a reminder not to get stuck," she added, "not to see the world outside through a glass cage."

The symbolism was obvious. Miley was no longer a pretty pet, caged up to be admired while under her keeper's control – she'd flown the comfortable, if unexciting, nest that was *Hannah Montana* and, while she hadn't abandoned the show, she wanted to venture further than its confines. This captured the spirit of what *Breakout* was all about.

True to the album's theme, she began experimenting with new projects. On *The Miley And Mandy Show*, for example, she turned amateur TV producer, teaming up with her close friend and back-up dancer Mandy Jiroux to create a playfully self-edited YouTube series. It gave fans a front row seat to the private life of Miley, who in her down time was surprisingly unselfconscious and down to earth. Unafraid to be silly, the pair would crack jokes, sing Christmas carols together and even conduct slapstick interviews with Miley's dogs, all the while casually dressed in T-shirts, tracksuits and jeans. This spelt that Miley had finally conquered her awkwardness about her image, as she was happy to appear on screen without her war paint.

However she was reprimanded for posting an episode that appeared to poke fun at Selena Gomez, interspersing parts of her love rival's music video with the YouTube show and talking about her with mocking undertones. It was speculated that the digs were made in retaliation for Selena's relationship with Nick and that Miley hadn't yet moved on.

Indeed, if tracks such as 'Full Circle' were anything to go by – about two people who were "always going to come back together, no matter what anyone says" – she hadn't given up on him and still secretly harboured the hope that they'd one day rekindle their affair.

Provocative YouTube videos aside, Miley had also been flying the flag for environmentalism. She'd been nagging her father repeatedly for a car, using the time he gave her a minor head injury at age two, in a collision with a tree branch, as material for emotional blackmail. Yet when she was finally gifted her mother's hand-me-down Porsche, she almost instantly traded it in for a greener model – a less gas-guzzling Prius. A humbled Billy Ray commented that the experience had taught him that "sometimes your kids are more conscientious and intelligent than you are". The theme also mirrored her album track 'Wake Up America', which urged others to take care of the Earth for the benefit of subsequent generations.

In her downtime, Miley would also lend her voice to the computer-animated film *Boly*, which would eventually be released in November. She didn't merely provide the voice of the character Penny, but also co-wrote a duet for the film with John Travolta, titled 'I Thought I Lost You'. Her efforts would even earn her a Golden Globe nomination.

Yet no matter how many new career achievements Miley could boast, they all seemed to pale in comparison to the public's continued appetite for scandal. Although she continued to donate to cancer charities and visit sick children, and even transformed her 16th birthday party into a non-profit ticketed event – Miley's Sweet 16: Join The Celebration – to raise money for an organisation called Youth Service America, earning it a million dollars, her more kind-hearted gestures were scarcely reported.

Regardless of how many good deeds she did, nothing would change the simple financial equation that made the media world go round – it was notoriety that sold newspapers, not niceties. Many seemed to derive pleasure from watching those who seemed to have it all crash and burn before their eyes – it perhaps gave the less fortunate a sadistic thrill that distracted them from the banality of their own lives. Over the years, celebrity-bashing had become almost a blood sport – a way of pseudo-legitimately projecting resentment onto the famous for the dubious crime of simply being more wealthy and successful than most. What was more, with Britney's recent admission to a psychiatric ward and Lindsay's stint in rehab and lesbian affairs, there was no shortage of fallen angels for the public to sink their teeth into.

Asked if being a role model was difficult, Miley would respond, "It's definitely challenging – you always have someone looking at you with a little microscope trying to figure out what you're doing wrong" – and indeed the micro-analytical scrutiny of her faults knew almost no bounds. After an innocent remark that she and her former boyfriend had enjoyed watching the animated children's film *Alice In Wonderland* – enjoyed by hundreds of thousands of young people every year – she was criticised for, by implication, advocating ecstasy. The story's hallucination-led plot was believed to have narcotic connotations, although author Lewis Carroll had penned the original book in the 1800s – long before ecstasy had become an officially recognised drug.

Next, Miley faced another phone-hacking scandal, where photos of her in the shower, intended for Nick, had been passed around. Rumours began that Miley's parents had been so enraged by the leak that they'd disowned her, while others countered that she was seeking emancipation from them and considering getting a court-backed "divorce", just as Frances Bean had done to escape from her allegedly abusive mother, Courtney Love.

The gossip took on an especially unpleasant tone when one hacker went as far as hijacking Miley's official website and reporting the false news that she was dead. Uploading a fake video alleging that she'd been killed in a drink-driving crash, the hacker added an audio clip of her song 'Goodbye' to play in the background. Unusually the culprit was little more than a child himself – a 19-year-old who'd also hacked into the pages of Chris Brown, Rihanna and Fallout Boy. As chilling as it was to hear a news report that chronicled her own death, Miley had by now developed a thick skin – and this time around there wasn't the same burning sense of humiliation and powerlessness. "I [now keep] my heart guarded," she explained simply, "to make sure I don't get hurt."

Her birthday would afford her a little time to escape the media circus and reacquaint herself with family – the people who she felt truly mattered in life. She'd been accused of turning her party into a money spinner despite the fact that, as all proceeds went to charity, she hadn't earned a penny.

However subsequently, on the actual date, she was doing something with which few could find fault – hosting the American Music Awards with her father. Over the same period, she also found time to collaborate with Trace on his showbiz ambitions. As her half-brother, he didn't share the Cyrus genes, but nonetheless he felt a strong affinity for music, having grown up around it, and, together with his band Metro Station, had a hankering for "world domination".

His journey had begun when Billy Ray – who affectionately regarded Trace as his own flesh and blood, had taken him on the set of *Hannah Montana*, where he met Mason Musso, a fellow aspiring musician. Mason was there to visit his brother Mitchel, who played Miley's friend Oliver on the show – and, besides both having showbiz siblings, he and Trace found they had a lot in common. They formed a band in which both sang and played guitar and soon recruited Blake Healey from Synthetic Joy on keyboard, synth and bass. Drummer Anthony Improgo, almost a decade their senior, followed. The latter had initially felt "creepy" at the prospect of socialising with 17-year-olds and, after doing a double take at the quality of the trio's songs, had needed to incredulously question his housemate, "Are these guys as good as I think they are?"

However, once he was on board, the group was quickly signed to Columbia Records. They'd stayed in the shadows to start with as, like Miley, they were keen to be recognised not for their connections, but on their own merit. Trace had been so secretive that the record label hadn't known he was a Cyrus until just before they signed the contract, while, were it not for a chance remark made by Mason, even Anthony would have been oblivious.

While he was afraid of accusations that he'd hitched a free ride on the coat-tails of his father and sister, there was another reason for him to distance himself from Disney – as teenagers, "all we wanted to write about was sex". Having outgrown the tween market, they'd hoped to avoid acquiring the patronising tag of "parent friendly". There was little chance of that, when their biggest song, 'Seventeen Forever', dealt with fighting the desire to be sexually involved with a child. Trace would later elaborate that it was "about wanting to be in a relationship with a girl who's under-age so bad".

While the theme might have raised eyebrows, Columbia had high hopes for them. In September 2007, they'd released a self-titled debut album, only for the first two singles, 'Kelsey' and 'Control', to flop. By March of the following year, however, their third offering, 'Shake It', had made it to the Top 10 of the *Billboard* charts. Now they were about to film the video for 'Seventeen Forever', the song that had got them signed.

Now that Trace had demonstrated he could attain success without reference to the family name, he was more relaxed about revealing his true identity – and Miley, who'd spoken of how she hated for her brother to be on tour without her, stepped in and insisted on a cameo role in the video. Set within the grounds of a carnival taken over by a group of teenagers, it depicted Trace about to score with a love interest, until Miley interrupted by bumping into him in a dodgem car. Meanwhile Billy Ray would appear as one of the carnival performers, encouraging revellers to see the show.

Ironically, the news that Miley was collaborating with her brother's band barely featured in the news at all – reporters were far more interested in shock value. (Interestingly they failed to pick up on the potentially explosive story that Trace – by now heavily tattooed and the visual signature of rebellion – had been singing about a wish for illicit love with an underage girl, while Miley's cameo ran in the background.) When the single was released on December 13, it attracted very little attention, and when Miley spent New Year's Eve performing at a small and unprofitable concert to raise awareness for breast cancer – in the gym of Beckham High School in Irvine, California – that story too failed to trend.

Her appearance at the Kids' Inaugural Concert in Washington D.C. on January 19, 2009, however, couldn't be ignored. A committed Democrat like her father, she'd joined him for renditions of new track 'The Climb' and 'See You Again' to celebrate Barack Obama's Presidential Inauguration. Meanwhile First Lady Michelle and her daughters, Malia and Sasha, had watched eagerly from the wings.

However, although the occasion was widely reported, even this publicity had slightly negative undertones – rumours circulated first that Obama's girls would play a guest role on *Hannah Montana* and then that it had been called off over his disapproval of Miley's behaviour. Magazines then added that model Cindy Crawford had forbidden her young daughter from even watching, claiming it would teach her prematurely how to be "sassy". Cindy herself spoke out to refute the gossip and insist she was a fan, but suffice to say Miley was no longer a fan of the media – and it looked like her February 12 single 'Fly On The Wall' had been well timed.

"It's about how [the media] think they know everything about me, when they don't," she revealed. "They want to be a fly on my wall and watch me 24/7." Illustrating that she was ill at ease with the constant attention, the video became a spoof of Michael Jackson's own iconic video 'Thriller'. The original had featured Michael terrifying a lady friend after a full-moon-lit date at the movie theatre by turning into a zombie at the end of the night. She had run away squealing, while Michael and an army of other zombies followed in hot pursuit. In Miley's case, her biggest fear was not fiendish, outlandish creatures, but persistent photographers.

The video begins in exactly the same way as 'Thriller', with Miley and a love interest leaving the cinema. She assumes she's incognito on a relaxed date but, just as a full moon peeks out from the clouds, her worst nightmare comes to life – her boyfriend starts a violent coughing fit before transforming before her eyes into a camera-armed paparazzi photographer. As she flees in horror, he protests, "Miley, come here! I just want a couple of shots!" Betrayed, she continues to run from a now growing mob of photographers. Eventually they surround her, only to frighten her even more when they break into their own synchronised dance moves to the tune of the song. Her boyfriend then returns – sans camera – in an apparent rescue bid. Yet as she climbs into the getaway car, unbeknown to her, a video camera is rolling to capture her complaints. The video ends with a screenshot of the footage her two-faced boyfriend posts online, with the title "Miley Cyrus Bugs At Paparazzi!"

The plot captured the general sense of betrayal Miley felt at the time, alongside the trauma of trying to deconstruct each hanger-on's agenda and never truly knowing who she could trust. The message was clear: trust no one and do not let your guard down.

Intriguingly, Lady Gaga's 'Paparazzi', which chronicled her own love-hate relationship with the press, was released later the same year. That video depicted her indulging in kissing and clothed foreplay with a boyfriend on her balcony, little knowing that he has secretly summoned photographers to the scene in return for a pay-off. When she catches sight of newspapers in the street, she starts to fight with her lover, only for him to seemingly hurl her to her death on the ground below. As the music starts, however, she is resurrected, springing from a wheelchair to begin the song – a martyr to her fame.

She would later state that the video had been inspired by Princess Diana (incidentally, a woman on whom Billy Ray had a long-term crush), recalling how she'd died in a car crash after being chased by photo-journalists and citing conspiracy theories that she'd been betrayed by her loved ones in the moments leading up to her death.

By the time 'Fly On The Wall' was released, Gaga's track had already been written – but the video followed five months later, in the summer of July 2009, suggesting she may have been inspired by Miley's own accounts of martyrdom for fame. On the other hand, perhaps both artists had been partly inspired by the story of Princess Diana?

Yet it may simply have been that Gaga's situation closely mirrored Miley's own, one that in the wake of her disastrous relationship break-down she knew all too well. After all, the former would state that it related to her struggle to make a choice between two competing wishes that could not co-exist – the desire for love and the desire for fame.

Chapter 7

THE love-fame conundrum was certainly one that had been outwitting Miley – having an authentic relationship that wasn't clouded by press intrusion and hidden agendas had thus far proved impossible. She was reluctantly beginning to see the wisdom in Nick Jonas' warning to keep their romance sacred and private in a showbiz world where almost nothing could be so. She'd begun a new relationship, with model Justin Gaston, but was predictably finding that media interest was taking its toll.

Justin was the archetypal gorgeous male model but someone who also, paradoxically, boasted family values and hidden depths. He was straight-edge, shunning all drugs and alcohol. His commitment stemmed from the Biblical phrase that a man's body was his temple and must be preserved as such. This made him a match for the equally abstinent Miley – and in any case, the constant pressure of parents on her tour bus meant she lacked any opportunity to imbibe. He was also respectful to his mother, which she had discovered by secretly reading the text messages on his phone. Her rationale was: "If a boy is mean to his mother, he'll also be mean to you." She could also tick off the God-fearing box, as his chest was even adorned with a passage from the Bible – Psalm 7.8, which read, "Judge me, O Lord, according to my righteousness." The reason for the inking? "I don't want to be judged," he would explain, "so I put it on my body in an attempt to become that bold." Little was said, however, of the Bible's contradictory warning not to tattoo oneself.

Nonetheless, Miley was won over – and to top it off, he was adored by her father. In fact, it was Billy Ray who'd introduced them. Justin's story had begun when, as a small town country boy from Pineville, Louisiana, he'd left his sleepy surrounds in New York in pursuit of becoming an actor. Within three months, the then 17-year-old had tired of the "shallow and fake" showbiz circuit there and relocated to LA. Naysayers might have regarded the move as one from the frying pan straight into the fire, but Justin was more optimistic – and he soon successfully auditioned for the show *Nashville Star*. That was where he met Billy Ray, who – disregarding the fact that, after just three episodes, he'd been fired – declared, "This guy's gonna be a big, big movie star. I'm calling it right now! Tom Cruise, look out!"

Unfortunately, this was one of his predictions that wouldn't come true, but he did manage to find him a guest slot on *Hannah Montana* as a guitar player. Justin welcomed the gig, as up to that point, financial strife had led him down a path he hadn't wanted to tread – modelling. While some of his work had been innocent enough, including bookings for Adidas and Hugo Boss, he'd also found himself posing in his underwear – something he'd later shuddered that his mother "would not be proud of". Duly, in September 2008 – just two months before Miley's 16th birthday – he had entered the *Hannah Montana* set. "It's like if you had a 16-year-old who said, 'Oh, daddy, he's so cute – I want to meet him!'" *Nashville Star* producer Ruby Cantin would reason. "That's exactly what happened."

And so romance blossomed – until, of course, media speculation killed it stone dead. Their dates were covertly filmed by photographers, who would then corner them at the exit of their chosen restaurant or theatre, clamouring and pleading with Miley to let them know who the mystery man was. At first, Justin hadn't been concerned – after all, he would be the first to admit he suffered from a craving for attention, making the peculiar admission in an interview with *Details* magazine that, for the same reason, he'd like to be a dog. "One of those little lap dogs that gets petted all day," he would divulge. "You know, they wake up, get fed, get affection – I like attention."

However, this wasn't the type of adoring, undemanding attention for which he'd hoped – rather, the attention took the form of cynical speculation. "[The relationship] seems like a de facto advertisement," pop culture columnist Courtney Hazlett of *MSNBC* would write. "Is Gaston a girl's first love or part of a stage dad's cynical ploy to help his multimillion dollar daughter forge a post-Disney career?"

The speculation was undermined a little by the fact that Miley hadn't been abandoned by Disney and that, at that time, the third series of *Hannah Montana* was still in full swing. Plus, as Justin was the anonymous part in their relationship – just one of many low-key models-slash-actors whose biggest claim to fame had been a minor cameo as Taylor Swift's fictional crush for the 2008 single 'Love Story' – it was hard to imagine how he could impact on her future career. It seemed as though she was thrusting him into the public eye, not the other way around – and photographers would refer to him, using derogatory tags such as "white shirt guy". Miley would laugh off questions as to his identity by teasing, "He's actually my mom's boyfriend. Hey, dad, I really hate to break it to you . . ." but unsurprisingly, Justin resisted the prospect of a life in which the highlight of his career was being "Miley Cyrus' boyfriend", or, even worse, just "white shirt guy". He started to resent the rumours – especially the criticism over the fact that he was three years her senior – and would mention in interviews that he'd started having nightmares about camera flashes, waking up in the night paranoid and sweating.

Although the pair didn't officially split until the summer, this relationship was over almost before it began – testament to the destructive influence of the press. The drama echoed Gaga's warnings that a celebrity had to choose – love or fame. As it turned out, the romantically minded Miley had been planning her dream wedding since the age of five, obsessively poring through bridal features in magazines and making photo montages of her favoured dresses and cakes that she'd cut out from them.

As one long-time friend revealed to the author, "She'd actually beg her mother to buy her wedding planning magazines. On one occasion, she literally dragged her into a bridal dress shop. The owner saw her charging through the aisles and assumed she was going to be a bridesmaid, so suggested a lilac or pink dress – and then this tiny little girl told her in a big, loud voice, "NO! I AM THE BRIDE! I must wear white!'" Chuckling, she added, "No matter what people think of Miley's exploits now, she's still a traditional country girl at heart, and as comical as it must have sounded from someone so young, the big wedding was – and I'm sure still is – a must."

Miley might not have changed much, but her life had – and it was no longer conducive to love. Marriage – and, some might argue, even short-term affairs – was one of the areas where celebrity status symbolised routine failure. Relationships lived in the public eye seemed to be characterised by shallowness and infidelity. If the romances weren't mere relationships of convenience, then others were accusing them of being so. Fame attracted people with the wrong motives and eroded relationships with those who had the right ones.

Miley had learnt this bitter lesson young – a boy she'd been infatuated with in sixth grade had been totally uninterested in her pre-fame, only to ask her out once he heard she'd landed the role of Hannah Montana. Finally she had the boy she wanted, only to be dumped almost immediately. As one classmate told the author, "It was all about bragging rights. The ego trip of sending a star packing was a bigger buzz than he would have got from a relationship with her."

Miley was starting to see, over time, why her friends – intimidated by the sheer scale and force of the hero worship – had said looking on had actually made them averse to living the stereotypical teenage dream and becoming famous.

Meanwhile those she knew she could trust to love her purely and unconditionally – her family – were rapidly losing patience. Whether it was at an eatery, a skating rink, a theme park, or a shopping mall, everywhere Miley went, she would feel obliged to pass the time of day with any fan that approached her – and coping with the continual stream of autograph hunters had begun to erode their private time together and invade their closeness. It had become so bad that her mother had even forbidden her from accepting such requests when, for example, they were eating. It seemed that it was only when away from the spotlight that love could survive – and that realisation tied in perfectly with the filming of her next project – *Hannah Montana: The Movie*. In the early years of her career, Lady Gaga had chosen fame over a boyfriend every time, bitterly chiding that her music would never wake her up in the morning and tell her it didn't love her any more, so it had to be her priority. For Miley, on the other hand, separating the two wasn't so easy – she loved both and that applied whether 'love' meant friends, family or romance. The movie addressed this dilemma head-on, centring around her exploration of what truly mattered in life.

The opening scene of the film highlights the sheer insanity of being Hannah, with monumental crowds of hysterically screaming fans sprinting through a car park to be first in line to collect tickets for her show. Backstage, Billy Ray is already musing the dark side of fame, glaring ominously at a row of Hannah dolls on the table beside him. Having lost the backstage pass that identifies her, Miley is forced to jump the queue at the ticket booth to get into her own show – and without success. She and best friend Emily end up hijacking an unattended golf cart, with security reprimanding them indignantly as they speed off. Finally she is reunited with her father back-stage, who sternly reminds her, "Your turn to do the dishes tonight!" When she protests that she did them the night before, he adds, "Hey, don't give me no lip – you're the one who wanted best of both worlds."

Yet could the best of both worlds actually have degraded to enjoyment of neither? As if to punctuate that thought, the scene then switches to an inter-view room where a glum Miley faces a grilling from yet another manipu-lative journalist. He is eventually sent packing, but not before he surreptitiously plants a camera, which – when he retrieves it later – reveals that she has an undisclosed "secret". When he relays the evidence to his editor, she isn't taking no for an answer, ordering, "I suggest you find out every sordid, juicy detail of Hannah Montana's glamorous, outrageous life."

Meanwhile an unsuspecting Miley is causing scandalous headlines all by herself when she starts a very undignified cat fight with model and TV show host Tyra Banks over a pair of heels. When photos of the drama are circulated to the media, Billy Ray is furious, but Miley – who had hung up on him days previously telling him he had the "wrong number" – insists she can't talk about it as she's scheduled to appear at an awards show in New York.

He reminds her that attending will mean missing his grandmother's birthday, but Miley merely runs off with her publicist, leaving a trail of excuses in her wake. Her dismayed father is left standing alone and forlorn on the beach but soon resolves to trick her, hiring a private jet that will allegedly take her to New York but in reality is headed for Tennessee.

When an unwitting Miley steps off the plane, she is aghast. "Your limo awaits!" Billy Ray tells her, gesturing towards an old battered truck approaching the makeshift runway. (The scenery that greets her – a seem-ingly infinite green landscape dotted with cows and horses – is in fact the location of her real-life childhood home.) An indignant Miley protests, "Hannah Montana is meant to be walking the red carpet in three hours!" However, her pleas of "I want to go home!" fall on deaf ears as he replies, simply, "You *are* home."

Feeling her soul has been corrupted by the giddy heights of fame, Billy Ray – becoming more authoritative than he'd ever had the heart to be in real life – prescribes a "Hannah detox". To him, it couldn't have come a moment sooner – she'd been alienating her friends and disregarding her family.

The glamour of the Hannah mirage is stripped down almost instantly – starting when her horse leans over and scoops off her wig. Meanwhile the huge gulf between stardom and simple country living is illustrated when Miley, still clad in bright yellow patent Dr Martens boots, struggles to ride her way to the house. In fact, within seconds, the horse – affectionately nicknamed Blue Jean – sends her flying. (Incidentally, as she grew up, Miley had lost her love of riding, believing it was cruel. She would tell one interviewer in explanation, "I want to pet them, not put them to work!" This was where her acting skills would come into play, allowing her to look totally at ease.)

Miley, still hankering after the red carpet, reluctantly agrees to stay for two weeks – and how far she's travelled from her roots becomes rapidly apparent. She gets up one morning to collect eggs from the chickens, only to flee screaming when she encounters their "poop". Seemingly even more persistent than the paparazzi, the flock follows and she is chased across the farm by them, ending up covered in egg yolk and feathers.

As well as comedy moments, there are serious lessons to be learnt from the journey back home. Now a pampered city girl, Miley realises she's at times guilty of looking down on her roots and the Southern customs with which she was raised. She is instantly attracted to a face from her past – Travis, whom she met in first grade – but inadvertently sneers at him for collecting eggs to sell at the local farmer's market, asking if trading the meagre produce is all he aspires to do with his life. His response, that he has to start somewhere, inspires Miley to realise that "life is a climb", inspiration for a new song.

While her urban lifestyle regularly shines through – for example, she commends Travis for his hard work installing a satellite dish only to be told that the structure is actually a bird bath – she grows to believe that his life, one of simplicity and Southern values, surrounded by loved ones, could teach her what real happiness is about.

When she finds out about a local campaign opposing plans for a shopping mall which many residents believe will blight the countryside, she agrees to recruit her "best friend" Hannah Montana to perform a fundraising concert. That's when she discovers that Travis – uninterested in fame and material things – is unimpressed by Hannah. Instead it's the down-to-earth Miley who is his ideal woman. When he unwittingly meets her in her guise as Hannah, she urges him to ask the real her out. Yet leading a double life in such a small town proves near impossible and, when Miley has a dinner date with Travis on the same day that Hannah is due to perform, she is forced to juggle two public identities – with disastrous consequences.

Earlier, she'd managed to dupe her father's new love interest into believing that her friend Emily was Hannah, lying that she was suffering jet-lag and covering her face with a towel. When she queries the fact that LA is just two hours flying time from Tennessee, Miley has no choice but to paint the star as an eccentric and demanding diva who "only flies West to East". Perhaps no more unusual than some of the outlandish requests rumoured to be on Mariah Carey and J-Lo's riders, the fairy story is accepted, but Travis is harder to fool – and before long Miley's cover is blown. Accusing her of making a mockery of him, he wants nothing more to do with her.

Realising the destructive effect the deception has on her personal life – wrecking her relationship with Travis and even her father's burgeoning romance – she decides she must make a choice and, live onstage at the fundraiser, she dramatically confesses to being Miley and rips off her wig. Asking those she has hurt for a second chance, she performs her song 'The Climb' – something "a little more personal" than the crowd might hear from Hannah. Cheered by her honesty, Travis forgives her, while he and the rest of the audience egg her on to continue the show as her alter ego. Finally, she obliges – after all, "The show must go on" – and the community agrees to keep her secret safe so that, outside of this small corner of Tennessee, her double life can continue. Yet although she is still performing as Hannah, she has learnt an important lesson – that family and solid, simple relationships are always a priority over fame.

That said, the real-life Miley hadn't needed quite as much convincing as her fictional character – she would loyally state that she found life on the farm far superior to being in LA. Nonetheless, the filming on home turf reinforced to her just how good it had felt to be home.

Musically, the film introduced fans to 'The Climb', but also saw her break into an unconventional hip-hop and rap-infused country tune combined with a line dance that first debuted on the *Hannah Montana* TV series – the Hoedown Showdown. Plus, as the first of two fundraisers, sandwiched between a performance by Miley and one by her father, was a guest spot from Taylor Swift – someone with whom Miley instantly hit it off.

Taylor and Miley had both entered showbiz early, with the former desperately walking up and down Nashville's Music Row to pitch her services to record labels as early as age 10. She'd also started composing her own lyrics and melodies, a move that made her Sony ATV's youngest ever staff writer at just 14. Already on the payroll, she would drop into the studio daily after school. Not only had both girls been regarded as child prodigies, but Miley could also relate to Taylor on an emotional level as – just like her – she'd been bullied relentlessly at school for pursuing her ambitions. Both had been ostracised from a group they'd formerly been part of and had endured the angst of false rumours. Every angry word to which Taylor had been a victim rang a bell in Miley's memory too – especially the accusations of being a snob whose showbiz inclinations meant she thought she was superior to the others.

The more they chatted both on and off set, the more the pair had in common and before long, they'd arranged to collaborate at the 2009 Grammy Awards, breaking away from filming for a day to do so. They'd shared a dressing room with a star-struck Katy Perry who, with their permission, had even cut off strands of their hair. "I asked them for a lock of their hair for each of them," she recalled, "which is totally creepy, but awesome. I put little bows on them individually and put them in my purse . . . I'm a freak!"

Onstage later that night, Miley and Taylor sang the latter's track 'Fifteen', as an ode to the growing pains of their teenage years. Naturally, turning 16 wouldn't make life any easier and Miley was still being reprimanded and scolded about how she should behave. One such incident surrounded a photo that emerged online of Miley posing with some "male companions". She had been pulling the skin on her face into a position that made her eyes appear slanty, which was instantly interpreted

Growing Up Fast: Miley, by now a figure of controversy with risqué leaked photos, arrives at the 2008 MTV VMAs in Hollywood hand-in-hand with Katy Perry – a rising star whose hit single 'I Kissed A Girl' has led to lesbian rumours. HUBERT BOESL/DPA/CORBIS

Miley enjoys a photo opportunity with mother Tish and elder sister Brandi at the 2008 American Music Awards in LA.
PHIL MCCARTEN/REUTERS/CORBIS

Now internationally notorious, Miley promotes *Hannah Montana: The Movie* at an April 2009 press event in the Spanish capital of Madrid. SERGIO PEREZ/REUTERS/CORBIS

Miley and fellow actress Kim Cattrall don matching dresses for an afternoon on the set of the *Sex And The City 2* movie in New York in October 2009. DENNIS VAN TINE /RETNA./CORBIS

Blurred Lines: reality and fiction combine when Miley shares a romantic moment with her on-screen and real-life lover Liam Hemsworth at a December 2009 photo shoot in Paris. The pair are promoting their co-starring movie *The Last Song*. KCSPRESSE/ SPLASH NEWS/CORBIS

Miley croons with fellow vocalist Justin Bieber at the 2010 Much Music Video Awards in Toronto, sparking rumours of a secret romance. Miley's response: "That's impossible. I'm engaged!" MIKE CASSESE/REUTERS/CORBIS

Clad in fashionably ripped jeans and a studded leather jacket, Miley embraces her rock roots, duetting with Guns 'N Roses rocker Bret Michaels at a 2010 concert in New York. Bret's alleged affair with Miley's mother would later be implicated as the reason for her father's decision to file for divorce. ROB KIM/RETNA LTD./CORBIS

Miley dons a glitzy floor-length ball-gown paired with Swarovski jewels for an appearance at LA's 2010 Academy Awards. Yet the cracks are already beginning to show as a secretly punky Miley uncomfortably plays the role of a red carpet princess.

FAIRCHILD PHOTO SERVICE/CONDÉ NAST/CORBIS

A Return To Her True Self: Miley channels a tomboy look as she straddles a motorbike with tousled hair to play a not-so-girly secret agent on the set of her third movie, *So Undercover*. AHMAD ELATAB/SPLASH NEWS/CORBIS

A thrilled Miley breaks into a grin, offering a Peace sign, as she accepts the honour of Favourite Movie Actress at the 2011 Nickelodeon Kids' Choice Awards in LA.
MARIO ANZUONI/REUTERS/CORBIS

A down-to-earth Miley, sporting plain black leggings and scraped back hair, takes her dog for a stroll at Toluca Lake in California's San Fernando Valley. Shunning diamonds, this girl would later describe her dogs as her "best friends". AKM IMAGES/SPLASH NEWS/CORBIS

Back To Glam: An immaculately turned out Miley plays the role she knows only too well at *Vanity Fair's* Oscars party in February 2012
FAIRCHILD PHOTO SERVICE/CONDÉ NAST/CORBIS

Jaws drop as Miley premieres her newly cropped blonde hairstyle while driving around Philadelphia with assistant and close pal Cheyne Thomas in August 2012. Miley was in town to film *LOL*, while boyfriend Liam was in the same city to shoot his own movie, *Paranoia*. SPLASH NEWS/CORBIS

Miley hits the shops in New York's trendy East Village and public shock continues as she sports a camouflage hoodie around her waist, chunky gold chains and a plethora of tattoos. Her transformation had only just begun. CHRISTOPHER PETERSON/SPLASH NEWS/CORBIS

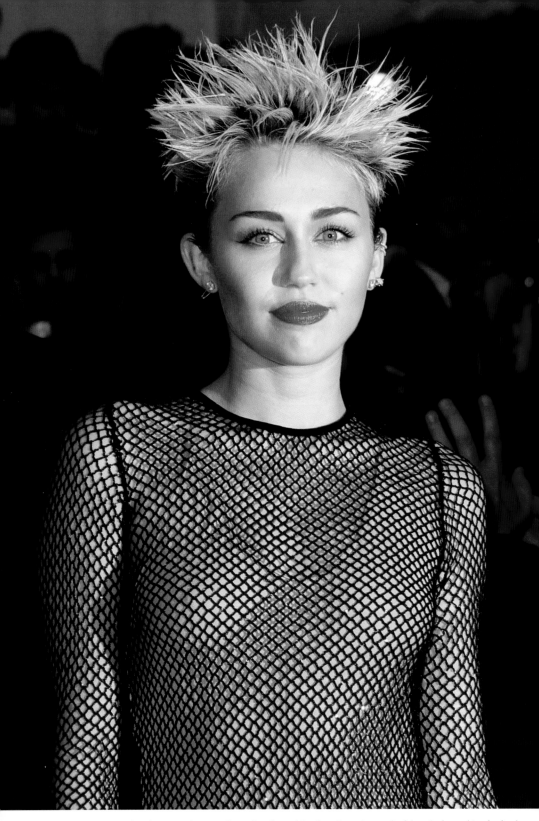

Miley's hair takes on a punk rock twist as she sports dramatic spikes, with safety pin earrings and a fishnet body-stocking (and only a thin opaque under-layer to preserve her modesty), to celebrate the May 2013 opening of the PUNK: Chaos To Couture exhibition at New York's Metropolitan Museum of Art Costume. LUCAS JACKSON/REUTERS/CORBIS as a racist joke intended to make a mockery of the appearance of Asian Americans.

An incredulous Miley released an online statement denying any such intent. "I've been told there are some people upset about some pictures taken of me with friends making goofy faces," she ranted. "Well, I'm sorry if those people looked at those pics and took them wrong and out of context. In NO way was I making fun of any ethnicity! I was simply making a goofy face. When did that become newsworthy? It seems someone is trying to make something out of nothing to me. If that would have been anyone else, it would have been overlooked! I definitely feel like the press is trying to make me out as the new 'BAD GIRL'!"

Unfortunately, an outright denial did little to calm the storm. Korean comedian Margaret Cho momentarily lost her sense of humour when she posted a song about Miley's indiscretions on her blog, with one verse venting, "All you have to do is pull at your face, to make your eyelids resemble our race. This kind of joke has no proper place, Miley Cyrus is a disgrace!"

Then a group called the Organisation for Chinese Americans followed on by demanding a public apology to their community. Yet one member of the public, Lucie J Kim, took her indignation a step further by filing a lawsuit. Claiming that the video had infringed the civil rights of her people, she asked for a multi-billion dollar payout to compensate every single Asian-Pacific Islander living in the state of California. Miley would react by asking her legal team to "sanction Kim's lawyers for filing a 'manifestly frivolous' lawsuit". Ultimately no action was taken by either party.

Better news followed in March when it was revealed that, in spite of the latest scandal, Miley's appeal had still not been extinguished with the Disney crowd. On March 28, when cartoon channel Nickelodeon held its annual Kids Choice Awards, she beat Beyoncé, Rihanna and Alicia Keys to the trophy of 'Favourite Female Singer'. As nearly every media source had speculated that her behaviour had alienated her tween fanbase for good, she hadn't expected to win and, overwhelmed, she'd burst into tears. In her acceptance speech, she'd insisted that "the kids are more important than anything in the world".

Yet in spite of her sentiments, Miley was growing up and moving on –

and the *Hannah Montana: The Movie Soundtrack* – released the same week – would provide the perfect way to symbolise that. According to film director Peter Chelsom, it was "an opportunity to move forwards with the music, to make it more sophisticated, to move with Miley's age".

The sound also marked the end of an era, with the Disney princess leaving her glamorous life behind and returning home to rediscover her Southern roots. In reflection of that, pop and rock were counterbalanced by country, with artists like Taylor Swift and Rascal Flatts featuring.

Then there was Billy Ray's heartfelt contribution, 'Back Home To Tennessee'. He'd suffered homesickness throughout his career, taking on his role in *Hannah Montana* purely to keep the family together. Prior to that, he'd relinquished his lead role in *Doc* due to the refusal of show bosses to relocate filming to Nashville. And there'd even been a time when he'd sacrificed shows for the Queen of England to be at home with Miley – his biggest inspiration and now the sole reason that Billy Ray, a country boy at heart, was living out his days in the big city. He'd fought tooth and nail for the movie to be filmed in his own state, which he'd argued would add authenticity, and 'Back To Tennessee' captured the delight he felt when producers agreed.

"After four years of *Hannah Montana* and living in LA and giving up my previous life and existence and who I am and where I came from," he would later evaluate, "you'll hear a guy who's immersed in music and my love and desire and need to go home. It's about remembering where you come from. It's always important to be aware of where you are and always be looking to where you wanna go, but most importantly, don't forget where you come from. That's what 'Back To Tennessee' is all about – it comes from the heart." To him, the track would be "the cornerstone of the film".

While Miley was younger and less sentimental, and lived a life that was ever changing by choice, there were times when she too craved home – and this track was one of the most authentic in describing her journey. However, unfortunately, not all attempts to blend Miley Stewart with Miley Cyrus had run as smoothly. The soundtrack's lead single, 'The Climb', released on March 9, exposed just how little autonomy she had when performing under the Disney name.

Intended as a candid expression of her feelings, it was in reality a second-hand song that had already been turned down by several other artists on its way to her. It was then the catalyst for a battle between the songwriters and the film director over whether the lyrics should appear in the first or third person. One of the original writers was adamant that altering this would see the song's entire meaning lost in translation. Yet as inflated egos waged war on each other, it poignantly seemed that Miley's was the one voice that nobody had heard.

"They wanted the big tearjerker that was going to be the highlight of the movie," one insider anonymously revealed. "The classic country ballad that would get adults listening, the one everyone would rush out to buy. Miley was just the vehicle for that song to be heard."

As if publicly being declared a puppet wasn't embarrassing enough, reviewers proved to be equally sceptical, with several commenting that the track was a little heavy emotionally and beyond her years. Meanwhile, in taking on the country genre – one traditionally dominated by male artists – Miley would have to brace herself for the impact of sexism. Her peer Taylor Swift had recalled that doors had been shut in her face purely on account of her age and gender, claiming that one or two industry bosses had even told her to her face that there was no place for a "little girl" in country music. Even beauty had blighted her, as the narrow-minded had automatically regarded her as the face of a song, rather than the brains behind it. Like Taylor, Miley was a keen writer who, as she matured, would feel growing frustration at the perception of young women in the business as Barbie dolls.

Of course, the fact that she hadn't played a part in creating 'The Climb' would only give ruthless critics further ammunition with which to shoot her down. Perhaps predictably, *Country Universe* would sneer that the track was "a soulless rephrasing of an extremely famous philosophical message (so famous it borders on cliché) that doesn't provide an emotionally coherent content or justification". To punctuate his disdain, the reviewer illustrated his words with two motivational posters. One, portraying the intended message of the song, read, "Life – it's not about the destination but the journey", while the second offered the critic's interpretation – "Success: Everything is easy when you're cute."

The implication was obvious: that Miley had used her looks as a fast track to progression and that the "hard work" she spoke of wasn't genuinely in her vocabulary. In terms of being taken seriously as a song-writer, the journey really had only just begun.

Yet while the track might not have resonated with the critics, its chart performance was another story. On the week ending March 7, it made its early debut on *Billboard*'s Hot Country Songs Chart at number 48 – the same week that Billy Ray's 'Back To Tennessee' had debuted at number 59. It marked the first time a father and daughter had achieved separate songs on the chart simultaneously in almost 20 years – preceded by Johnny and Roseanne Cash in 1990 with the tracks 'Silver Stallion' and 'One Step Over The Line' respectively.

'The Climb' would peak at number four on the mainstream *Billboard* chart, making it the highest-charting song Miley had yet released in her own name, and it would go on to become the eighth bestselling song of 2009.

Next came 'Hoedown Throwdown', which was released just a few days later on March 10. The dance that inspired the song's name combined Miley's new showbiz lifestyle (via its hip-hop elements) with her old-school country roots (symbolised by the barn-style line dancing). Director Peter Chelsom had his heart set on transforming the unusual mash-up into a worldwide dance craze, similar to the 1995 'Macarena'. While it might not have reached those heights, failing to break the Top 15, after the movie's release, viewers could often be seen in their dozens jumping out of their seats to recreate the dance moves in the aisles.

By March 20, Taylor Swift's 'Crazier' hit the charts, making the soundtrack a triple threat. Three days later, the album followed, peaking at number one in Austria, Canada, Portugal, Spain, New Zealand and the USA. Finally, all the fanfare culminated in the theatrical release of the movie, which earned $35 million in its first weekend.

The release also led to animal rights organisation PETA presenting Miley with its Compassionate Citizens Award, after it became public knowledge that she'd rescued several of the chickens from the movie set. Sad that they were destined for a life of performance, she offered several to her mother, lamenting that they were "sad to be working", and even kept one for herself.

Yet while the accolades for the movie kept coming, Miley found herself squirrelled away planning a "transitioning album" – and, according to rumour, her escape from *Hannah Montana*. Filming for the third season concluded in June, but cutting the ties wouldn't be that simple, as Disney had taken up the clause in its contract offering the option of a fourth series. However, Miley was branching out into new projects all the while and, by July, she'd begin filming on a tailor-made movie called *The Last Song*.

She teamed up with prolific novelist Nicholas Sparks – who at that time had 13 published books to his name – and asked him to write a customised plot for her that could be modelled into a film. The plan was for Sparks to be the author of both the book and the screenplay. Association with him almost guaranteed success – every one of his novels had featured on the *New York Times* Bestseller List, and there were 89 million copies of them in print across 50 different languages.

Miley had been intrigued by the way the film adaptation of one of his stories, *A Walk To Remember*, had transformed formerly one-dimensional pop starlet Mandy Moore into a serious actress – and she was keen for him to work the same magic on her. However, Sparks hadn't written a "young love story" since – by his own admission, the proposed plot took him out of his comfort zone as he had to assume knowledge of what it felt like to be "an angry teenage girl".

However, Miley was ecstatic with the finished product. She'd jokingly given him the brief that she liked "animals, music and hot Australians" – and, to her delight, the plot gave her an excuse to indulge in all three.

She was to play Ronnie Miller, an angry young rebel enraged by her parents' divorce. Determined to show them how they have hurt her, she embarks on a masochistic self-destruct mission that threatens to destroy her future. Her musician father, who has moved from New York back to small-town Georgia where he grew up, is considered dead to her on account of his abandonment. Under his wing, she had shown great promise of becoming a classical pianist, but had demonstratively refused to play since the day he left three years previously, even shunning a scholarship at a prestigious music school.

At her wits' end, her mother arranges for her and her brother Jonas to spend the summer holidays with her estranged father, hoping they can make peace. However, when a sullen, standoffish and miserable Ronnie first arrives, she makes it clear that peace is the last thing on her mind – in

Georgia purely under duress, she'd prefer to be at home clubbing with her friends.

Meanwhile her father – falsely framed for accidentally setting fire to the local church – is creating a new stained-glass window to replace one that was burnt in the wreckage. Ronnie is coolly uninterested in his project and, in a bid to avoid him, she spends much of her time out of the house.

While at a beach volleyball match, she first encounters boyfriend-to-be Will Blakelee, but when he spills her drink over her by way of a greeting, she is equally cold towards him. However, unbeknown to her, the pair have a shared affinity with sea life, with Blake volunteering at a local aquarium, and they end up bonding over a nest of loggerhead sea turtles. One night they camp out on the beach to keep a watchful eye on the nest and protect the eggs from predators until they finally hatch safely and swim out to sea – and while doing so, she realises Blake is not the enemy she'd originally thought.

The day the eggs hatch, love blossoms between the two, but the affair is blighted almost before it has begun, with the collapse of Ronnie's father. To her horror, it emerges that he has terminal cancer and limited time to live. Consequently at the end of the summer, she extends her stay in Georgia to make the most of what little time they have left to repair their relationship. He's been working on a piano composition dedicated to her, but, as the disease ravages his body, he becomes too frail to continue. Ronnie takes over, but he dies just as she finishes it.

Consumed with grief, she has also fallen out with Will after discovering that his best friend was the culprit who set fire to the church and had knowingly allowed her father to take the blame. However, they reconcile after the funeral and Will resolves to move to New York so that they can be together.

Although Miley strived for an edgier, more adult role, she wouldn't be completely gratified just yet due to Sparks' conservative personality. "My teenagers don't do bad things," he explained. "I don't even write profanity. Why? Because my grandparents are still alive. They read my books!"

Once again, Miley had been relegated to the suitable-for-parents-and-children category. However she did get to experience a few self-indulgent tantrums that she had been too polite to unleash in real life. "I just got to drop the guard for a little while and throw all the fits that I wanted to for the past year, on screen," she recalled. "It was fun!"

Although on one level the storyline hadn't been a drastic departure from the usual Disney fare, carrying the grandparent-friendly tag, the role did challenge Miley as an actress more than ever before. While *Hannah Montana* bosses had cut an episode about diabetes, deeming the subject matter too intense for young children, *The Last Song* was unafraid to tackle serious issues such as depression and terminal illness. Miley would be flexing her acting muscles – in fact, so much so that Sparks had feared she would struggle to cope. "The first thing I thought when I finished the screenplay," he confessed, "was, 'Wow, I hope she can do this! This is a tough role because I'm bringing you through a whole gamut of emotion and you're just a 16-year-old girl who's done the Disney Channel. Are you able to do this as an actress?'"

This attitude was exactly what infuriated Miley – she was weary of being written off as "just a teenager" and dismissed as a mere pretty face, and this was her opportunity to unleash some of her inner Ronnie and prove Sparks wrong. Fortunately, thanks to her break-up with Justin Gaston just after the start of filming, she was able to conjure up tears on demand with little effort. "How many tears are in there?" Miley would ask plaintively on Twitter, giving her fans a running online commentary. "They've gotta run out soon, right? Why does saying goodbye hurt so much?" She would later add, "Daddy's giving me therapy. This is worth 10,000,000 dollars!"

She was also able to summon up sadness by recalling the death of Vanessa, the young cystic fibrosis patient who'd passed away while she was on tour two years earlier. Every time she was grieving for her dying father, she replaced his fictional image with her real one. "I remember moments when I couldn't breathe and I felt sick. I couldn't even switch on the TV because I couldn't think of anything else," Miley recalled. "It was way too early for her to go. You're so hurt that you push everything away – and that's exactly what my character does in the movie. That scene made me think about things I have been through in my life and I was able to put those sad feelings into something good. Everyone goes through a period where they lose a friend or a family member and I didn't want to sugar-coat the emotions. I wanted to keep it as real as possible."

To personalise her feelings even more, she chose her character's name herself, picking Ronnie in honour of grandfather Ron. Plus when her mother won the role of executive producer, they were able to work together to make adaptations to the script until Ronnie more closely resembled the real Miley.

That wasn't to say there weren't enormous challenges – as it was her first serious film, she at first struggled to find a way to express intense and complex emotions without simply turning on the tears. Soon director Julie Ann Robinson scolded that her reactions were too predictable. "The first thing I did when I saw a sad scene was think, 'Oh, my character would cry!'" Miley confessed. "And she was like, 'No, the whole end of the film can't just be crying. There has to be some type of dimension to it.' That was the biggest thing that I learnt. You have to go deeper than that. When you are watching an hour and a half of film, you don't just want to see one type of emotion. You want to see her getting through it, putting up her guard and trying to have strength. The crying scenes were easy, but it's a little harder to find something beyond that and be able to see it in your eyes and your body language – and not necessarily just the obvious."

The role also called for intensive sessions with a dialect coach to rid Miley of her persistent Tennessee accent and teach her a different twang. Finally, portraying an authentic piano prodigy meant taking lessons – something an impetuous Miley couldn't wait to terminate. "It's so different! It takes so long!" she would complain to her director, whose mouth would drop open in admiration when she learnt the star had mastered the skills in just two lessons. "I guess it's 'cause I'm just used to playing instruments," she joked, "and I'm not really scared to sound like crap at the beginning."

Yet there was another fear for appearance-conscious Miley to overcome too – the prospect of shooting with a naked face. One scene involved total immersion in a fish tank with the aquarium's whale sharks, for whom any form of make-up is toxic. Yet facing her fear of removing the ultra-glamorous Hannah mask and being exposed to the world as 'ugly' was strangely therapeutic, allowing her to come to terms with her ambivalence about her looks and achieve self-acceptance.

That was just as well, as playing Ronnie wasn't for the bashful – the very first day of filming required her to spend the afternoon kissing a complete stranger on the beach, moments after being introduced to him as an onscreen lover. However, Miley had begged for a "hot Australian" and she wouldn't be disappointed – Liam Hemsworth, two years her senior, was something of a sex symbol in his own country.

His start in life had been anything but glamorous – the son of an English teacher mother and a social services counsellor father, his family was the epitome of average – and his first job had involved taking home a modest wage for carpeting floors. Yet after seeing his elder brother Luke win a role in TV soap *Neighbours*, he began to seriously consider following in his footsteps – and by 2007, he'd been given his own part as athletic paraplegic Josh.

As he'd previously worked almost entirely in Australia, he was only vaguely aware of who Hannah Montana was and consequently was not intimidated by Miley's celebrity – particularly when he found out he had significantly more acting experience. Miley, on the other hand, was scared stiff. Plus, at 6ft 4in, he was an entire 12 inches taller than her, prompting her to joke that they'd have to shoot the entire movie with her "standing on apple boxes". Regardless, that first day's kiss in the ocean "definitely triggered something" and before long, life was imitating art again, with the pair becoming real-life partners.

Chapter 8

IN contrast to the name of her movie, it was far from the last song for Miley. In fact, she'd had to disentangle herself from Liam the moment filming was over and hurry back to the US to release an album and fashion line.

She'd teamed up with Max Azria – the brand that had brought BCBG and bandage-dress pioneer Herve Leger to the masses – for a budget-conscious range at department store Walmart. While Max Azria's usual pieces would set buyers back by up to thousands of pounds each, this line came with young Miley fans in mind – every item would be priced under $20. Yet when it reached the shelves, she was less than impressed. She'd envisaged edgy fashion items, whereas she felt Walmart was stocking clichéd 'cute' items she'd seen far too many times before.

Miley might have been an animal lover, for instance, but she drew the line at endorsing a kitsch T-shirt with a puppy's face printed on it – and when she saw the type of clothing that now publicly bore her name, she recoiled in horror.

"I was like, 'This is not what I wanted!'" she told *Harper's Bazaar* indignantly. "I wanted skinny jeans. I wanted to bless Walmart with jeggings!" Yet it was too late – and Miley now found herself in the awkward position of being a contractually obligated brand ambassador for a line she despised.

Meanwhile the album, which Miley claimed had been released purely to promote the clothing range, was even less representative of her. The time constraints, complicated by her summer filming commitments on Tybee Island, Georgia, had led to a hasty collection of tracks being compiled while Miley admitted her involvement had amounted to almost zero.

The strongest track, 'Party In The USA', had been earmarked as the lead single and yet it had originally been penned with Jessie J in mind. Jessie had written elements of the song herself while on her first extended

138

work trip from London to LA. Without her friends or family, she'd felt lonely and alienated, but when she heard familiar and much-loved tracks booming from the speakers of a taxi cab's radio, it coaxed her out of her shell and made her feel more at home – ready, in fact, for a party in the USA.

Producers had taken the concept and substituted a move from London with a move from Nashville, but they had neglected to change any of the lines. Consequently, despite singing with enthusiasm about a Jay-Z song, Miley barely knew who the artist she was praising was. And, asked by a reporter which of the rapper's songs had inspired the tune, she didn't hold back. "I don't know – I didn't write the song, so I have no idea," she replied bluntly. As the incredulous journalist's mouth dropped open, she continued, "Honestly, I picked that song because I needed something to go with my clothing line. I didn't write it and I didn't expect it to be popular . . . I [just] needed some songs." Openly dismissive of Jay-Z and seemingly confused even about his genre, she elaborated, "I've never heard a Jay-Z song. I don't listen to pop music. 'Party In The USA' is not even my style of music."

Yet while that might have seemed like a revelation, it was nothing compared to the shock value of her August 9 performance at the Teen Choice Awards. The stage show was intended to be a spoof of growing up in Tennessee, depicting Miley as playfully contemptuous of the cooler-than-thou posturing she'd encountered in Hollywood. While some girls oozed rock'n'roll glamour with "their big glasses", she would shoo them away and remain true to her roots.

That element, however, might have been lost in translation, as all parents saw that night was Miley gyrating on a pole. Controversially, the performance blended adult sexuality with symbols of child-like frivolity in the unusual pairing of an ice-cream cart and a stripper pole – and onlookers were enraged. The reason for their indignation? Over a million of the show's US viewers were believed to be under 18. The concerns were that presenting sexual imagery on a normally family-friendly awards show would influence children to imitate the moves, or, even worse, develop low self-esteem or eating disorders as a result of feeling they didn't measure up to Miley physically.

On the other hand, some argued that taking to the pole didn't always imply erotic intentions, pointing out that pole-dancing lessons were offered by mainstream gyms as part of fitness training. Yet according to the conservative majority, the moral fabric of the nation was rapidly unravelling – and it was all down to Miley Cyrus.

When approached for a statement, Disney execs were deliberately evasive, taking care to distance themselves from the controversy. Their only formal response was "Disney Channel won't be commenting on that performance, although parents can rest assured that all content presented on the Disney Channel is age-appropriate for our audience – kids 6–14 – and consistent with what our brand values are."

Meanwhile Miley's father, who was seen clapping proudly in the audience, was perhaps the least perturbed of all. "You know what?" he challenged. "I just think that Miley loves entertaining people."

The pre-recorded awards show aired on August 10 and the single 'Party In The USA' followed a day later. Debuting at number two on the *Billboard* chart, it would become the fastest and bestselling single Hollywood Records had ever made. Not only that, but the song – certified six times platinum – would become one of the bestselling singles of all time, across any record label or genre.

The irony, of course, was that Miley felt almost no personal attachment to the song. However, she injected some of her own personality in the video, approaching director Chris Applebaum to ask if she could emulate a scene from *Grease*. She'd been impressed by the moment John Travolta had sung 'Sandie' on a swing in a jungle gym with projections in the background behind him, and wanted 'Party In The USA' to have the same feel. The video would begin with Miley arriving at a drive-in theatre, which was named the Corral Drive-In in dedication to her parents, who – back in Kentucky in their youth – had regularly dated at a place of the same name. Her mother would have arrived in a '79 black Pontiac Trans Am – her car of choice at the time – and so that was the car that Miley rocked in the video.

According to Applebaum, who'd also worked with Rihanna, Usher, the Pussycat Dolls and Demi Lovato, Miley was "no cookie-cutter star" – but now that she'd seen the perils of manufactured music first-hand, she faced trying to prove that to herself.

Her mini album, *The Time Of Our Lives*, was released exclusively in

Walmart stores on August 28 – and yet just one of the tracks featured Miley as a co-writer. 'Party In The USA' had been a perfect song, previously turned down by Jessie J because it wasn't edgy enough for her tastes – and Miley now felt the same way. Meanwhile, although she loved the punky, rock guitar-infused 'Kicking And Screaming', it too was a recycled song – Ashlee Simpson had recorded it first, back in 2005. 'Before The Storm' – a song co-written and co-performed with the Jonas Brothers – was a crowd-pleaser when the live rendition made its way on to the album, but even that felt awkward, as it brought back all the memories of a failed relationship.

There was just one track to which she felt she could truly relate, 'Obsessed' – but persuading producers to include it had been nothing short of a battle. She related to the "romantic" tale of passionate and addictive love, capturing how it felt not to be able to erase someone from your thoughts, day or night. It was natural that, as Miley matured, these topics would resonate with her – after all, she'd just met in Liam the man she regarded as her "first serious love" – and yet, enchained to all of her contracts, it was a continual struggle just to be herself.

This didn't go unnoticed as, after catching one of her live shows, a reviewer from the *LA Times* remarked, "Once again, the make believe Miley is more compelling than the real thing. [We lack] a deeper idea of who she is and what her music means." Meanwhile AllMusic had stated, "If *Breakout* began to establish Miley Cyrus as a singing star in her own right, free of Hannah baggage, then this EP is another confident step in that direction." Little did the critics know, of course, that the Hannah baggage had simply been replaced by another type – and a miserable Miley was even more weighed down than before.

She had little time to consider her woes, however, as, after participating in the charity single 'Just Stand Up!' to raise funds and awareness for cancer sufferers, it was time to get back on the road. Her Wonderworld tour, which ran from September to December, was an eagerly anticipated one, with European dates selling out in entirety in just 10 minutes. Plus while the UK was crippled by recession, her concert at London's 02 Arena attracted the biggest turnout in the venue's history.

Sponsored by Walmart, it seemed that no expense was spared in creating lavishly detailed props, costumes and choreography. The now rockier element to her music was emphasised with a huge Harley Davidson motorbike which Miley would mount and ride across the stage and she'd also perform a nightly cover of Arrows track 'I Love Rock 'N' Roll'. Of course this invited further comparisons to Britney Spears, who in 2001 had covered the song formally and released it as a single.

Her Teen Choice Awards performance had also seen her compared to her rival – no stranger to scandal, either – but Miley chose to ignore the connotations of a twin meltdown, laughing that the comparison was a compliment.

Meanwhile, during interludes, her dancers would perform an imitation of the choreography in Michael Jackson's 'Thriller', which of course accompanied 'Fly On The Wall'. They even incorporated part of the Black Eyed Peas' 'Boom Boom Pow'. Yet the biggest highlight for Miley was sharing the stage with her brother Trace, whose band Metro Station was the tour's designated support act.

On the first leg of the tour, disaster struck when the crew bus lost control, struck an embankment and rolled over several times on its side, killing the driver almost instantly. Although Miley was not on board, she was deeply shaken by the experience, asking her fans in North Carolina that night to pay tribute.

Later, Miley was able to fulfil her father's suppressed ambition of meeting the Queen, when she was one of several artists invited to take part in the annual gala evening the Royal Variety Performance. The event was famed for the presence of figures of senior royalty and in recent times, both Queen Elizabeth and the Prince of Wales had been taking it in turns to attend on alternate years. On the day of the event – December 7 – she was scheduled to perform 'Party In The USA', but again, in a growing trend for Miley, it wasn't the music that did the talking.

Gaga might have been the proud wearer of a predictably ludicrous costume – this time a red latex full-length gown with a solid Edwardian-style neck ruffle and matching crystal eye patches, garb the Queen seemed barely able to keep a straight face about – but this time it was Miley towards whom the finger of complaint was pointed. Onstage, she'd worn a comparatively tame outfit of black leather hot-pants, crop top and matching jacket, but it prompted the *Daily Mirror* to dub it "the sluttiest outfit we've ever seen".

To greet the Queen and shake her hand, she'd changed into a more modest floor-length orange gown, but even that attracted criticism, due to complaints that it showed too much cleavage – something onlookers insisted was "disrespectful and totally inappropriate" in the presence of a then 83-year-old woman.

Yet Miley was a rebel, rather like John Lennon before her, who'd poked fun at the pomp and snobbery he believed the event consisted of, with the cutting onstage words, "Will the people in the cheap seats clap your hands? For the rest of you, just shake your jewellery!"

Meanwhile an increasingly brash Miley seemed unconcerned about public opinion, shortly afterwards unleashing a less than subtle critique of the city that hosted the event. "Blackpool is one of the strangest places I've ever been in my entire life," she insisted. "I was performing for the Queen, in Blackpool of all places. I got there and I was like, 'This is the weirdest place!' There was this amusement fair but nobody was there because it wasn't summertime. It reminded me of *Zombieland*. There was literally nobody. I didn't think if I was ever going to perform for the Queen *this* is where I'd have to go." She added, "I was even staying in a creepy motel."

Of course her candour did little to spare the feelings of Blackpool residents, some of whom were incandescent with patriotic fury, others of whom wearily agreed, adding that the city was a drug addict-riddled eyesore. Fortunately for Miley's ego, her fast-paced schedule left little time to dwell on the negative press. In fact, she didn't even make it home for Christmas, but as soon as she returned to LA, she took what for many pop stars spells the first step on the road to rebellion – getting her first tattoo.

Her grandfather Ron had succumbed to lung cancer, while Vanessa's death had been due to cystic fibrosis, but both had suffered severe breathing difficulties towards the end and, in honour of their fight, Miley had the phrase 'Just Breathe' inked beneath her left breast. The tattoo was with both her parents' blessing, although it spelt one of the few things that they did agree on.

Miley should have looked forward to coming home for New Year after her prolonged absence, but in fact the entire family was dreading the break – and placing work temporarily into the background only amplified the fact that the household was fraught with tension.

Billy Ray had started to suspect that showbiz was "driving a wedge between us" and even publicly wondered if he'd made a mistake by shying away from disciplining his children. Meanwhile as close as Miley was to her mother, living and working with her, day in day out, had regularly caused tempers to flare. "I can't stand when she tells me, 'Do the scene again like this!'", Miley had admitted. "Then I tell her, 'Mom, you're not an actor – leave it to me and the director!'"

Hailing from a Southern background, she regarded Miley's dismissiveness of her advice as rude and self-important and there were fears that fame, not to mention the LA lifestyle in itself, had eroded her values. Sometimes Tish and Billy Ray looked at her and simply saw a spoilt princess with a penchant for tantrums – someone who, at just 17, already thought she knew it all. This, of course, might have been a reaction of defiance to protect her feelings from the constant criticism offered up in the media. "You can't do anything without people commenting on people saying whatever they feel like you did wrong and pointing the finger at you. I never cared to say I'm perfect. I never wanted to be. That wasn't my selling point, because I want people to like me for me."

Yet Disney – whose vast empire counted on painting landscapes of innocence – might have disagreed. She *had* been marketed as perfect – for many years – and now everything that she did in deviation from that image was gleefully dissected by her detractors. That had been one of the reasons for taking a hiatus from Twitter. Her mother had long since banished tabloids from the house, so her only remaining vice had been the ever-present temptation to tweet or google herself on her phone.

Troll risks aside, her updates had become so prolific that she was spending more time writing about her life than actually living it. Realising it could become an obsession, Miley took a step back from the virtual world, even closing her account on Twitter altogether.

"I'm on my phone a lot less," she would reveal to one interviewer of her digital detox. "I have a lot more real friends, rather than friends that I'm talking to on the internet. That's not cool, not safe, not fun and most likely not real. Everything is just better when you're not wrapped up in that . . . it's lame. I feel like I hang out with my friends and they're so busy taking pictures of what they're doing to put on Facebook that they're not really enjoying what they're doing. You're going to look back and have

10 million pictures, but not be in one of them because you weren't having fun. You were too busy clicking away. You have to just enjoy the moment you're in for yourself and stop telling people about it."

She would take these views a step further by advising young people not to use social media at all. "I'm telling kids not to be on the internet," she reiterated. "It's dangerous . . . it wastes your life. You should just be outside playing sports, instead of sitting in front of any type of screen!"

Twitter aside, however, Miley still lacked the luxury of a normal teenage life, and working so closely with both her parents meant all three ran the risk of simply lashing out and taking out their frustrations on each other.

In January, it was back to work shooting Hannah Montana's final series, but that period was scarcely much easier. "Season four, it was a disaster," Billy Ray later confessed. "I was going to work every single day knowing that my family had fallen apart, but yet I had to sit in front of that camera . . . how did I ever make it through that? I must be a better actor than I thought."

Meanwhile Miley was juggling filming during the day with songwriting and recording tracks for her second full-length album. In addition, she was struggling with the impact of being thousands of miles away from her new love, Liam. 'When I Look At You' – their song from the film, which had appeared on both the movie's soundtrack and Miley's own 2009 EP – was released on February 16, and served as a bittersweet reminder of the distance that separated them. The video had been shot in Georgia back in August, just before filming commitments drew to a close – and had featured the pair sitting at a grand piano with the ocean lapping in the background behind them. It was a success, peaking at number 16 in the USA, although Miley's aggressive promotion of it may have been key. Throughout her Wonderworld tour the previous year, she'd played piano and sung the track each night while giant video screens projected a trailer for the movie behind her.

By March 31, the film had made its US debut at the box office, earning over $36 million by the end of the first weekend. It proved a success in the UK too although, owing to the Icelandic volcano Eyjafjallajökull, which saw almost all flights stranded and left Europe blanketed in volcanic ash, she was unable to attend the London premiere.

The following month, Miley stirred deep controversy when 'Nothing

To Lose', her collaboration with Bret Michaels – formerly of the rock group Poison – was premiered. The pairing certainly raised some eyebrows. At 47, Bret was 30 years her senior and almost three times her age. He was also notorious for his womanising shenanigans back in the eighties and nineties – behaviour he himself described in such terms. Even some of his work in the studio had been X-rated – on one track he'd recorded himself having sex with a succession of groupies so that he could use their orgasmic moans as a form of backing vocals. He'd also been recorded scolding one woman for faking.

Perhaps unsurprisingly, then, the lyrics of 'Nothing To Lose' bordered on the soft-core pornographic. If Miley had wanted to shed some skin, she'd succeeded, because this was about as far away from the tame world of *Hannah Montana* as it was possible to get. To make matters stranger, Miley's mother had been in the studio while they recorded it.

However, unbeknown to the public, Bret had been a long-time family friend and Miley's first ever concert had been to see Poison. In fact he had known her since she was a little girl named Destiny Hope and regarded her as his unofficial niece – so much so that any vibe between them other than a platonic one was off limits and would have almost felt like incest.

Their duet on the provocative track had happened by chance, when he was recording tracks for his own solo album *Custom Built*, and discovered that Miley was sharing the same studio. One of her all-time favourite songs was the Poison track 'Every Rose Has Its Thorn' and, taking advantage of their proximity, she'd suggested they record a rendition of it together. He instantly agreed, but then Miley heard him nostalgically rehearse 'Nothing To Lose' – a track from his archives that he'd shelved years ago without releasing – and she became hysterical with excitement. She started begging him to let her record some harmonies and, in spite of the fact that the lyrics described a sexual encounter, he was as enthusiastic about the collaboration as she was. "I guess in hindsight I should have looked more at the maturity of the song," he would later admit, "but she was never singing it to me, so I never thought about it. As God is my witness, I have nothing to be defensive about. It got really controversial for no reason." In Bret's mind, it was entirely innocent, but for others, it had conjured up visions of a barely legal teenage girl sexualised and exploited by the industry – and perhaps even involved with Bret in the scenes the song spoke of.

There was more age-gap drama the following month when a video surfaced online of *The Last Song*'s wrap party, featuring Miley giving producer Adam Shankman a lap dance. Yet again, it was gossip gold, with headlines screaming, "Miley Cyrus Dirty Dances With 44-Year-Old Man". Apparently oblivious to the cameras, she'd been filmed first lap dancing for him, and then peeling open the top of her shirt as if to expose her breasts, while Shankman grinded up against her, simulating sex.

The fact that her co-worker – renowned for producing the film *Hairspray*, as well as for his high-profile judging slot on TV show *So You Think You Can Dance?* – was openly gay did little to quell the disapproval. According to the revellers who filmed the footage, children in single figures sat just a few feet away. In fact, some were instantly pulled out of the party by their parents.

The timing was significant because, in spite of being filmed almost nine months earlier, the video had only just come to light. Had it truly been leaked or was this a mischievous Miley's attempt to drum up publicity for her radical new image, to be unveiled later that month? Perhaps her new adage when faced with press intrusion was, "If you can't beat 'em, join 'em."

Either way, when 'Can't Be Tamed' made its debut on May 14, the world was watching. The single was a celebration of self-discovery and of her breakout from metaphorical captivity to start to claim her own identity – but it was also an acknowledgment of how difficult the transition had been. "I've lost my sense of self a lot," she'd admitted. "There's times when you hear what you should be so much that you lose who you actually are." The single aimed to express that feeling, while also setting the imbalance straight – and as such, shooting the video had been empowering and therapeutic.

The opening scene sees a smartly suited museum curator lead an excited audience to his most prized exhibit, introducing Miley as "the rarest creature on Earth, Avis Cyrus". Describing her as "a creature so rare it was believed to be extinct", he unveils a giant cage, revealing Miley slumbering inside a nest – a sort of Sleeping Beauty in bird form. The cage symbolises her entrapment at the hands of Disney, which has imprisoned her behind the bars to control her and ensure her compliance. It sees her exotic plumage – or, in reality, her rare talents – as a lucrative benefit to be captured and exploited. However, she must be handled carefully and the nest represents her captors' desire to infantilise her and forbid her to fly. Keeping her safely swathed in the nest – a confined environment where she is constantly on call to be admired – means they can maintain the image of innocence, perfection and naivety. She plays the proverbial untouched virgin who is of the most value before she has been tarnished.

The video provides a way for Miley to express her agitation at those who had been holding her back. She feels they have wanted to stunt her growth, preserve her innocence and own her beauty, all for financial gain – and the only way for them to do so is to turn her into a tightly controlled metaphorical museum exhibit.

She resembles a peacock, courtesy of her green tinted feathers, but her predicament also bears resemblance to that of other captive birds. For instance, like a parrot who memorises and repeats words told to them by others, Miley would soon confess that she had been instructed on what to do and say in almost every aspect of her life in the five years since she'd joined *Hannah Montana*. She would tell of how she felt thoroughly sick of conforming to a prescribed character – and that she'd felt manipulated. Feeling tied to the persona of a child, she had even advised little sister Noah to stay well away from acting in her youth lest she fell prey to the same manipulation. "I say, 'Just wait, dude,'" she recalled. "The way you're going to be when you're my age and the way you are right now are so different. Don't put yourself in a situation where people are going to think of you as only one thing – you're going to change a lot. It interferes with your growing up if you're not strong and you're not sure who you want to be."

Miley, of course, knew from bitter experience that she was far from strong – and the video portrayed that struggle. For instance, when a camera flash startles her, she sweeps her enormous peacock feathers in front of her face to shield her eyes from the impact. This action symbolises her vulnerability when faced with attention, while her position of passivity as a caged bird disables her from evading it. The way she recoils at the sight of the flash illustrates the many times she had tried to break free of the cage, but been too blinded by the press intrusion to find her way. Like a trafficked woman, with all eyes focused on her, she has become almost a victim of her own beauty.

Yet in an instant, Miley – whose delicate, fragile prettiness renders her impotent in the eyes of underestimating spectators – makes a move no one could have anticipated. She breaks free from the cage, flees the nest and, with over 40 backing dancers flanking her, goes on a violent rampage around the museum. Powerful energy appears to transform her as she runs, fists punching the air, into the path of freedom. Now unimpeded, she dances sexually, exchanging provocative glances with both male and female co-dancers, often stopping teasingly just on the brink of swooping in for a kiss.

Miley's costumes for the video – besides expansive feathers – included a black leather ensemble and a lavish silver corset handmade from over 2,000 metallic pieces. The latter was created by the Blonds, who also designed custom costumes for Lady Gaga's onstage wardrobe. To make her exotic plumage complete, she was also endowed with peacock feather claws. Burlesque performers such as Dita Von Teese typically incorporated a bird cage into their stage routines, giving the prop an air of eroticism.

However, while the video expressed strong sexuality, according to Miley that was pure coincidence – the real message was liberation from a life as Hannah. "It isn't about being sexy, or who can wear the best clothes," she insisted. "It's about explaining the song and living the lyrics."

The track debuted at number eight on the US chart, to cries that it was "like 'Party In The USA' on steroids". Meanwhile, it even had reviewers talking as far afield as Ireland, where the *Irish Times* asserted, "Miley's taken a sexy electro edge. Less 'Party In The USA', more Party With My Parents Away. We like this. A LOT."

Perhaps it was unsurprising that the video invited comparisons with Christina Aguilera's 'Not Myself Tonight' – not just due to her flirtation with electronica mimicking that sound, but also because her pop rival had felt stifled and repressed when transitioning from a preteen on the Mickey Mouse Club to a sexually charged and more adult performer. In fact, a video from Christina's archives, 'Stronger', also depicted a metamorphosis – in her case, depicting her turning from a moth into a butterfly. Both girls had shed old skin to become the people they felt they truly were at heart, beneath the layers of manufactured faux personas.

That said, Miley – who'd taken an active role in the direction of the video – had been adamant that she didn't want to take inspiration from anyone. In fact, she had resisted watching other material at all as she'd sought to avoid her or her co-creators being influenced by creative styles that already existed. Instead, she'd promised ahead of release that the song would present as her "diary", so that fans could see the real her, rather than the squeaky clean, airbrushed version – and at large, they hadn't been disappointed.

Her only source of frustration was hearing people talk of the "new Miley", when the message she'd been desperate to get across was that this was no new persona – rather, she now simply had more freedom to be the person she was meant to be in the first place. "I didn't want to be a character," she explained. "I wanted to be myself. I think that's why the video is so unique."

Later in the month, as if to punctuate that point, she recorded the Rockangeles remix of the song with rapper Lil Jon. Now there was no question that her image was changing. The rap world was seen as tough and "street" and was often associated by mere implication with guns, gangs and violence – a brush with which a company of Disney's ilk wouldn't want to be tarred. Yet the lyrics of 'Can't Be Tamed' already offered a defiant retort to that suggestion, with Miley informing that she "wasn't here to sell ya".

The same month, she made a brief cameo appearance in *Sex And The City 2*, fulfilling a long-standing wish to take part. Due to her busy schedule, she'd come in to shoot her segment for just two hours before being whisked away again. Despite the brevity of it, she was well-liked by the cast; Kim Cattrall affectionately referred to her as a "princess". Rapper and producer Timbaland too joined the long queue of people waiting to praise her when he called her "the female Justin Timberlake".

Yet the hype surrounding her wasn't to last and, after the initial public-ity surge, the heat surrounding her began to cool. When the album, also titled *Can't Be Tamed*, made it to the shelves on June 18, it charted poorly and, while it made the Top 10 of several charts internationally, the position was fleeting.

Meanwhile, when she attempted to showcase the album in the UK by performing its title track on *Britain's Got Talent*, she was met by conserva-tive attitudes and a part of the choreography which involved simulating a kiss with a female back-up dancer was met with fury. Miley, who by now

150

had given in to temptation and reinstated her Twitter account, released an equally impassioned statement defending, "It is ridiculous that two entertainers can't even rock out with each other without the media making it some type of story. I really hope my fans are not disappointed in me because the truth is, I did nothing wrong. I got up there and did my job, which is to perform to the best of my ability."

Perhaps as a distraction from the negativity, Miley went back to the tattoo parlour for her second inking – this time getting the word 'Love' emblazoned across her inner right ear. The decision was prompted by a desire to let the love of the people she cared about override the petty hatred of outsiders and to keep that love around her as a barricade against the negativity of others.

She followed this up in September with a tattoo on her right hand little finger of a heart. The message behind this one was her need to show solidarity with her family, as it exactly matched tattoos that both of her parents had. However her desperate will to keep them together seemed to be too little too late, as the following month Billy Ray would file for divorce.

A traditionalist at heart who knew only too well the stigma he'd acquired when he became the only person in his class at school to be the son of divorcees, he'd been reluctant to break up the family – put simply, he believed in the institute of marriage and took the commitment seriously. However, he felt the relationship he had with Tish was irreparably damaged.

As if the moment wasn't already painful enough, a rumour soon swept the media offering a less than wholesome explanation for the split – that Tish had been having an affair. The culprit, headlines read, was Bret Michaels of Poison and Billy Ray, painted as the victim, had been oblivious.

Bret issued a point blank denial, reiterating that he'd worked with Miley on two songs, had approached Tish about the possibility of her production company making his book, *Roses And Thorns*, into a film, and that he'd known the Cyruses for as long as he could remember. Although it was far from surprising that Bret had denied the potentially career-destroying allegations, there was another clue that seemed to prove his innocence – he'd been in hospital through much of the period when the affair was claimed to have happened, in recovery from a brain haemorrhage.

The story became all the more ludicrous with the allegation that Billy Ray had heard the news from Tish's eldest child, Brandi. It seemed unusual that Tish would have chosen to share the details with her daughter – she would surely have gone to even greater lengths to hide the infidelity from a minor than she would from her own husband, suggesting that it was a fabricated twist invented to add shock value.

As her mother's sordid adventures, implied or otherwise, were gaudily bandied about for the world to see, Miley was struggling with the muted reception to her album. Even worse was the embarrassment of having her new, more sexualised image dissected, psychoanalysed and then attributed to a "cry for help" aimed at getting her parents back together.

Psychotherapist Dr Gilda Carle placed Miley on the metaphorical couch without so much as a word of consent when she gave an in-depth interview about her "subconscious motives" to *Hollywood Life*. "Exposing herself is an act of defiance," the doctor claimed in reference to Miley's recent penchant for flashing mischievous hints of cleavage at events, including an infamous braless side-boob shot. "She's acting out – acting like a bad girl, so sexualised, because she wants to force her parents to jump back in and act like her parents again and stop her. Children of divorce, like Miley, often take it upon themselves to try and manoeuvre their parents back together and that's exactly what Miley is trying to do. She has a lot of guilt and the only way she can remove it is if she can get her parents back together by forcing them to discipline her in unison."

She also dismissed Miley's accounts of breaking free from an ill-fitting, wholesome image that had been forced upon her, countering, "She wants to destroy it because she blames her career for breaking up her family and, in her subconscious mind, if she screws up her career, it can't be to blame any more and mommy and daddy can get back together."

Miley chose not to respond to this interpretation of her antics, instead focusing on promotion for her October 22 single, 'Who Owns My Heart?' Asking whether love or art held the key to her heart, it revisited the classic Lady Gaga 'heartbroken but wiser' theme, echoing a statement she'd made that she was too much in love with her music to commit to a man. Miley would admit that she'd been inspired by Gaga on the track, but it had taken on a personalised meaning too, as she was battling lovesickness for a man who lived on the opposite side of the world. Realising that she can't serve two masters, she lives out her dilemma before concluding that her relationship is an art within itself.

The video continued the theme that 'Can't Be Tamed' had started, featuring Miley writhing provocatively on a bed – initially blindfolded, giving rise to bondage play connotations – before getting ready to make her appearance at a sexy dance party. The imagery led the Parents' Television Council to release a statement of chastisement which read, "It is unfortunate that Miley would participate in such a sexualised video like this one. It sends messages to her fanbase that are diametrically opposed to everything she has done up to that point. Miley built her fame and fortune entirely on the backs of young girls and it saddens [us] that she seems so eager to distance herself from that fanbase so rapidly."

Miley's indirect response? As someone who was only human, she was "always going to have temptation". She expressed this in her performance of the track at the 2010 MTV Europe Music Awards in Spain, held on November 7, when she devised a routine inspired by the 2000 film *Angels And Demons*. The female dancers were dressed in white, complete with Victorian-style lace and ruffles to convey innocence, while the men that served as their temptresses, compelling them to misbehave, were all in black.

This single spelt an end to the promotion for *Can't Be Tamed*. Although successful albums would typically spawn four or more single releases, the reception for this one overall had been poor – and a disappointed Hollywood Records had slashed the marketing budget. Although Miley had amassed a fortune of $48 million that year, which had seen her earn a repeat mention in *Forbes* as the 18th Highest Hollywood Earner for 2010, *Can't Be Tamed* hadn't been the reason for that status. In fact, in the USA, she had barely scraped 350,000 album sales – by her usual standards, a point-blank failure. Plus 'Who Owns My Heart?' lacked the fanfare surrounding the women who'd inspired it – aside from a few blink-and-you'll-miss-it mentions on selected European charts, it disappeared almost as quickly as it had come.

Perhaps Miley had by now alienated fans of the clean-living Disney girl but hadn't yet become raunchy or mature enough to win kudos in the edgier market, placing her in a lonely no-man's-land between the two.

Yet it wasn't the poor chart performance that irked her the most – after all, she would regularly boast that she had enough money in the bank to no longer care whether she made a profit – it was the sense that she hadn't been sufficiently true to herself on the album.

Some elements were very adept at portraying her at that time – for example, 'Robot', which depicted her "desire to escape from the machine everyone thinks you should be" and 'My Heart Beats For Love' – a song in support of her gay hairdresser, championing his efforts to find equal footing in a homophobic world. Yet not all songs were a snapshot of the true Miley.

For example, while the video for 'Can't Be Tamed' symbolised her struggle accurately, some of the lyrics – featuring bragging and bravado about her beauty and her 'perfect 10' status with the men – read more like a Fergie track such as 'Fergilicious'. The boasts were at total odds with the Miley who, not long before, had been terrified to get out of bed in the morning because she despised her looks. 'Can't Be Tamed' didn't speak of a girl who'd been incapable of feeling beautiful – rather it featured phrases that might be more at home with the ego-driven Kanye West. Some part of Miley, who continued to claim in interviews that the war women like her waged on their looks might never be won, might have felt that the track was misrepresentative and dishonest and, while there was an empowering element to it, it might also have inspired a slight cringe.

Working with a team of co-writers, all of whom had their own ideas about what was best for her career, had meant the message wouldn't always come through crystal clear. However, above all, Miley had felt she'd compromised herself by creating an album that was so unabashedly pop. She hinted that the intention behind it had been purely to please her young, pop-loving audience when she told *GMTV*, "I want this to be my last record for a little while . . . in a few years, as I grow up, so will all my fans and I won't have to focus on pop music so much and I'll be able to have more of the sound of music that I'm into."

It seemed to be an outright admission that she sang on certain tracks half-heartedly, was compromising her own desires to make a profit and that, musically, she'd effectively become a puppet for mainstream publicity. She would add earnestly, "The more I make music that doesn't truly inspire me, the more I feel like I'm blending in with everyone else."

Later laughing that she may previously have been, incongruously, younger and wiser, she joked that her 13-year-old self "would have beaten up my 17-year-old self for being a sell-out". At that moment, pop was too commonplace for a sensation-seeking Miley – and she was longing for a change. While one reviewer of 'Who Owns My Heart?', at *The Guardian*, delivered a controversial put-down about her past, answering, "Probably that creepy guy from the Disney Channel who went about violating your Godliness" – *Pop Matters* offered a theory, caustic as it may have been, that resonated about her present: "It's commerce that owns your heart, Miley, and always will be."

Determined that it would be the last time such a comment was made about her, she announced to the world that she was taking some time off and, moreover, that they'd just witnessed the last pop album of her career.

Chapter 9

"PEOPLE would be shocked to know that my career is not my priority," Miley announced. "It's not my life any more. I really just want to enjoy life and become who I am to the fullest."

These were normal emotions for a teenager – especially for one who'd never experienced a gap year or the comparatively lazy pace of high school – but inevitably, it was how she did so that would cause concern. Miley was entitled to a break – after all, she'd barely had one in seven years – but the camera-wielding reporters her nightmares were made of weren't about to take one, and she would soon learn that, even in her private life, nothing was off limits.

In December, a film emerged on the internet, filmed just five days before her 18th birthday, that depicted Miley surrounded by a group of friends, inhaling deeply from a bong. Wide-eyed and giggling hysterically, she then mistakes a random object across the room for a person – namely her boyfriend – and slurs, "Is that a fucking Liam lookalike, or is that my boyfriend?" Seconds later, she concedes that she might be having a bad trip.

Fans automatically assumed it was cannabis, but Miley corrected that it was salvia – a legalised high free for all to purchase in California. It had been labelled a cross between marijuana and LCD, due to possessing more intense hallucinogenic properties than the former. Although the drug was technically legal, it was frowned upon nonetheless, not least because it had not been proved safe, and experts pointed out that Miley was inhaling a cocktail of chemicals more potent than if she'd been smoking a cigarette.

When the news broke, she'd felt a surge of embarrassment. She would bitterly declare that "your party friends don't give a fuck about you", but the damage was already done – the instant she'd let her guard down, the video clip was on the internet and the headlines emblazoned across the newspapers. Although she'd made a point of being unapologetic about many recent events of her career – from provocative poses to implied lesbian kisses – in this case, she issued an unreserved apology.

Hoping to coax a more rock'n'roll response out of her through trickery, one *Marie Claire* reporter questioned casually whether the episode had truly been a mistake. After all, she reasoned, statistics showed that nearly two million Americans over 12 had experimented with salvia at some time in their lives – was this really any different? Miley instantly responded, "But they're not Miley Cyrus. They're not role models. So for me it was a bad decision, because of my fans and because of what I stand for."

Even more poignantly, she'd promised less than two years earlier that even cigarettes would be permanently off her radar, for the sake of her health and her voice. "A good party is someone getting their face smashed in a cake – not getting smashed," she'd insisted. "I don't drink and I would never smoke. I always say that for me, smoking would be like smashing my guitar and expecting it to play. I'd never do that to my voice, not to mention the rest of my body." She then continued vociferously, "My mum wants me to be careful – not just about smoking but about second-hand smoke too. What mum doesn't? Both of my granddads died of lung cancer, so I understand why Mum is extra worried."

Yet it seemed that, all too quickly, Miley had turned her back on her own advice, and the news hit Billy Ray particularly hard. "Sorry, guys, I had no idea," he posted on Twitter. "Just saw this stuff for the first time myself. I'm so sad. There is so much beyond my control right now."

Yet if, as psychotherapist Dr Gilda Carle had a little patronisingly theorised, Miley had indeed been acting up to bring her parents back together, she'd succeeded. By March, their divorce had been called off. "I want to put my family together," Billy Ray duly announced. "I feel like I got my Miley back in a way. I just feel like we were the daddy and daughter that we were before *Hannah Montana* happened."

Yet the euphoria might have been short-lived, as one thing threatened to shake the equilibrium he'd strived to create – a six-page confessional interview for the March 2011 edition of *GQ*.

Openly contemptuous of the show that had brought his daughter to worldwide notoriety and fame – and the handlers he said had mismanaged her – Billy Ray gave an exposé that would keep the gossip columns alive for weeks. Firstly, he claimed he'd only taken the role in *Hannah Montana* for Miley's sake, in the knowledge that he was being financially exploited. "I knew I was working for peanuts," he insisted. "I'm not the smartest man in the world, but I know the difference. I went from $12,000 a week to, after four years and the millions that they make, $15,000 a week. Hell, yeah."

He added, "The damn show destroyed my family . . . I hate to say it, but I wish it had never happened. I'd take it back in a second, for my family to be here and just for everybody to be OK, safe, sound and happy and normal . . . I'd erase it all in a second if I could."

Sounding embittered about the blame that had been placed on him over the years each time a new scandal erupted, he even began to compare himself to Jesus Christ, painting a vivid image of his own martyrdom. "Every time the train went off the track – *Vanity Fair*, pole dancing, whatever scandal it was – her people, or as they say in today's news, her handlers, every time they'd put me . . . 'Somebody's shooting at Miley! Put the old man up there!' Well, I took it because I'm her daddy and that's what daddies do. 'OK, nail me to the cross, I'll take it!'" he groaned. "All those people around, they used me every time. It became so obvious that, man, no matter what happens, they're going to put you up there and let you take the bullet. Some of these handlers are perhaps more interested in handling Miley's money than her safety and career."

For instance, in November, Miley had been photographed drinking beer and partying in Madrid while she was there to perform for the MTV European Music Awards, while her 18th birthday party the same month had been held in a bar – news that would send a cold chill down Billy Ray's spine. Anticipating a backlash, he'd chosen not to attend at all. "It was wrong!" he decided. "It was for 21 years old and up. People wanted me to fly out so that then when all the bad press came, they could say, 'Daddy endorsed this stuff.' I started realising I'm being used."

Yet the worst was yet to come – the last straw was when handlers were involved in an FBI-style mission to track down teenagers with incriminating evidence of Miley's exploits and, possibly using bribery, "make their computers and phones disappear". In their eyes, her minders had callously dismissed his concern, swatting him away like a fly. "I didn't know what the footage was – they told me it was none of my business," he recalled with indignation. "I'm dealing with somebody that had only known my daughter for possibly four years – and I'm her daddy. I was pretty damn insulted – and I took that as the ultimate alarm. 'It's none of your business!' None of my business that you're running around LA trying to buy kids' computers and phones because there's something about my daughter?!"

Meanwhile Miley's own refusal to shed light on the events that had inspired such secrecy caused an even bigger rift between them. Not for the first time, he began to question his permissive parenting style. "How many interviews did I give and say, 'You know, what's important between Miley and I is I try to be a friend to my kids'? I said it a lot – and sometimes I would even read other parents might say, 'You don't need to be a friend, you need to be a parent.' Well, I'm the first guy to say to them right now: you were right. I should have been a better parent [and said], 'This is dangerous and somebody's going to get hurt', [but] I didn't know the ball was out of bounds until it was way up in the stands somewhere."

On release, the interview's impact was explosive – and in the absence of any formal statement from Miley about her father's words, other sources presumptuously spoke out for her. The headlines that had once read, ludicrously, "Miley flashes her boobs to try to stop her parents' divorce" were now replaced by attention-grabbers about her fury with – and deliberate estrangement from – her father. "To say she is angry is an understatement," one friend was quoted as saying. "She's furious that her own flesh and blood would make a private matter so public. Who does he think he is, Michael Lohan? He never said a bad word about *Hannah Montana* all those years it made millions for the family, and now that Miley has turned 18 and is making her own decisions, he does this. Unforgivable."

It was true that Billy Ray's candour had perhaps been excessive – and more than a journalist could dare to hope for from the average tight-lipped celebrity. Yet his words were those of a man bitterly disappointed at his inability to protect his daughter, powerless to stop fame derailing their relationship. Reading his comments that there was no doubt that his family was "under attack from Satan", the public wondered whether he, rather than his child, was the one approaching a breakdown.

Nonetheless, it was safe to say that his open ambivalence towards *Hannah Montana* had spelt the end of Miley's working relationship with Disney. In fact, the fallout from the turbulent year the Cyruses had suffered was so extreme that she'd felt compelled to omit the USA from her touring schedule altogether, unsure of whether she'd even be welcome. "I just think right now America has gotten to a place where I don't know if they want me to tour or not," she had explained. "I just want to go to the places where I am getting the most love."

As her promotional commitments for *Can't Be Tamed* drew to a close, she therefore chose to spend the last few months on the road in territories such as Australia, the Far East and South America. Most of the cities in her schedule were places she'd never been before and Miley made no secret of the fact that, now that her career was no longer her top priority, she'd organised the tour "mainly because I wanted to travel".

On her instructions, her aides scheduled two days off between each show to allow her time to explore – and, while some cities inspired hysteria of Beatlemania proportions, meaning Miley was unable to walk around freely even with her handlers in tow, other regions had a more laid-back vibe.

Venezuela fell into the latter category and, after a day of adventure there, she was inked with her fifth tattoo – a large dream-catcher symbol with four beaded feathers to honour each of her four siblings. Perhaps inked in a nod to her father's part native North American Indian heritage, dream-catchers are traditional, feather-adorned hoops, typically hung over someone's bedside. The concept is that any negativity that haunts them in their dreams will be forever trapped in the hoops and unable to trouble them again. Tattooed on the right-hand side of her rib cage, the symbol was intended by Miley to keep herself and her family safe from evil. After all, it was embracing superstition and spirituality that had lifted her through tough times.

The tattoo followed hot on the heels of a black cross, which had been inked to her finger to symbolise her Christian faith. Meanwhile in Brazil, she'd added a sailor-themed anchor tattoo to her collection to remind her of the importance of staying true to her roots. It symbolised having a safe port to go to – an antithesis of the stormy weather at sea – and warned her to keep her feet on the ground in any times of trouble. It was all the more poignant in the wake of Billy Ray's comments to GQ that he was keen to "shelter her from the storm", suggesting that the anchor was a reminder of the safe base she had with him, and a signature of her gratitude. The word 'karma' was also added to an index finger, indicating that those who spoke negatively of her in the press might just get their comeuppance one day.

As the tour continued, she serenaded Panama, the Philippines, Costa Rica and Ecuador to name but a few – but it was her visit to Australia that she cherished the most. Now, for the first time she would see the place where her beau had grown up. "He's a 6ft 4in tall Australian surfer and I'm 5ft 4in from Tennessee and I couldn't surf if someone gave me 10 million dollars," Miley had joked of their differences, "so we couldn't be more opposite. But [when] I went to Australia to visit him and his family, I was like, 'Ohmigod, this looks like Nashville!' There are cows everywhere. I'm like, 'How are you from the opposite side of the planet and your world is just like mine?'" She would describe the trip as the ultimate "bonding experience".

Of course, part of the attraction lay in presenting herself to the potential in-laws as a superstar. She chuckled, "It looks really good if your boyfriend is from there and it's like, 'I sold this place out!' That makes you feel pretty awesome."

However, it was telling that Miley had described her trip to Australia purely in terms of visiting the Hemsworths – it was as though the sell-out show was a mere afterthought. Clearly it had been no publicity stunt when she had defiantly announced her career would from now on be taking a back seat.

However that didn't mean she no longer had a voice, and – a far cry from yesterday's Miley, who'd claimed she was the last person on Earth to be opinionated – she used her fame to raise awareness for a political cause: the defence of homosexuality. In August 2011, she even used her body as an advertising campaign, unveiling a photo on Twitter of her ring finger, which now bore the equality symbol, alongside the phrase 'All Love Is Equal'.

It had been her fourth tattoo in under a year. However, she hadn't anticipated the backlash about the political message. Referring to Biblical messages implying that homosexuality was a sin – including one that many interpreted to advocate stoning people to death for taking part in gay sex – some of Miley's followers mocked that her views meant she was no longer God-fearing.

Many hard-line Christians believe that being gay is a lifestyle choice rather than a biologically hard-wired predisposition and that same-sex urges, if they arose, could reliably be 'cured' through the use of prayer and therapy.

Miley, on the other hand, regarded their stance as ignorant, and set out on the war path to prove them wrong. "A lot of people said, 'What happened to you? You used to be a Christian girl!'" she recalled, "and I said, 'Well, if you were a true Christian, you would have your facts straight. Christianity is about love." However, others begged to differ – and, as the debate intensified, Miley and her supporters even received death threats.

The Bible's true stance on homosexuality is ambiguous. The book of Leviticus was one of several references that opponents of gay rights used to support their views, which included lines like, "If a man also lie with mankind as he lieth with a woman, both of them have committed an abomination – they shall surely be put to death, their blood shall be upon them." However, the same book suggested that giving birth made a woman unholy and unclean and advocated sacrifice of one's own sons to comply with religious ritual.

The Bible also made statements about nature and science that are demonstrably known to be false. Yet numerous high-profile celebrities have had their say on the topic, including Beyoncé, who infamously claimed that she could never kiss a girl as it was a sin, and would mean going to Hell.

Miley, however, found her stance incomprehensible. Even if homosexuality was a sin – and she believed otherwise – surely it was contrary to Christian culture not to show compassion and forgiveness? "Imagine finding somebody you love more than anything in the world, who you would risk your life for, but couldn't marry," she challenged in an interview with *Glamour*, "and you couldn't have your special day the way your friends do – you know, wear the ring on your finger and have it mean the same thing as everybody else. Just put yourself in that person's shoes. It makes me feel sick to my stomach."

She continued vociferously, "I believe that every American should be allowed the same rights and civil liberties. Without legalised same-sex marriage, most of the time you cannot share the same health benefits, you're not considered next of kin and you're not granted the same securities as a heterosexual couple. How is this different than having someone sit in the back of the bus because of their skin colour?"

She was also keen to point out that even the stereotypical committed Christian wasn't necessarily opposed to gay couples. "My dad, who is a real man's man, lives on the farm and is as Southern and straight as they come," she mused, "but he loves my gay friends and even supports same-sex marriage. If my father can do it, anyone can. This is America, the nation of dreams. We're so proud of that and yet certain people are excluded. It's just not right."

She would also launch a campaign against the clothing store Urban Outfitters, whose CEO, Richard Hayne, had donated $13,000 to Catholic fundamentalist Rick Santorum in his bid for presidency.

Described by one journalist as "a Bible-obsessed buffoon who has no grasp on American history" and by another as "a frothy mixture of hate, bigotry, stupidity, insanity and danger that America doesn't ever need", it seemed safe to say that Santorum faced some stiff opposition – and it wasn't hard to see why. He sought to make abortion a criminal offence, advocated a point-blank ban on the contraceptive pill, wanted passion to be replaced by prohibition and disapprovingly dubbed women in employment "radical feminists".

One of his most memorable quotes demonstrated a desire to ban premarital sex altogether, seeing him insist, "Contraception is not OK. It's a licence to do things in a sexual realm that is counter to how things are supposed to be. Sex is supposed to be within marriage."

He also believed that entrusting childcare to a nanny was irresponsible, blasting, "What happened in America so that mothers and fathers who leave their children in the care of someone else – or worse yet, home alone after school – find themselves more affirmed by society? Here we can thank the influence of radical feminism."

Equally, he seemed hell-bent on making a country of liberty unworthy of its name, sarcastically sniping, "The idea is that the state doesn't have rights to limit individuals' wants and passions. I disagree with that. I think we absolutely have rights because there are consequences to letting people live out whatever wants or passions they desire."

Yet in spite of holding extremist views that had made him deeply unpopular with the more liberal majority, it seemed that America did have something to fear, as Santorum would go on to almost claim victory in the state of Iowa, losing out to fellow Republican Mitt Romney by just eight votes.

And what had infuriated Miley most of all was hearing him compare consensual gay relationships to "man-on-dog sex", claiming that indulging would be a springboard to illicit activity such as bestiality and paedophilia. "If the Supreme Court says that you have the right to consensual gay sex within your home," he'd added, "then you have the right to bigamy, you have the right to polygamy, you have the right to incest, you have the right to adultery. You have the right to anything [and that undermines] the fabric of our society."

Tweeting one of Santorum's infamous quotes – "If we allow gay marriage, next thing you know, people will be marrying goldfish" – she warned, "Every time you give Urban Outfitters money, you help finance a campaign against gay equality." As Miley had over a million Twitter followers at that time, many young fashion-conscious women included, the announcement wasn't an auspicious one for the firm – especially as her words came hot on the heels of claims that it had stolen jewellery prototypes from independent designers and passed them off as its own. However, in case anyone had missed the news, she reiterated it again in an interview with *Glamour*, adding, "I was shocked and disappointed that a company with such diversity would exclude such a large group of people. I can no longer bring myself to shop there."

She continued her stand by being photographed for the No H8 campaign, posing with duct tape sealing her mouth, to symbolise the belief that gay people had been metaphorically gagged and denied a voice, and with the words "No H8" emblazoned on her cheek. The campaign was a protest against Proposition 8, which had overturned the short-lived right for gay people to be legally married in the state of California.

Then, by November 23, she'd made another foray into politics by publishing an unofficial video for the RockMafia remix of her song 'Liberty Walk'. A track about "breaking free", it featured news footage of the political movement Occupy Wall Street. The organisation had been protesting against corruption in the banking world, and income equality for all but a privileged minority. Its catchphrase – "We are the 99%" – was a reference to the disparity statistically between the highest earning 1% of the country and the remainder of America.

Unfortunately the police took a less than sympathetic stance and a mass protest on Brooklyn Bridge resulted in over 700 arrests. Each received a criminal court summons for their peaceful but firm campaign, causing a group of the protestors to file a lawsuit against New York City for not giving sufficient notice that crossing the bridge would result in their arrest. Even Barack Obama offered words of support, claiming, "I think it expresses the frustrations the American people feel that we had the biggest financial crisis since the Great Depression, huge collateral damage all throughout the country . . . and yet you're still seeing some of the same folks who acted irresponsibly trying to fight efforts to crack down on the abusive practices that got us into this in the first place."

The following year, a federal judge ruled in favour of the protest group, acknowledging that they had not received sufficient notice of the chance of arrest, but at the time Miley released the video, the sense of anger and injustice still hung thick in the air, allowing her to reinvent 'Liberty Walk' as a protest song. In fact, with her democratic, anti-capitalist views, it seemed as if Miley was starting to take after her father.

A third foray into politics came when she offered her services free of charge for a Bob Dylan tribute album, *Chimes Of Freedom*. The CD, which featured artists such as Adele, Maroon 5 and Ke$ha covering Dylan classics, honoured the 50th anniversary of Amnesty International, but it also served as a battle cry against online piracy, an industry that cost musicians billions of dollars per year. With illegal downloads on the rise, sometimes even world-famous artists now regarded live shows as their main source of income, and in support of the bid to raise awareness, Dylan donated all of his publishing royalties. For Miley's part, she contributed a cover of 'You're Gonna Make Me Lonesome When You Go' – and, like the other artists, declined payment.

Hot on the heels of its January 2012 release was an appearance on *Punk'd* with Kelly Osbourne, seeing the pair trick socialite and reality star Khloe Kardashian into believing that the pizza delivery man has trapped his privates in his zipper. Screaming in faux agony, he prompts Khloe to make a panic-stricken emergency call to 911 for advice – only to discover that, courtesy of Miley and Kelly's prank, the joke is on her.

The theme of jokes continued with the release of *LOL*, the film adaptation of a novel about the tribulations of teenage romance in the Facebook era. Seeing the finished product brought back memories for Miley of her own awakening back in 2010, when she'd flown to Detroit during a blink-and-you'll-miss-it break from relentless touring and taken her first steps without the bane of parental guidance. "Detroit's where I felt like I really grew up," she later recalled. "It was only for a summer, but that's where I started going to clubs, where I got my first tattoo – well, not my first tattoo, but my first without my mom's consent. I got it on 8 Mile! I lied to the guy and told him I was 18. I got a heart on my finger and wore a Band Aid for months, so my mom wouldn't find out."

Detroit, home to some of the worst scenes of poverty in North America, was gritty and far from glamorous – in fact it was unlike anywhere she'd ever been before – but Miley thrived on the danger. It was also in this city, the birthplace of Eminem, where she discovered her love of rap. She'd thrown herself into the music scene on the very first night of her arrival, thanks to an impromptu and spontaneous collaboration with a local rapper.

Anticipating some serious partying, hotel staff had cordoned off the entire restaurant for the actors' use after hours and Miley didn't waste the opportunity, indulging until five o'clock in the morning. As it turned out, the gesture had been aimed entirely at damage limitation, as staff feared the wrath of fellow guests if the noise from the party had reached their bedrooms.

Meanwhile the following morning had proved to be a rude awakening for Miley, when her lead character, Lola, was obliged to kick off proceedings with a sex scene.

Although the film – which had hit India in February 2012, Singapore in March and finally the USA in May – embarrassingly failed to break even, the joy for Miley had been reminiscing. After all, *LOL* had represented the first fork in the road to womanhood.

With the exception of pre-agreed promotion for the film, she had followed through on her threat to withdraw from showbiz – and she was almost nowhere to be found during 2012. Following the advice of her onscreen mother, Demi Moore, she'd decided to create a fortress, free from prying eyes, to work on her relationship. "Demi really taught me to have one place that's yours, that no one can come into," she revealed. "Everybody needs their own space . . . that's why lions have a den. They're the fiercest of them all, but even they go back and they protect their babies and they go into the den and that is like their safe zone. Me and Demi always say that we go out and we act like we're the strongest ones in the jungle, but at the end of the day, you've got to go and have that little safe haven."

Thus, disdainfully labelling LA a "war zone" and shuddering at the thought of over-intrusive paparazzi, she moved into her parents' secluded home in the San Fernando Valley. They'd moved out of the 8,000 square foot villa just months earlier to relocate two doors down and Miley had acted quickly to make it a love nest for herself and Liam. "We both have somewhere that is like our own little piece of heaven," she recounted. "No one can come here. No one can talk about us. No one can judge us. This is for whatever we want to do and whoever we want to be with and each other!" She added playfully of the safety the villa's isolation provided, "It's kind of a black hole – and no one is going to fuck with me when P Diddy lives right across the street!"

However, there was one regular intruder – her father, who'd been known to scale gates and trespass over neighbours' property, including the lawn of Bob Hope's widow – to easily access Miley for a visit. While unannounced parental visits might have caused tension between some couples, Liam actively welcomed Billy Ray's presence. With his own family at the opposite end of the planet, he came to regard him as a substitute father figure – and by May 31, that connection would become official. Liam would get down on bended knee to present her with a yellow gold-banded 3.5 carat diamond ring dating back to the 1880s and, although his proposal was a "complete surprise", she didn't hesitate in saying "yes".

"Life is too short to not be with the person you want to be with," she'd explained, in the face of public disapproval from critics who claimed she was too young to marry. After all, she had relatives who'd fallen in love and married within days, while – incongruously for the showbiz setting, characterised by short-lived, superficial relationships and messy and chaotic break-ups – her parents were still going strong almost two decades after she was born. With the exception of their hiccup two years previously, they were more in love with ever – and her engagement was something to which both gave their full blessing.

"My [grandmother] met her husband on a Monday and they got married on a Friday," Miley recalled. "They were together for 27 years. My mum doesn't believe there's any such thing as being too young or too naïve to be in love. In my family, when you fall in love, that's it."

Miley Cyrus

Thus, whether or not Liam would prove in the long-term to be a keeper, Miley was freeing herself to follow her heart. What was more, the honeymoon period didn't look set to end any time soon. "All the time, I'll literally look at him and be like, 'You are hot, dear God!'", Miley confessed to *Cosmopolitan* of her lust. "The other day, I turned on the pool heater and it was steaming and he walked outside and took off his clothes and jumped in the pool. I was like, 'I'm gonna faint – the hottest guy of my life is in a steaming pool. This looks like a *Playgirl* shoot!' So I took a photo and made it the background on my phone. My best friend grabbed my phone and was like, 'Who's that? He is so hot!' That's my hubby!"

That summer, she turned housewife prematurely when, having placed her own career on the back burner, she accompanied her fiancé to Philadephia, where he was scheduled to start filming a new movie. Yet, just like in Detroit, the change of scenery freed Miley to step out of her comfort zone and undergo another transformation. It was there – while totally incognito – that she would develop what would soon become a controversial trademark style. "I was away from people for a minute," she explained simply, "and I just started feeling my own vibe. I bought a pair of Doctor Martens. I shaved my head. Driving a fucking Ford Explorer around – just blending in."

For Miley, cutting her hair was a deliberate act of defiance. In her eyes, she'd been the uber-feminine Disney princess in a bouffant dress for far too long. "I'm trying to break out of that long hair, big boobs stereotype that women feel they have to conform to," she expressed. "I mean, we're not living in the freaking fifties – short hair is OK. Have people got so little imagination?" She added, "Every morning I look in the mirror and I feel like a blank canvas and I choose who I want to be. In a normal job, you have to live by someone else's rules, but I'm in a job where my work is play and I don't have to pretend to be something I'm not."

She saw herself as above the need to please other people with her looks and, in an era of carbon-copy blonde, Barbie-inspired beauties with long, flowing waist-length hair, this new style was a way for her to assert her individuality. "From the beginning of time, any woman considered hot has had long hair," she groaned, "[but] I think that is so off, because if someone has the confidence to cut their hair, that automatically makes them more relatable, because they're not shy, they have a sense of who they are."

168

To her, it was unimaginative to simply copy centuries-old unspoken rules about what constituted sex appeal. What was more, she felt that deviating from those rules would be a symbol of feminist empowerment for her fans, urging them to reject conformity and not to value themselves based on how physically desirable their exterior might be. While she could have chosen the look of the inaccessible ice princess flaunting her superior beauty with every flick of her elegantly coiffured mane, she'd had the confidence to counter that image and do something that, in the eyes of many men, instantly reduced her sex appeal by far. Yet her attitude bordered on total indifference and in that sense, the harsh crop demonstrated how confident Miley was with herself – a message she hoped to pass on.

There was an added bonus about the new look too – it safeguarded her against becoming the stereotypical sex object. Miley had become increasingly frustrated with the public's penchant for judging her on her external beauty rather than her talent or inner qualities. Her godmother, Dolly Parton, was one of those who had fallen prey to that trap and was forever being seen as a bimbo, whose hair, face and breasts seemingly attracted more attention than anything she might have had to say. Yet Miley would indignantly counter, "She's smart. She's not just a blonde with big titties – she is a genius under there." The moral of the tale? "Don't let people's judgment define who you are – know who you are." That was a statement that applied to everyone – fans or famous peers alike.

Her aim above all was for people to look first and foremost at her art – whether it be the music, the fashion, the stage projections or even her controversial twerk fests, rather than merely placing her in a generic fantasy category. In principle, removing the superficial beauty might encourage people to look past the surface and embrace the more meaningful message beneath, although Miley had read too many lurid headlines constructed at her expense to hold her breath for that outcome.

However, either way, her attitude symbolised a refusal to compromise her identity or self-expression. "I read that 80% of what people think of you is made off the first 10 seconds they meet you, and you look at someone and you say, 'Are they competent, are they this, are they that?' They're going to think they know who I am, so . . . I want everything to be representing who I am."

The same went for fashion – and Miley's appetite for her own distinct style was only just beginning to emerge. Increasingly, she was becoming equally counter-cultural in her dress sense – and for the same reasons. So-called high fashion was so named not due to the towering stature of the models sporting it, but because donning couture so bizarre and left-field that the average person would simply never wear it was symbolic of occupying a powerful, influential position in society. Its wearer – usually wealthy – would be above feeling the need to conform to social norms or to strive for approval from higher places – rather, they would hold a privileged enough rank not to feel obliged to take others' opinions into account.

For Miley, defiantly parading her own style without heed to how others perceived her was the ultimate mark of empowerment, indicating someone strong and secure enough in themselves not to care.

Consequently Miley would soon be seen in outfits such as orange, black and turquoise brocade chain leggings – items the fashion pack wouldn't previously have been seen dead in – and proudly posting the evidence on Twitter. The bizarre ensembles of oversized football jumpers, fetish-inspired leather leggings, loud geometric prints and long Doctor Martens boots that followed might have induced horror, causing some to shudder with embarrassment in memory of the nineties grunge era – but Miley was a leader rather than a follower, and she was about to make the impossible seem cool.

Plus on the red carpet, she would shun couture gowns, joking that she'd only end up paying for the ludicrously expensive loan pieces if someone accidentally stepped on and ripped the train. Given that her father apparently had two left feet, it was something that she spoke of from bitter experience. Confident enough not to hide behind stereotypical symbols of femininity, such as swathes of silk and lace, she instead donned razor-sharp trouser suits that complemented her hair.

Her powerful dress sense and cropped cut would even lead to rumours that she was a lesbian, leaving a bemused Miley asking why that was classed as an insult. The expectation for women – and, of course, celebrities in particular – to be uncompromisingly elegant and feminine in their attire was so ingrained in popular culture that when Miley was seen stepping off a plane wearing pyjamas and fluffy unicorn slippers (albeit alongside a Chanel handbag), it caused newspapers to accuse that she might have been on the verge of a mental health crisis. Statements like that, however, merely strengthened her resolve to, at all costs, refuse to give in to the pressure, and continue being herself.

She was contradicting beliefs that women moulded their appearance purely with the aim of attracting men. In stark contrast, for Miley – and, she hoped, many women like her – the body was a blank canvas, a vehicle through which to express art, mood and personal style. "I'm such a fashion junkie," she admitted, "and I feel like I express myself perfectly by the way I dress."

Miley was now shaking up social norms before she'd so much as released any new material – and indeed, the most controversial part of her overhaul was yet to come.

Chapter 10

To execute her transformation, not to mention fulfil her potential as an adult artist, Miley knew it was time to free herself of old ties, and start afresh. Her goal was to "set a new standard for pop music" and product something as timeless as Michael Jackson's *Bad* – ambitions which were by no means for the faint-hearted – and she lacked confidence in her then management to deliver. The solution was simple. "I basically cut off all ties," she explained. "I got rid of my manager, I got rid of my label. I just started over. I really wanted to stay . . . but I felt like [my evolution] would have scared them."

That evolution included a new tattoo bearing the word 'Bad' – etched on a now permanently raised middle finger – the impassioned slogan 'Love Never Dies' on her lower chest and a miniature sugar skull on her foot, which formed part of a matching pair symbolising the commitment between herself and Liam. Meanwhile the Roman numerals VIIXCI, also inked that year, paid homage to July 1991, the month and year when her parents first met.

Then, in a wry jibe at her critics, she'd had words from a 1910 speech delivered by former President Teddy Roosevelt at the Sorbonne in Paris inked onto her left forearm. Challenging that those who so readily passed judgment had never been brave or accomplished enough to walk in her shoes, it read, "So that his place shall never be with those cold and timid souls who neither know victory nor defeat."

In a show of solidarity with his fiancée, Liam had the preceding line of the speech tattooed on his own arm, reading, "If he fails, at least fails while daring greatly." Unfortunately, the tattooist seemed to have omitted the word "he" from the passage, but the message was clear.

Other lines from the same speech summed up Miley's sentiment exactly, including, "It is not the critic who counts: not the man who points out how the strong man stumbles or where the doer of deeds could have done better. The credit belongs to the man who is actually in the arena, whose face is marred by dust and sweat and blood, who strives valiantly, who errs and comes up short again and again, because there is no effort without error or shortcoming, but who knows the great enthusiasms, the great devotions, who spends himself for a worthy cause; who, at the best, knows, in the end, the triumph of high achievement."

A part-defiant, part-defensive Miley would confirm to the media, "It's about how people judge who wins and who loses, but they're not the ones in there fighting."

That summer, she would take another step to shield herself from the acid-tongued critics to which she made reference by adding an eyeball to her collection – a traditional Middle Eastern symbol representing protection from the "evil eye" of others' envy. With the symbol on one's person, ancient tradition dictated, any negative thoughts coming her way would be barricaded out.

While Miley's growing tally of tattoos might have seemed tame in comparison to those of her brother Trace, who had by now transformed his entire face into art, they were a sure signature of rebellion – Miley was changing fast. "[Not only am I] not the same person I was six months ago," she clarified, "I'm not even the same person I was two weeks ago."

Adding that she already felt alienated and totally "disconnected" from the version of herself she'd showcased on the *Can't Be Tamed* album, she continued, "When people go to iTunes and listen to my old music, it's so irritating to me because I can't just erase that stuff and start over."

Perhaps not – but securing herself new management might have been a good start. In an industry as fickle as showbiz, where by 25 many artists could already be considered has-beens, Miley knew she had little margin for error when it came to her comeback. After much deliberation, she approached Larry Rudolph, someone who specialised in helping artists transition from child stars into adult entertainers. Originally an entertainment lawyer with high-profile clients like Justin Timberlake on his books, he'd then moved into representing artists, beginning with Miley's idol Britney Spears. Britney's mother had asked him to listen to her then 15-year-old daughter sing, which had led to him helping her secure her first record deal. Not only had he guided her through huge changes, but he'd done the same for Christina Aguilera and Jessica Simpson – and his track record had Miley hooked.

What was more, he insisted he was immune from the temptation to manufacture his artists, instead merely facilitating their own voices to be heard. "There's no such thing as, 'OK, let's figure out the plan for growing up.' It doesn't work," he asserted. "The public sees through it in five seconds and every artist who's tried to do it has failed."

This was a sentiment to which Miley could entirely relate. "Everyone has to work on the things they don't care about to get where they want to be," she mused. "I worked for five years on something that was a character where I didn't really get to be the creative person that I wanted to be. I had to make my money [but now] I can just make music because I love it. It doesn't really have to be driven by, 'I wanna build up my fanbase', because I have an amazing fanbase that's followed me. Now because I [finally] don't have any more responsibilities or have anyone that I have to really answer to, I can [just be myself]."

It seemed that Larry might be the man to help her realise that dream. He was offering her a chance to expose her true self to the world – and if he could turn Britney from an innocent, pig-tailed schoolgirl into a writhing temptress with a snake wrapped around her body as she sang 'I'm A Slave 4 U', what might he be able to do for Miley?

She signed on the dotted line, simultaneously setting the wheels in motion to change labels from Hollywood Records to RCA, and Larry instantly introduced her to Pharrell, the man who'd play a leading role in shaping her comeback album. A songwriter and recording artist in his own right, Pharrell had even produced 'I'm A Slave 4 U', the song that had unleashed Britney's sexy side for the first time.

Not everyone had seen the potential at first, however. "People weren't getting it," Miley recalled with agitation. "They were like, 'He doesn't have anything out right now.' I was like, 'Who the fuck cares? He's Pharrell!" He reciprocated her affection and, having heard about the salvia scandal, sensed automatically that she was craving liberation. "That bitch is actually living," he would remark admiringly. "She's not sitting there with her Momager's chain on her door. I want to free that bitch. I want her out of her cage."

Plus, while some urban producers might have thought that Miley's farm-girl accent would damage their street cred, Pharrell was more open-minded, urging her to stay true to her country roots and twang – the one thing that set her apart from her rivals. Telling her to "be what no one else can be", he insisted that blending both country and hip-hop influences together would result in an album unlike any of the urban acts by which she was inspired, creating a new genre in itself. Her fusion might result in a hybrid which fans of both genres would scornfully reject, but it was a risk she was willing to take. "I've made my money," she reiterated, "[so] if no one buys my album, it's cool. It's fine. I've got a house and I've got dogs that I love. I don't need anything else!"

Consequently she took the plunge into new territory, inviting rappers such as Ludacris, Nelly and Big Sean to collaborate with her, as well as lesser-known up-and-coming artists such as Future and French Montana. While many tracks would feature hard-hitting rap vocals by Miley and partners, even polar opposite Britney was added to the mix, contributing guest vocals to the Salt-N-Pepa-inspired feminist anthem 'SMS Bangerz'.

As the album developed, it would boast rap, R&B and "Dirty South hip-hop" with an incongruous country twist. The small group of producers who aided the sound included Mike Will Made It, who'd previously worked with 2 Chainz, Ciara and Kanye West, not to mention Rihanna on her pole-dancing anthem, 'Pour It Up', and Sean Garrett, who'd worked extensively with Beyoncé and Nicki Minaj. Miley had all the big names she needed to ensure a controversial comeback – and for months, she'd barely ventured out of the studio.

Of course, she made an exception to appear in the video for Borgore's 'Decisions', a dubstep track to which she'd secretly lent her vocals that summer. Anxious to avoid stereotypes based on her pop reputation, Miley had initially kept totally quiet about her involvement, instead allowing Borgore – a vocalist, producer and nightclub DJ – to unleash it on unsuspecting revellers all summer. It had also appeared on his independent EP of the same name – and those who prided themselves on being edgy and counter-cultural, who might have automatically branded the track uncool if they'd known who was singing, were online in their droves to express their love of it. It wasn't until September, when the video was released, that Miley finally came clean, forcing onlookers to question their unswerving 'Fuck the mainstream' attitude and perhaps wonder whether they might have been missing out.

Even the media was shocked, one *Entertainment Weekly* journalist writing in astonishment, "If you had told me five years ago that Miley Cyrus would one day be featured on an Israeli DJ's dubstep track, I would have scoffed and replied, 'Hannah Montana? Are you serious?!'"

The wheels were being set in motion for Miley's transition, aided by the track's accompanying video. With the repetitive refrain of "Bitches love cake", the track was a wry take on groupies with a superficial interest in those who could boast success, money and fame. Cynically, it featured a successful singer struggling to choose between real love and a family or "fake" love with a glamorous porn star – perhaps a dig at Borgore's porn actress ex-girlfriend Jessie Andrews, who, bizarrely, also made an appearance in the video. For Miley's part, she emerged from a giant cake, à la Madonna, before breaking into a kiss with a unicorn – who, underneath his disguise, was her real-life boyfriend.

The 'cosplay' element had been what had persuaded Liam – who rejected the idea of a stereotypical nightclub scene – to take part. "He didn't just want to be in a video partying," Miley recounted, "so I said, 'Wear a disguise! Be a unicorn and make out with me!' It was very weird kissing a unicorn – my tongue was just going into a plastic unicorn mask all night!"

'Decisions' was the public's first introduction to Miley's cropped haircut – and, just as she'd predicted, not everyone was a fan. In fact, one of Pharrell's closest friends, fellow producer Tyler The Creator, teasingly taunted on Twitter that she should "kill her barber for what he did to her". Miley's competitive instinct instantly came into play and she fired back, "Nothing can match what God already did to your face. By the way I love your music. Smiley face!" Pharrell, who by now regarded Miley as a little sister, was proud at how feisty she'd become, marvelling, "The ovaries! The sophistication to end it with, 'But I love your music. Smiley face.' 'Yes, I will nuke you. I'm not afraid – but I like your music.' That was a very proud moment for me. Name another pop artist under 21 who would have responded like that."

Aside from stepping out on Twitter to effortlessly annihilate her opponents, Miley then remained holed away at home or in the studio and barely appeared in the public eye until the release of her third movie, *So*

Miley twerks against fellow vocalist Robin Thicke for a performance the pair had vowed would make history, while she suggestively gestures at her crotch with a giant foam finger. The location? New York's 2013 VMAs. AKM-GSI/SPLASH NEWS/CORBIS

Miley arrives at the 2013 VMAs, sticking out her tongue to launch what would become her trademark gesture.
NATE BECKETT/SPLASH NEWS/CORBIS

Miley steps out with Blackeyed Peas star Will.i.am for a performance on the *Jimmy Kimmel Live!* show in June 2013.
CLINT BREWER/SPLASH NEWS/CORBIS

Miley and Liam make a strained final public appearance together as she shows support for the August 2013 premiere of her fiancé's film, *Paranoia*, in LA. Despite a desperate attempt to patch up their affair, the pair would announce their break-up just days later.
COLLIN/CELEBRITY MONITOR/SPLASH NEWS/CORBIS

A newly unattached Miley enjoys the single life with an appearance at the September 2013 iHeart Radio Music Festival in Las Vegas. Her outfit – a white fishnet dress with contrasting black nipple pasties – leaves little to the imagination.
AKM-GSI/SPLASH NEWS/CORBIS

Pairing a casual cheerleading shirt with a contrasting bangle and handbag from high fashion brand Chanel, Miley makes her appearance at the August 2013 filming of producer Mike Will Made-It's video single '23'. WALIK GOSHORN/RETNA LTD./CORBIS

Miley arrives at the November 2013 MTV VMAs in Amsterdam in a dress emblazoned with the faces of hip-hop legends Biggie and 2-Pac. She would later celebrate the liberal location by lighting up a joint onstage. BROCK MILLER/SPLASH NEWS/CORBIS

Miley shows off the three-wheeler motorbike that beloved father Billy Ray gifted her for her 21st birthday, riding around the streets of LA. CLINT BREWER/SPLASH NEWS/CORBIS

Miley belts out 'Wrecking Ball' with an explosion of emotion at the November 2013 American Music Awards. Her costume for the night would be a bralet and high-waisted shorts set emblazoned with cat faces. LUCY NICHOLSON/REUTERS/CORBIS

Miley dons a festive outfit and twerks with Santa Claus live at New York's December 2013 Z-100 Jingle Ball.
WALIK GOSHORN/RETNA LTD./CORBIS

Miley unleashes her famous tongue in celebration of the opening night of nightclub-cum-circus Beacher's Madhouse in Las Vegas.
PETER FOLEY/EPA/CORBIS

Miley finds herself back on stage to see in the New Year at New York's Times Square on December 31, 2013. PETER FOLEY/EPA/CORBIS

On stage in Vancouver in February 2014, a cowboy hat-clad Miley pulls out a comedy set of decaying false teeth – used to embellish her final encore, a rendition of 'Party In The USA'. R CHIANG/SPLASH NEWS/CORBIS

Miley straddles a giant hot dog prop suspended from the ceiling – although the stunt was perhaps less offensive to Muslims than pal Katy Perry's stunt of burning an 'Allah' necklace in a promo video the same year. R CHIANG/SPLASH NEWS/CORBIS

Miley spanks the voluptuous spandex-clad bottom of her aptly named backing dancer Amazon Ashley who, at 6' 7", is over a foot taller than her. OBERON/SPLASH NEWS/CORBIS

Miley wows LA in a marijuana leaf-adorned bodysuit as she sings her heart out atop an onstage car, February 22, 2014.
AKM-GSI/SPLASH NEWS/CORBIS

Undercover, in March 2013. In the film, she starred as Molly, a teenager who drops out of high school to join her former police officer father on his adventures as a private investigator. At first their work together is barely challenging – for example, cornering petty thieves or humiliating unfaithful partners by catching them red-handed – but life changes when an FBI agent becomes a client, approaching Molly to take on a guise no man or adult woman could ever hope to pull off – that of a teenage sorority sister at college.

While Molly was miles apart from Miley, the movie did mirror the latter's real-life feelings about being obliged to play a role with which she simply couldn't identify. Molly has two personas – that of the street-wise, tough-talking tomboy with a stereotypically masculine career and that of the faux affluent sorority girl whose superficial life is filled with make-up, fake nails and obligatory fits of giggles. Just as Miley had been failing her Hannah role, Molly, too, struggles to become a girly girl, but is forced to do so believably in order to protect fellow sorority sister Alex, whose father's plans to testify against dangerous criminals have placed her life in danger. To complicate matters further, she finds herself falling for the man she suspects may be under orders to take Alex's life.

Molly, who had shunned university in favour of work, is forced to navigate a world she knows little to nothing about while, surrounded by con-men with ulterior motives, she is able to trust no one in the process. In real life, however, Miley was given some help as she and co-star Kelly Osbourne were sent to shadow an actual sorority group in New Orleans as research for the film. Miley's verdict? It might have been fun, but the experience had merely confirmed to her that she was glad never to have had to share a dorm room at university. "A girl room-mate? I don't think it would've ended well," she joked. "I'd be throwing things . . . I couldn't handle not having my own space."

Of much more appeal was the opportunity to play an undercover agent, although some of the stunts left her father with his heart in his mouth. Miley, who admired the powerful persona of Angelina Jolie and her ability to "flip a car while [simultaneously] giving the hottest look to camera", and sought to emulate her tough-girl brand of sex appeal, had been forced to reassure him – and herself.

"In the opening scene, I'm dangling off the side of a building in New

Orleans, which is 100% real," she bragged, although she confessed that her heart had been pounding. "In the first shot, I was supposed to stand up on this flowerpot to climb onto the side of the building and the flowerpot tipped over. I was so scared. My dad had his arms wrapped around his chair and he was like, 'No, you can't do this!' I was literally walking on the side of the building, which is one of the coolest things I've ever done."

The following month, she continued to showcase her edgier side when she collaborated with Snoop Dogg, who was appearing under his alter ego, Snoop Lion, for a reggae concept album called *Reincarnated*. She lent her vocals to the track 'Ashtrays And Heartbreaks', which Snoop, perhaps unwittingly revealing a secret, told the media was about a woman mourning the death of a relationship that "no longer exists".

By some accounts, Miley's relationship with Liam had been a notoriously on-off affair, although she would on occasion take to Twitter to vociferously deny that the engagement was off. However, for most, the real scoop was Miley's involvement with unusual musical partner Snoop Dogg. His other collaborators on the album, such as Drake and Rita Ora, already firmly fitted into the urban category, whereas Miley was clearly the odd one out – and for some, for her even to share the same sentence with the joint-toting gangsta rapper was shocking.

However, she was quick to point out that a love of illicit smoking was something they definitely shared in common. From the salvia scandal to the party at which she'd been the proud recipient of a Bob Marley birthday cake, publicly chuckling of the gift, "That's how you know you smoke way too much fucking weed." Miley had by now advocated marijuana for years and thus the title of the song was perhaps more apt than *Hannah Montana* fans knew.

As for the meaning behind the track, if the romance between her and Liam had indeed been in trouble, perhaps it was down to the total immersion in music that her career demanded in the lead up to an album she considered to be her "debut" – the first time that the public would see the real, adult Miley.

Yet was the public ready? The reaction to first single 'We Can't Stop' firmly suggested otherwise. Production duo Rock City had originally intended the track for Rihanna but, believing that it deserved to take centre stage as an album's debut single, they were deterred by the success she'd already had with 'Diamonds'. Consequently, they then offered it to fellow producer Mike Will Made It, who decided the track was perfect for Miley.

Although she'd historically been ambivalent about taking on others' songs, feeling that it was a less than authentic measure, 'We Can't Stop' had instantly resonated with her. The song, with its tales of hard partying and coming of age, increasingly represented Miley's life – and the lives of those just like her, who "stayed out all night long". This fact was illustrated by a subsequent epic two-day party where sleep was forbidden, towards the end of which an exhausted Miley finally succumbed to shut eye in front of an open fireplace and unwittingly melted her brand new Doctor Martens boots. By dawn on the second night, the group had shifted the party to the rooftop to watch the sun rise, and Miley began to sing the track that would soon become her new single, substituting the line, "This is our house, these are our rules" for "This is our house, this is our roof", to honour the occasion.

That sentiment was met with a deafening roar of drunken approval – and yet when the song hit the charts, on June 3, 2013, not everyone was as tolerant. Campaigners were instantly enraged by the drug-fuelled imagery – firstly of cocaine, when Miley sang about clubbers queuing to "get a line" in the bathroom, and secondly of ecstasy, when she spoke of dancing with "molly". Yet although the word represented the street slang for potentially deadly MDMA, the word also resembled the sound of Miley's own name – an ambiguity she was quick to exploit and hide behind. "If you're aged 10, then it's Miley," she admitted to *The Sun*, [but] if you know what I'm talking about, then you know." Of her concession to "Miley", she added, "I just wanted [to make sure it would be] played on the radio."

Although she'd temporarily felt gagged by radio regulations against drug references, she would notably make up for the concession later by speaking candidly of her various vices in the media. "I think weed is the best drug on earth," she asserted to *Rolling Stone*. "One time I smoked a joint with peyote in it and I saw a wolf howling at the moon. Hollywood is a coke town, but weed is so much better. Those are happy drugs – social drugs. They make you want to be with friends . . . I really don't like coke. It's so gross and so dark. It's like, what are you from, the nineties? Ew."

Evidently, Miley had changed her stance not just on smoking, but on shock value. Just a couple of years earlier, she'd told of how it annoyed her when people falsely thought that she would deliberately court shock value, insisting angelically, "I'd never do that" – and yet now she was making an admission of the exact opposite.

"I know what I'm doing, I know I'm shocking you," an older and perhaps wiser Miley now teased. "The more that [people] are wondering, 'What the hell is she doing?', the more they're going to want to listen to my record." She'd later add, "It's all marketing – if a website is like, 'We love Miley's performance!', I don't think people are gonna click on it. 'Miley's cute performance with teddy bears!' – no one is gonna click on that."

With that in mind, she knew the single's accompanying video had to follow the same sensation-seeking rules as she'd seen in headlines in the media. With each new admission, the layers of the Hannah Montana illusion were slowly being peeled away – and yet an attention-craving Miley felt compelled to take things a few steps further.

After all, with free content more readily available on the internet than ever before, the watching public had become almost desensitised – in her eyes, even yet another kitsch animal video was more likely to go viral than new material from a singer. "People are watching, like, 'Cute cat plays with yarn' for three hours a lot more than they're watching anyone else's music video," she would comment sardonically – and if the craze for gimmicky multimillionaire felines such as Grumpy Cat was anything to go by, she was probably right.

Thus, by Miley's account, she had promptly taken charge of the creative reins for the 'We Can't Stop' video, promising that she would be her sceptical label's "little puppet" for ever more if she wasn't able to prove the first time round that she knew exactly what was hot.

The aim of the video was to depict the legendary party that the song's lyrics spoke of – one that was a cross between the film *Project X* and a *Nylon* high-fashion shoot. According to Miley, "Everyone is going to wish they were at this party."

To achieve her vision, she enlisted the help of video director Diane Martel – also responsible for Robin Thicke and Pharrell's number one hit 'Blurred Lines' – and together they resolved to make a "trippy, fucked-up video" the whole world would remember, one that posed as a "giant selfie".

Yet the world might not have been ready for Miley's candour. The first indication that she could have taken things too far came when horrified bosses at MTV UK forwarded a monumental 18-page list of edits that they insisted must be made before they'd even consider transmitting the video over the airwaves. Some of the more extreme gyration was instantly cut, while a large 'X' would have to censor Miley's mouth to hide a gesture she made symbolising oral sex.

As the list continued, Miley saw entire scenes crumbling to dust before her eyes. "It's so lame," she sighed, "because you can shoot people in a movie but you can't show someone [simulating oral sex]. The world is in such a fucked-up place." There was plenty of evidence in support of her argument – for instance, computer games such as *Call Of Duty* depicted graphic violence and yet they were regularly accessed even by children, while in the UK news it would emerge that a 13-year-old boy had raped his eight-year-old sister after downloading rape scenes on his X-Box. Meanwhile, when the 'Blurred Lines' video suffered the same prejudice, Robin Thicke's wife spoke out to echo Miley's point of view, publicly announcing, "Violence is ugly [but] nudity is beautiful and 'Blurred Lines' makes me wanna fuck."

Miley's indignation raged on, provoked even more by the "hypo-critical" moral values of her home country. "I was watching *Breaking Bad* the other day and they were cooking [illegal drug crystal meth]," she recalled. "I could literally cook meth because of that show – it's a how-to – and then they bleeped out the word 'fuck'. And I'm like, really? They killed a guy and disintegrated his body in acid, but you're not allowed to say 'fuck'? It's like when they bleeped 'molly' [in my song]. America is just so weird in what they think is right and wrong."

The video finally premiered on June 19 and, despite the artistic censor-ship, it went viral nonetheless, receiving 10.7 million views on Vevo in just 24 hours. Already breaking the record for most-viewed video on the site, it then reached 100 million views in 37 days.

The public delighted in gory images such as a skull made of French fries, which was then shattered and booted across the floor – another example, perhaps, of violence triumphing in the authorities' eyes over com-paratively tame expressions of sexuality. With visual artist Christopher Chiappa in charge of its creation – a man whose former projects included the Knife Factory, where he assembled scores of his own model knifes in an artist's booth – it was always going to be macabre. Viewers would also see a male friend of Miley's bite into a bread roll filled with dollar bills, followed by scenes of her submerged in a swimming pool which deliberately paid homage to a similar photo, 'Rushing River', by Ryan McGinley, a man who'd shot the album cover for Katy Perry's *Prism*. (Notably, Ryan had also collaborated with Miley's producer Pharrell on an advertising campaign for the 2012 relaunch of MySpace.)

Meanwhile the scene of Miley smooching a Barbie doll was inspired by the work of fashion photographer Helmut Newton, whose "obsession" with mannequins, blow-up dolls and plastic toys had dated back to the sixties. The photo Diane had sought to emulate featured a model lying on the beach on her back simulating a French kiss with a male doll, while another loomed just behind her.

Back on the macabre side, the world witnessed an array of deceased dogs, stuffed and posing with sunglasses, including one that a fur-clad Miley dragged behind her as she walked. The taxidermy theme – partly seeming to have been inspired by aspects of Lady Gaga's 'Bad Romance' – had been Miley's idea. Then there was a vision of a woman simulating the amputation of her own fingers with a knife, before candy-pink-coloured blood oozed out.

Yet, as if to prove Miley's point, it wasn't the scenes of gore that piqued the public's disgust, but merely those of a sexual nature – especially those which depicted her 'twerking'. The controversial dance move, which involved bending over and sexually gyrating the buttocks at speed, was deemed distasteful – and yet the wave of outrage wasn't just from those covering their children's eyes.

She also stood accused of objectifying black people, many of whom staked a claim on the move as an integral part of their racial identity. For these individuals, the twerk was not just a dance move, but a political gesture. Seeing Miley, a privileged white woman, emulate it had cut open long-standing wounds about racial prejudice and some of the more voluptuous girls, sneering that Miley was "a skinny white girl with a flat ass who couldn't twerk to save her life", were using it as an open invitation to incite race wars.

Miley would laugh the insults off, giggling in agreement, "I know! I'm only 108 pounds!" Yet the words were symptomatic of a deep-rooted resentment towards her and the oppression she represented. While many black Americans felt marginalised and looked down on for their "ratchet" culture – considered primitive and unsophisticated – Miley, one of the wealthiest young women in the city, was able to posture at being "hood" for fun before returning to her lifestyle of opulence and without needing to face the realities of being discriminated against as a member of the race she was portraying. They felt she was misappropriating their culture – and even making a mockery out of them.

Black women's magazine *Jezebel* summed up these sentiments when it blasted, "A lesson from Miley Cyrus' new video – if you want to look 'cool' and 'edgy' and 'tough', just steal the styles and dance moves of black people."

Accusing her also of copying their hand gestures and stereotypical penchant for wearing gold grills on their teeth, it added, "She can play at blackness without being burdened by the reality of it. Miley and her ilk need to be reminded that the stuff they think is cool, the accoutrements they're borrowing, have been birthed in an environment where people are under-educated, oppressed, under-represented, disenfranchised, systematically discriminated against and struggling in a system set up to ensure they fail."

It was true that "ratchet" – a slang term deriving from the word "wretched", which referenced a low-class, "ghetto" and often contemptible lifestyle – had racial connotations. Yet was the bitterness of those who felt tarred with that brush merely causing even greater segregation between the races, as they sought to exclude whites from their world? Plus might it not be equally racist to insist that specific dance moves belonged exclusively to a specific race and that entire styles of behaviour should be divided strictly by skin colour?

Regardless, many were steadfast in their disapproval of Miley – and fuel was added to the fire when a track called '4x4' leaked from her then yet to be released album. Lyrically it depicted her speeding in a getaway car so fast that she was about to "piss myself" in a bid to help her assumed romantic partner – black rapper Nelly – escape from the police who want to "put him in jail". Some might have felt that she was glorifying gangsta rap culture by making the danger appear cool and, in doing so, being insensitive to those actually living the nightmare of crime and jail. The fact that Miley was so detached from this lifestyle herself and was using it merely as an attention-grabbing plot, would only have added insult to injury. It could have been argued that gang culture was so ingrained into the fabric of certain poverty-stricken ghetto neighbourhoods that many of those born into them had little chance of ever "going straight". Thus for Miley to turn their plight into a theatrical song that could earn her millions, without having paid her dues by actually experiencing it, was a controversial choice. By portraying herself as a "ride or die" gangster's moll, she'd transformed the dark, gritty reality of such a lifestyle into something exciting, glamorous and decadent.

To make matters worse, the track arrived hot on the heels of an inconveniently timed *Newsweek* article, which had quoted that there were more African Americans in the US corrections system today – in jail, on probation, or on parole – than there were enslaved in 1850.

Meanwhile Miley found herself accused of metaphorical slavery herself when a twerking session during 'We Can't Stop' had seen her surrounded by black women who were watching her in awe. *Jezebel* claimed that portraying a white woman in the middle of the room, with her darker-skinned peers at the sides, communicated "a powerful, disrespectful message [giving the impression that] she is in charge and they are in service to her". Of course, as the starring vocalist, it was only natural that Miley should be at the forefront and centre, but the question was why all of the girls crouching subserviently at each side of her were of an ethnic minority.

She dismissed their concerns however, pointing out defiantly, "I'm not Disney where they have, like, an Asian girl, a black girl and a white girl just to be politically correct. I'm not trying to make any kind of statement." Plus because Miley had never viewed black people as being worth less than whites, it hadn't occurred to her to give them compensatory special treatment.

Yet she would also have to explain away the fact that she'd spanked a black girl on camera. The recipient of her playful dominatrix-inspired posturing, Amazon Ashley – a burlesque dancer who, at 6ft 7in, had branded herself "the world's tallest stripper" – had insisted that Miley had treated her with "the utmost of respect". The pair, who had been friends

184

for years, had a demonstrably affectionate, tactile relationship, illustrated by videos Ashley posted on Instagram of Miley simulating sucking her breasts while singing an impromptu version of 'Wrecking Ball' to her. Meanwhile to add even more fuel to the speculation, Ashley was openly bisexual.

All of the photos she'd posted of the two showed them partying together on equal terms – and even outside of the video set, she didn't seem to mind using her ample derriere as a walking advertising aid, posing in a pair of pants that featured bright red lips and an extended tongue, emblazoned with the title of Miley's album, *Bangerz*. She then posted on Instagram a photo of Miley rocking the same design.

Was it really racially demeaning for Miley to spank her friend on film when the smack had been reciprocated – and if so, was it equally racist that some photos depicted Ashley scooping Miley – someone almost 15 inches shorter than her – up in the air, almost holding her above her head? Arguably, this too was a symbol of domination.

Then there was the photo she'd posted of a very statesque black Barbie doll towering over a diminutive blonde doll who stood at her feet, her lips just about level with her companion's knee? She'd jokingly insinuated that the dolls in the photos were intended to represent herself and Miley. Was this demeaning to white people, or did racism only apply to a group that had historically been discriminated against, making whites immune from harm? Furthermore, did the pair perhaps merely have a 21st century friendship free from the restraints of racial connotations, or even conscious awareness of the skin colour that divided them?

Miley's goal was a world where, in the decades to come, people would ask incredulously whether gay people had really once been forbidden to marry and whether in the past black Americans had really been discriminated against. For, unbeknown to her detractors, she'd secretly been travelling to Atlanta for years to take part in ethnic-minority-heavy parking lot dance-offs – and not only had she perfected her dance moves, she'd also been an active champion of racial integration. In stark contrast to the atmosphere in Atlanta – a state renowned for record amounts of slavery, where blacks still typically had a much lower income and status, and mixing with whites remained taboo – she'd refused to see skin colour. In fact, she felt that those who distinguished between the races, singling out blacks for special treatment to escape connotations of slavery and white supremacy – notions from an era that had died a long time previously – were the truly racist ones. As she was young and lived by modern values, she automatically assumed equality – and the concept of degrading the race of another by her unconscious actions hadn't even entered her head.

However, a conversation with her producer, Mike Will Made It, offered a reality check. "He said, 'For me, my biggest achievement has been working with a white girl, but for a white girl to work and associate with black producers, you're being ratchet,'" Miley recounted. "He's like, 'Why am I on the come-up if I work with you, but if you work with me, you're trying to be 'hood?' It's a double standard. I didn't realise it, but people are still racist." Yet Miley's opponents were adamant that she was merely passing the buck and in the media, she would regularly be forced to defend that her black co-stars were not her "accessories", but "my homies".

That was just the beginning. While some argued that she didn't respect her dancers, an increasing number of people taunted that she barely respected herself. One journalist summed up public criticism when he commented that Miley and her peers sounded like singers, but aesthetically might be mistaken for porn stars. "Their message to girls is, 'Forget talent – what counts is being hot and available,'" he asserted. "No wonder they are sexting topless pictures, pouting on Facebook and feeling pressure to service boys' needs too young."

However, he omitted from his argument the notion that girls had needs too and that, as they matured, a desire to express their sexuality – with or without the influence of pop stars – was perhaps inevitable. Could it be that those unable to cope with their "babies" growing up at high speed were passing the buck to celebrities to parent their children, to absolve themselves of the guilty burden of responsibility when things went wrong?

Moreover, the theory that sexualised celebrities dissuaded girls from prioritising talent raised the question of why, in the 21st century, any woman should feel obliged to choose between good looks and accomplishment. As a growing number of critics questioned Miley's credibility, sneering that she couldn't be taken seriously because she'd demeaned herself with her "undignified" twerk, it raised another question: would David Beckham still be taken seriously in football after posing provocatively on billboards in his underpants?

At first sight, it might well have seemed that she was the victim of sexism and misogyny – a young woman with a strong sexuality whose liberation was being crushed by pressure to adhere to an unfair double standard. After all, her defiantly cropped haircut and quotes in the media suggested her demeanour was about anything but pandering to the needs of men. Perhaps the true pressure came from people trying to extinguish her sex appeal, rather than from those promoting it.

However, Miley was also giving mixed signals. While she certainly seemed to be having fun, how much of her image was based on external advice? The occasional off-guard comment might suggest that even with her vast wealth and strong sense of self, she was not entirely immune. "It used to be if you're a woman, you do not sing about sex," she told *Lifetime TV*, "and now if that's not what you're singing about, if that's not your entire image, you won't get played on radio." With that comment in mind, was her current look what she truly wanted, or, on the other hand, was it part of a desperate bid to remain relevant in an increasingly sexually saturated music scene?

There were other inconsistencies in Miley's words too. For instance, she'd been adamant that she wanted to embrace her sex appeal on her own terms, citing a love of Khia's 'My Neck, My Back' because the lyrics emphasised a man pleasing a woman, instead of the other way round, due to the vocalist's demand that her lover satisfies her. "It's like, 'I'm not going to do all this to you – you please me!'" Miley chuckled admiringly. She'd then added, "I want my music to be like, 'Me and my girls are going to get drunk and have a good time, not the guys going, 'We're going out to bang a bunch of chicks!'"

However, her words didn't match her actions when she appeared onstage at a Juicy J concert that June 4 for no other purpose than to twerk to the track 'Bandz A Make Her Dance', which boasted of "bitches" who are "like porn stars" and featured additional lyrics about "popping pussy". Not only did the song appear derogatory to women, but Juicy J had formerly been a member of Three 6 Mafia, a group that rose to fame with tracks like 'Slob On My Knob' and 'It's Hard Out Here For A Pimp'. Perhaps the words of *Jezebel* magazine when it accused Miley's music of being "Dirty South/crunk hip-hop associated with strip clubs, pimps and drug dealers" weren't as rash as they might originally have seemed.

Although she opposed sexism, she was giving mixed signals by twerking at the concert of someone who, judging by his track record, seemed to view women as objects.

Clearly there was more to her complex psyche than met the eye, but she was unfazed by all the negative publicity, as it only served to raise 'We Can't Stop' to number two in the USA, with over two million copies sold, and the top spot in the UK. "Haters are gonna hate," Miley taunted, "but haters are also going to clock on your YouTube video just to watch it so I really don't care. You helped me break the record [for most views in 24 hours], even if you were watching just to hate on me – and now I hold the record, so I win!"

She added, "I like it when people say, 'How are they not talking about these real world issues right now and Miley's just about twerking?' I'm like, 'What do you want me to do?'" she laughed. "You're the one clicking the damn page. Go read the news about real shit in the world and don't keep clicking on my page – you're the one that's making it keep coming back and the reason why people won't quit talking about it! I already did it and I've got bigger and naughtier things to be thinking about – my mind's a fun place to be!"

True to her word, she did unveil something bigger and better, with the August 25 release of the single 'Wrecking Ball'. This time, she even broke her previous record by attracting almost double the number of views – 19.3 million – in the first 24 hours. Gleefully, she knocked One Direction off the top spot.

The total antithesis of the party vibe of its predecessor, 'Wrecking Ball' was a dark and depressive anthem that, according to Miley, mirrored "how it feels when everything around you is destroyed". She'd chosen to release a track that was the polar opposite of 'We Can't Stop' in a deliberate effort to confound viewers' expectations, turn stereotypes on their head and keep the public guessing.

Then, for her second shock tactic of the summer, she chose infamous photographer Terry Richardson to direct the video. He was a controversial choice – not least because of multiple claims he'd raped and sexually assaulted various models on photo-shoots. He'd also created some less than wholesome artwork, including borderline pornographic shots where he'd persuaded even professional fashion models to give him oral sex on camera.

There'd even been photos where a woman had fellated him while sitting inside a rubbish bin, giving the impression she was regarded as "trashy", clad in a tiara branded with the word "SLUT". Another model who refused to get naked on set due to her period alleged he'd nonchalantly responded, "I love tampons" and asked her to put her bloodied tampon in his tea. Meanwhile, Terry's work had even extended to photographing a crystal-meth-addicted prostitute with two black eyes, inflicted by an abusive client from whom she'd escaped. By many accounts, this wasn't someone with whom a self-respecting woman should even consider being associated – but Miley, perhaps unaware of the stories, had been convinced he was the right choice for her.

She'd asked him to create scenes similar to Sinead O' Connor's 1990 number one hit 'Nothing Compares 2 U', which had featured close-ups of the Irish singer's weeping face – but for this video Miley would not just be crying, but "naked and vulnerable", straddling a giant demolition ball of the variety used to destruct houses while clad in nothing more than a pair of faded red Doctor Martens boots. Brandishing a sledgehammer, she was set to prove it was more than records she could break. Yet what had inspired the stormy scene?

In spite of previous self-confessed heartache with Nick Jonas, Miley was now countering that her heart had never been broken and by now the emotional hiccup that was that relationship had long since been relegated to distant memory – so how would she conjure up genuine tears in the spirit of the theme? Was she thinking about her deceased grandfather, or the cruelty of the mass media? On the contrary, the surprisingly soft-hearted Miley was blubbing over the death of her beloved Yorkshire terrier, Lila. "I love dogs more than I love people," she confessed, "[so] I kept this image of Lila in my head and the tears just fell."

Portraying the tough, gritty, darker side of life was important to her. After all, "Sure, I could go put on a gown and have some beauty pictures taken of me, but where's the honesty in that?!" This was apparently where Terry came in handy – traditionally someone who'd shied away from the bog-standard beauty image. In Miley's eyes, he was singularly adept at capturing the paradox of "strength versus vulnerability".

The same day that 'Wrecking Ball' was released, she took to the stage at the MTV VMAs for a planned medley with Robin Thicke comprising both 'We Can't Stop' and his own chart topper, 'Blurred Lines'. The choice had been a controversial one before there'd been so much as a single twerk, on account of Robin's back story. 'Blurred Lines' – which spoke of ambiguity over whether or not a woman wanted sex, suggesting she was saying "no" when she meant "yes" purely to keep up appearances of being a "good girl" – was banned by some universities' student unions over claims that it condoned rape. Other critics complained that while the women in the video were fully clothed, placing them in the power position, the women writhed around in flesh-coloured lingerie while being physically appraised by the lustful eyes of the others. If ever there had been a blatant example of objectification and misogyny in pop culture, the critics flamed, this was it.

Director Diane Martel, on the other hand, was the first to defend the video, insisting it was completely harmless, portraying the men as "playful" rather than predatory – and even foolish. She added that she, as a woman, had even originally demanded they do a nude video. She reiterated that the song was never meant to be degrading to women. Robin, however, had gleefully admitted to the media that he'd had other intentions. "What a pleasure it is to degrade a woman," he'd announced. "I'd never gotten to do that before . . . We tried to do everything that was taboo. Bestiality, drug injections and everything that is completely derogatory towards women." Would he view his performance with Miley in the same way?

In just a few moments onstage, the pair managed to leave much of the nation open-mouthed. Initially the giant teddy bears that paraded around during the performance were more of a puzzle than a provocation, but Miley later seemed to confess to paedophile-like tendencies when she reflected, "I had this obsession about this character that's like an adult baby . . . there's something creepily hot about it. When I'm in that teddy-bear suit, I'm like a creepy, sexy baby. But I forget that it's, like, people in Kansas watching the show – that people sit their kid in front of the TV and are like, 'Oh, an awards show! Let's watch!'"

Miley also repeated her playful S&M-style spanking routine with her black backing dancers, which reignited the race debate and saw *The Guardian* accuse Miley of leading a politically incorrect "minstrel show".

Yet the part of the act that enraged viewers most of all was her twerk against Robin Thicke, seeing her simultaneously stick out her tongue and simulate masturbation with the aid of the finger of a larger-than-life foam hand. Even Steve Chmelar, the original creator of the finger, had a bone to pick, raging that she'd "defiled and degraded an icon".

All of the criticism revived a debate that the dust had barely settled on from the first time around – that of whether Miley was demeaning herself with her performance style. Even Brooke Shields – former guest star in *Hannah Montana* as Miley's mother – waded in, condemning the show as "desperate" and demanding to know who was advising her. Miley brushed her words aside, suspecting hypocrisy, as after all, "Brooke was in a movie where she was a prostitute at age 12!"

Meanwhile did some of the criticism have sexist undertones? For instance, Catholic *Fox News* presenter Bill O'Reilly – who had historically taken a less than healthy interest in the preservation of Miley's virginity – had publicly scolded her for the twerking while absolving the fully complicit Robin of any blame – and the fact that he'd openly admitted his song was degrading to women went totally without mention. The implicit message seemed to be, "Boys will be boys but Miley is a slut." O'Reilly's attitude echoed that of many of Miley's foes – and it hadn't gone unnoticed. "No one is talking about the man behind the ass," she pointed out. "It was a lot of 'Miley twerks on Robin Thicke', but never 'Robin Thicke grinds up on Miley.' They're only talking about the one that bent over – so obviously there's a double standard."

It seemed that Miley was expected to conform to traditional gender roles which dictated that boys were merely victims of their natural instincts, while women were at fault for projecting themselves as sinful objects of desire. While promiscuous or sexualised men might be regarded as studs, women behaving the same way were merely shameless. Feminist writer Julie Burchill summed up this attitude when she commented, "Men in music have always been handsomely rewarded for getting wasted and getting down – but let a young woman act like she actually owns and enjoys the body she has and all hell breaks loose."

Intriguingly, it emerged that the reaction to MTV was a subtle reflection of that, with TV bosses screening females being spanked during the VMA performance, but censoring parts that saw Miley reversing the roles. "I was trying to slap Robin's ass," Miley revealed, "but no one saw it. Believe me, MTV edited so much, they cut almost everything I did."

This mimicked the reaction to Christina Aguilera's 'Can't Hold Us Down', released a decade earlier. The feminist empowerment anthem, featuring a rap from Lil Kim, which aimed to expose double standards in society, depicted women's fury when men groped them or disrespected them. It then illustrated the women getting their own back, but MTV had heavily edited that part of the video, noting that anything portraying the objectification of men had to be censored. The scenes of men grabbing Christina's derriere, however, remained. A petition from fans had protested the decision, but to no avail.

Fast forward to 2013 and it seemed that the playing field was exactly the same. Thus for some feminists, Miley's performance had raised important questions – for example, was society at large intimidated by a woman who depicted a strong sexuality? After all, it placed the onus on men to provide their partners with satisfaction, while other women might have been envious of their body confidence. The argument was that some men only found female sexuality acceptable and palatable when it was presented in a non-threatening package – one of submissive, feminine, compliant and doll-like passivity.

That was certainly the imagery of Miley some projected when they interpreted her stage shows as "a cry for help". In the weeks and even months that followed the VMAs, from tabloid newspapers such as *The Sun* to gossip magazines like *Heat*, entire double page spreads were devoted to speculation over Miley's mental state. To some, it was inconceivable that she could have independently chosen to sexualise her image and the wilful destruction of the *Hannah Montana* career she'd insisted was past its sell-by date would only mean that she was deeply troubled.

It was reported that she was on the verge of a "meltdown", with speculation rife that her compulsions were down to undiagnosed bipolar disorder. Meanwhile another pop argument was that Miley was "a little girl lost, exploited by male music executives". Yet was it, again, sexist to assume that Miley, as a woman, was a fragile, delicate little flower who desperately needed to be protected from herself – someone whose expression of sexuality could not be legitimate and could only be symptomatic of a mental illness? That was the argument of Julie Burchill, who challenged,

"Men in music who get trashed and show off are "trouble" – with all the enjoyable and attractive implications of that word – while women are "troubled", meaning they are victims in need of protection . . . we can't admit to envy, so we dress it up as feminist ethics."

The increasingly lurid reputations of unsavoury-sounding men such as Robin Thicke and Terry Richardson gave understandable cause for concern, but on the other hand, would a woman with a worth of almost £100 million, voted as one of the most powerful in America, not be immune from exploitation? After all, she scarcely needed the extra money and was surely free to do as she pleased.

So the argument began between two opposing breeds of feminists – those who believed Miley was pandering to male desires and losing all self-respect in the process, and those who felt the only sexist part of the equation was the attempt to restrict her freedom. The first group regarded Miley as "cheap", although that word in itself had roots in a culture that was discriminatory to women and, to the second group, harked back to a bygone era where bride prices were assigned to women. In that world, a higher value was placed on those who were chaste, virginal, dressed modestly and whose secrets had never been seen.

To liberal feminists, Miley's actions were commendable because they were the exact antithesis of that, rejecting being viewed as property and seeing her claim her sexuality for herself. Miley had acknowledged that "sex sells" – but how was exploiting that herself any more demeaning than selling one's brain in an academic role, or one's singing voice as a vocalist? Plus should the onus not have been on challenging sexist attitudes, educating that sex appeal didn't diminish or detract from someone's talents in everyday life, rather than on the women to cover up for fear of being unfairly judged?

Clearly the performance had opened the floodgates for political debate – the missing puzzle piece being whether or not Miley had truly been exploited. When she appeared on her producer Mike Will Made It's single '23' – released on September 10 and featuring alleged misogynists Wiz Khalifa and Juicy J – while dressed in a skimpy cheerleading uniform, surrounded by lyrics about "bitches" and "pussy", it added further fuel to the debate.

This aside, the public reaction to Miley had been astonishing. Two chart-topping singles in one summer, a worth of almost £100 million, and all the world was talking about was her twerk – but she had the last laugh. With her name on everyone's lips, there was no chance of being forgotten by showbiz any time soon.

Chapter 11

MILEY'S career was accelerating faster than ever before – but at a cost. Within weeks of her controversial VMA appearance, her relationship with Liam was over for good. In stark contrast, at the start of 2013, Miley had shared with the media that, of all the things in her life, her romance was the one in which she felt happiest and most confident. In her words, her fiancé was her "number one priority".

Yet of all the shows she would perform that year, solidarity would soon no longer be one of them – and the cracks quickly began to show. In February, after the Oscars, Liam had been spotted kissing and embracing *Mad Men* star January Jones – who, with her short, blonde crop, bore a striking resemblance to Miley – before leaving with her in a taxi.

The subsequent post-Oscars parties had seen a subdued Miley attend solo, leading to speculation that Liam and January had been caught having an affair. If so, she swiftly forgave his indiscretions, but a string of songs she penned revealed her true emotional state.

Snoop Dogg had accidentally spilled the beans about her break-up when he'd explained the meaning behind their collaboration, 'Ashtrays And Heartbreaks', while subsequent tracks created for Miley's forthcoming album echoed the dark vibe. 'Drive' had been written on Valentine's Day, "about needing to leave someone but not really wanting to completely cut yourself off from the relationship. It's a time when you want to leave, but you can't."

'My Darlin'' then saw Miley break free and graduate to grieving for her loss – and duly in May, she performed at the Met Ball in New York with her engagement ring notably absent. Although she took to Twitter to deny the rumours that her relationship was in trouble, angrily declaring plans to take another break from "emotionally draining" social media, many felt she was protesting a little too much.

It was intriguing to note that the Met Ball performance had been the moment, visually, that her public transformation had begun in earnest, seeing her step out in a fishnet dress sporting a spiky, punk-inspired hair-style. In contrast, when Liam had first met her, she'd been a sweet, com-paratively innocent 16-year-old – a loyal girlfriend and, as someone who was then still part of the Disney franchise, an iconic role model. He'd been proud to introduce this self-styled "good girl" to his parents. Yet in a few short years, she had become the polar opposite of the person he'd fallen for.

Although Miley had recalled appreciatively that her boyfriend had "been great" about her deviating from typical Hollywood beauty standards by chopping off her long locks – unthinkable in some showbiz circles – the change had been more than just physical. On turning 20, her trans-formation to an edgy punk-rock chick whose promiscuous posturing had earned headlines worldwide had allegedly become too much for Liam to bear.

To add to that, it was also insinuated that, following his alleged affair, Miley had become increasingly clingy and possessive – and that, feeling smothered by her insecurity, Liam had seen a none too complimentary snapshot of exactly what marriage to her might be like.

Yet another factor rumoured to have been a problem was Miley's "verbal diarrhoea". Fiercely private, Liam barely tweeted at all and fought to keep his personal life shrouded from the media. Miley, on the other hand, was a prolific social networker and, although she often complained about the internet's "evils", her self-imposed absences from it were never long. Miley was almost addicted to the adrenalin rush of near-instant feed-back from her fans and Twitter was one vice that she'd loved to hate. Yet Liam felt her continual tweets and status updates drew unwanted attention to the couple, encouraging media intrusion – something which had already been on the increase due to her onstage antics. Her penchant for over-sharing had been what had divided her from Nick Jonas, and now it looked set to wreck her relationship with Liam, too.

Plus while they'd once been on the same page, seeing their home as a sanctuary strictly for their nearest and dearest, it was claimed that it had gradually become an open house for Miley's producers and party friends – a motley crew that had included drug dealers and strippers. Liam felt that Miley was slowly becoming a caricature of her former self, but this was no illustration – it was reality. This wasn't the life he'd signed up for and both parties apparently began to question the validity of their loyalty to each other.

Yet speculation aside, there was no question that Miley and Liam had grown apart – and during an interview that Miley gave to *Rolling Stone* at the end of August, that reality had been illuminated more than ever. Turning even the interview into a performance, she earnestly declared that she had to "keep doing stuff that's really crazy", before duly having the words "Rolling Stone" tattooed to the soles of her feet.

Despite howling in agony as the tattooist's needle probed tender nerve pathways, just hours afterwards she had recovered and, journalist in tow, her appetite for sensation-seeking resumed. This time it led her to the desert, were she proceeded to do a 12,500ft high skydive from a plane.

Leafing through the indemnity forms with barely a gulp, she jokingly scrawled "unemployed" next to the job category box – and indeed, life and career really was a game for Miley now, albeit a very lucrative one. When she descended safely to the ground, she called her mother to tell her she was safe, noting, "The one thing about skydiving is you really know who you love, based on who you call." The journalist present enquired quizzically as to whether she had already contacted her boyfriend. "Oh, shit!" she exclaimed, instantly fishing her phone back out. Her actions said it all – perhaps Liam, who was notable at the VMAs only by his absence – was no longer among those she truly loved.

Barely two weeks later, she announced that their engagement was off. Perhaps the separation was inevitable – after all, teenage romances rarely lasted the distance as, at their tender ages, both were still finding themselves and learning about what they truly wanted from life. For Miley's part, she'd changed enormously – allegedly in a way that Liam could not embrace – and she'd started to feel she could no longer be herself around him. It had reached the point where she had a choice between clinging to her safe, familiar love affair or staying true to the Miley she'd become, enjoying her new sexually driven image guilt-free. In the end, she'd chosen the latter.

"Sometimes," she'd mused, "it takes separating yourself from someone else to really be happy with who you are." She added that, towards the end, she'd remained with Liam for no other reason than a fear of loneliness. "I was so scared of ever being alone," she confided in one interview, "[that] conquering that fear was actually bigger than any other transition that I had."

Both had recognised that something once beautiful had turned toxic and that they had to let it die to save themselves. Due to this realisation, the split had been amicable – after all, they were now so far apart that there was no desire for vengeful vendettas – and there were no acrimonious demands from Liam that she return the ring. He'd insisted that she kept it as a "memento" of their affair, during which he reiterated that he'd genuinely been in love.

Yet when questioned on live TV about where the £250,000 diamond gem was now, a nonchalant Miley had been decidedly less sentimental, responding, "I don't know. It might be in the shower." As the horrified studio audience visibly gulped at visions of a ring expensive enough to trade in for a small house descending down the plug hole, it seemed that Miley might have been following her own metaphorical advice from archive track 'Bottom Of The Ocean' – scooping up her feelings for someone she was no longer able to love and plunging them into a safe, undisturbed place beneath the water.

She proceeded to move on fast and, just days later, was centre stage at the iHeart Radio Music Festival in Las Vegas. She'd worn a furry gorilla outfit while clutching a banana-shaped microphone, which some could have interpreted as a racist dig at black stereotypes, following as it had done on the heels of the "ratchet culture" debate she'd incited. On the other hand, it could have been a parody or an entirely unrelated coincidence, but Miley was still commanding headlines while keeping her worldwide audience guessing.

At around the same time, she attracted the contempt of ex-Oasis star Noel Gallagher, who'd sneered, "Don't make a provocative video – write a good fucking song. Adele and Emeli Sandé – that music to me is like music for fucking grannies, but at least it's got some kind of credibility. Miley is just embarrassing."

If Miley had smarted at Noel's choice insults, she didn't show, although she did feel compelled to offer a response to a long and impassioned public letter from Sinead O'Connor. Following a string of media requests to speak on the similarity between 'Wrecking Ball' and her hit 'Nothing

Compares 2 U', the singer had decided to hit Miley with what she regarded as some home truths. Claiming that she'd "been in the business long enough to know that men are making more money than you are from you getting naked", she begged Miley not to send "dangerous signals" to her fans by continuing to "prostitute" herself.

"In the spirit of motherliness and love, I am extremely concerned for you that those around you have led you to believe or encouraged you in your own belief that it is in any way 'cool' to be naked and licking sledge-hammers in your videos," she wrote. "It is in fact the case that you will obscure your talent by allowing yourself to be pimped. Nothing but harm will come in the long run from allowing yourself to be exploited and it is absolutely NOT in ANY way an empowerment of yourself or any other young women for you to send across the message that you would be valued (even by you) more for your sexual appeal than for your obvious talent."

Claiming that at Miley's age, she'd deliberately chosen a traditionally masculine haircut to protect herself from male lust and build a career that saw her valued purely for her music, she continued, "The music business doesn't give a shit about you, or any of us. They will prostitute you for all you are worth and cleverly make you think it's what YOU wanted – and when you end up in rehab as a result, they will be sunning themselves on their yachts in Antigua, which they bought by selling your body, and you will find yourself very alone."

She added in no uncertain terms, "No one who cares about you could support your being pimped – and that includes you yourself. Yes, I'm suggesting you don't care for yourself. That has to change. You ought to be protected as a precious young lady [because] you are worth more than your body." She then added her view that Miley's youthful naiveté and "innocent heart" had made her prey to the media, who had also earned their money by exploiting her "youth and beauty" under false pretences.

The letter was articulate and respectful, but in Miley's eyes, the views she put forward were archaic and the scolding was nothing short of a public humiliation. On one hand, the letter offered motherly nurture and advice, while on the other it chastised her for being a bad role model. Perhaps feeling under attack, Miley lashed out in response.

Her first retaliatory tweet poked fun at bipolar sufferer Sinead's publicly documented battle with mental health issues, comparing her to former child actress Amanda Bynes, who at that times was in treatment for the same issue. She then posted a screenshot of several of Sinead's tweets from two years previously, when she'd been desperately seeking a psychiatrist to save her from being admitted to hospital – and in a further attempt to imply her insanity, and therefore invalidate the contents of her letter, Miley also posted a picture of her ripping a photo of the Pope to shreds.

Even in the eyes of some of Miley's biggest fans, the tweets were perceived as an unnecessarily low blow, a rash and immature response to a debate that might have been better solved by reasoned argument. They also questioned her departure from her impassioned anti-bullying campaign from just a few years earlier.

Needless to say, Sinead was furious. She penned a second letter – and this time she was no longer holding back. "Taking me on is even more fucking stupid than behaving like a prostitute and calling it feminism," she blasted. Pointing out that Miley had "exposed me to abuse for seeking help to save my life when experiencing suicidal compulsions as a side-effect of a medication called Tegretol," she claimed that large numbers of Miley's supporters had "urged me to commit suicide" as a means of defending their idol. She claimed that in the aftermath of tweets, she'd been the subject of "literally thousands of abusive articles and/or comments left after articles that I and therefore all perceived mentally ill people, should be bullied and invalidated."

The string of posts Miley had retweeted were from her distant archives, implying that her suicidal thoughts and then fragile mental health were current. However, Sinead's biggest concern was the impact that Miley's nonchalant attitude might have had on those in the wider world who were vulnerable, as she'd mocked someone for asking for help.

Commenting that seven out of every 100,000 people aged 15–19 in the USA commit suicide each year, that statistically one person stateside takes their life every 16.2 minutes, she urged Miley, "There are people who will not die tonight if you are brave enough to state that there is nothing whatsoever wrong with any person seeking help in order to stay alive." She would also elaborate, "You've acknowledged most of your fans are very young and you might therefore consider being careful regarding what signals you send those of them who may be feeling suicidal and would not be afraid to say so . . . mockery causes death, period. It is an unacceptable form of bullying."

Meanwhile she clarified that she'd ripped up a photo of the Pope for a reason – it was part of a long-standing campaign against the Catholic Church for its sexual abuse of children. Sinead insisted it hadn't merely been a slur against her alone, but equally against "every child who suffered sexual abuse at the hands of priests and had it covered up by the Vatican". "You could really do with educating yourself," she added, "that is, if you're not busy getting your tits out to read."

Miley had briefly tweeted in what had seemed to be a backhanded putdown at Sinead's lack of recent work, "I don't have time to write u an open letter cause I'm hosting and performing on SNL this week, so if you'd like to meet up and talk, lemme know in your next letter."

Sinead responded equally icily that she had no time to meet as she had a family to raise. However, she added, "You can take five minutes today between fucking g-string changes to publicly apologise to Amanda and myself all mental health sufferers as well as all those who were abused by priests. If you end up in the psych ward or rehab, I'll be happy to visit you and would not lower myself to mock you."

Sinead, who had gone as far as to threaten legal action over the episode, continued to write pleading public messages urging Miley to reverse the damage done by using her celebrity to destigmatise mental ill health. However, she was met by total silence.

Plus in spite of Sinead's insistence in her original letter that Miley did not need to shed the Hannah Montana image by getting naked and that the character was "waaaaaay gone by now – because you make good records", Miley felt the need to hold a public funeral that week on *Saturday Night Live*, playfully declaring Hannah dead and buried.

The skit show also screened a miniature remake of the Steve McQueen film *12 Years A Slave*, which parodied the race row surrounding Miley. The movie featured a recently freed black slave readjusting to life in the outside world, but in the remake, the slave – played by Jay Pharoah – was discouraged from dancing as actor Edward Norton warned, "Do not let white people see you dance. Once they see you dance, they will try to dance like you." Cue the arrival of Miley, dressed in full-on colonial clothing, for a ceremonial twerk. It was controversial humour, but for her, it was just the beginning.

Equally outrageous in the eyes of the public was a photo shoot with infamous Terry Richardson the same month, which saw her expose her breasts and, when clad in a red bodysuit, the frontal crotch of which was almost as skimpy as the back of a thong, she came dangerously close to exposing her labia.

However it was far from just the moral implications of near-nudity for which Miley found herself vilified. When the photos surfaced, she was ridiculed for her "boyish" and "child-like" physique and perceived lack of womanly hips and breasts – ironically the opposite of the problem the rapidly developing star had suffered years back on *Hannah Montana*. Some went as far as to state that they felt as dirty as if they'd viewed child porn, in spite of the fact that she was an adult woman. The backlash that had ensued was a symptom of a worldwide verbal war in which words wounded as painfully as bullets and both the perpetrators and targets were women. It involved endless criticism by females of both their own bodies and each other's. Curvy women allegedly looked fat, while slimmer ones were dubbed prepubescent. Now, as Miley's name entered the arena, it seemed as if, suddenly, being called a "slut" for stripping was the least of her worries.

In an attempt to de-stigmatise the female body and discourage people from viewing it as an object of secrecy and shame, that year Miley joined the controversial New York-based Free The Nipple Campaign. With a supporting film planned for 2014, the organisation, whose members described themselves as "a mass movement of topless women", campaigned against censorship and fought for the right of women to bear their naked breasts. Pointing out that men were allowed to go topless, they aimed to decriminalise female nudity through protest and prevent "sexist" treatment of women, who they claimed were looked down on even for breast-feeding in public.

The argument was along the same lines as Miley's reaction when the video for 'We Can't Stop' was edited by MTV. Like her, the group demanded to know why the female body was censored in films, while "blood and gore" was not, and why Facebook had lifted a ban on videos featuring real-life decapitation but still strictly forbade photos that revealed a woman's nipples. In their opinion, female nudity was depicted as sordid and shameful, but the same people holding those views turned a blind eye to morbid violence. Unsurprisingly, Miley had immediately lent her name to the cause.

Meanwhile her boundary-breaking exhibitionism continued – all good publicity, of course, for the October 4 release of her album *Bangerz* – so-called because she and her producers believed every track was guaranteed to be a hit. The exploits even continued during her downtime, seeing her first grind with producer Mike Will Made It and provocatively kiss his neck – all the while at the album's launch party at a New York club – and indulge in a three-way lesbian kiss between herself, a female friend and a dwarf who doubled as a backing dancer. Meanwhile her use of "little people" as "props" onstage would prompt aghast media sources to exclaim that the already immoral Miley had "sunk to a whole new low".

Of course at the other end of the height spectrum, Miley's friend Amazon Ashley was present at the party too, and she would thrust her face into the statuesque stripper's breasts by way of greeting, before enthusiastically "waterboarding" them while cameras flashed around the pair. Rumoured to have also kissed at least one man who was twice her age that night, a newly single Miley was certainly making up for lost time.

Bangerz was another chart topper, peaking at number one in the UK, the USA and several other territories, but by November, Miley had already returned to the singles charts. On November 5, her vocals appeared on 'Real And True', an R&B track by Future featuring Mr Hudson about "everlasting love". Following 'My Darlin'', it would be her second collaboration with the rapper. The video, which was thematically and visually somewhat similar to Katy Perry's 'Alien', depicted Future as an astronaut discovering the lifeless-looking corpse of Miley floating in space. Yet on closer inspection, it emerges that her eyelids are flickering and, in a bid to revive her, she is placed on a futuristic metal operating table. Miley, covered in glitter and seeming to be stark naked but for her body sprinkles, eventually rises to sing a romantic verse to Future, but it seems she is destined to remain in the cosmos, where she feels at home, as before long he has to retreat to his spaceship and sadly leave her behind.

Yet days later, Miley would give the public a real reason to believe she was "spaced out", when – taking full advantage of the fact that the 2013

EMAs were held in Amsterdam – she lit up a marijuana joint onstage. She even accepted her Best Video trophy for 'Wrecking Ball' while puffing on it, fishing the drug out of her classic Chanel handbag. Her actions represented who Miley was – liberal, decadent and rebellious – but drug charities blasted her decision to light up, claiming that although it had been legal due to the location of the ceremony, to do so at such a public event, which would be viewed worldwide, sent out an irresponsible message to millions of impressionable children. That said, Barbra Streisand had famously claimed to be smoking the same drug onstage at a concert all the way back in 1972, asking incredulously whether it was still illegal.

The dust had scarcely settled when, on November 26, another single was released – this time 'Feelin' Myself', a collaboration between Miley, Will.i.am, French Montana and Wiz Khalifa. Will.i.am had initially sought out the fellow "stoner" after hearing an early version of 'Wrecking Ball' and falling in love with her voice, while she'd subsequently made a brief appearance on 'Fall Down' for his album *#willpower*. He'd returned the favour by co-writing and producing 'Do My Thang' for *Bangerz*. Now they were together for a third time and the collaboration hit the number two spot in the UK. It featured Miley talking of popping molly and twerking her booty, although the gyrations on video were less intense than usual.

By December, Miley continued her relentless domination of the charts with her third single in less than two months – this time 'Adore You' from her own album. The video – a raunchier version of J-Lo's 'Baby I Love You' – featured a natural-looking Miley in minimal make-up writhing around on a bed and running her hands over her naked body before slipping them between her legs as if to simulate masturbation. Predictably, the track again attracted the disapproval of the morality police, although it did provide one positive message, "Love Thyself" – albeit in more ways than one. Whether or not one could jokingly interpret Miley's message as a campaign for safe sex perhaps wasn't a wise issue to broach with campaigners, who blasted that she had "betrayed" her younger fans by distancing herself from a wholesome image so quickly.

However she now had a campaign of her own to support – Free The Nipple – and, timed to coincide with the single's release, Miley held a plastic breast over her eye in symbolic protest against censorship. She also treated her fans to a bare-breasted Christmas card, featuring strategically placed seasonal greetings to disguise the so-called "incriminating" areas.

Miley's mission had the full support of Madonna – a long-time supporter of women's liberation and politically minded, self-styled feminist – and in January, the pair would even collaborate for Miley's MTV Unplugged show. Performing a medley of 'We Can't Stop' and Madonna's 2000 hit 'Don't Tell Me', the pair both wore giant, rhinestone-embellished cowboy hats in keeping with the country and western theme of the show, while Miley was clad in a Dolly Parton-inspired denim blouse, which – courtesy of some strategic rips – had an incongruous punk feel too. Miley's verdict? "Pretty fucking cool. I got to perform with Madonna in bedazzled cowboy boots, so I can't really complain."

While Madonna had long been renowned for stunts where she shared the stage with younger female performers – perhaps most famously of all at the VMAs a decade earlier when she kissed both Britney Spears and Christina Aguilera on the lips – but she seemed to be particularly on Miley's wavelength, even sticking her tongue out in unison with her co-star. The gesture had become the latter's trademark and some might joke that it was as much about liberating the tongue as freeing the nipple.

However a more sophisticated look was to come and by March, Miley adorned the front cover of German *Vogue* with the tag "Blonde Angel". It was quite a coup for Miley, as her sexually charged stunt at the VMAs had apparently cost her a *Vogue* cover in her own country – but even more so when she discovered that the theme called for her to channel Marilyn Monroe. Seeing her platinum blonde curls and pillar-box red lipstick, readers were shocked by the similarity between Miley and the real-life Marilyn. The shoot demonstrated her ability to be versatile – glamorous one minute and punk the next – while the polished look came in stark contrast to her penchant for tattoos.

In the months preceding it, she'd added to her collection a Native American crossed arrows tribal symbol on her arm, an anatomical heart inspired by Leonardo Da Vinci – a slap in the face to those who had seen her flashing the flesh and automatically doubted her intelligence – and a claw by legendary tattoo artist Kat Von D. The biggest and perhaps most meaningful of all, however, was a large vintage portrait of her maternal grandmother, Loretta, below the heart on her right forearm – chosen because, as Miley revealed on Twitter, "I am her favourite and she is mine."

She had the opportunity to show off her body art for the March 2014 issue of *W* magazine, which featured her totally naked, save for a strategically placed pillow. In one shot, it had been removed from her upper body entirely to expose her bare breasts. As her earlier shoot with Terry Richardson had merely shown them beneath a transparent top, this would be her first topless shoot – and British newspaper *The Sun* had made her an honorary member of Page Three to celebrate. They'd especially adapted one day's paper to include a snapshot of "Miley, 21, from Nashville" as a substitute for one of their usual girls.

Miley had officially become a glamour model – but that news paled in comparison to the shot that had everyone talking, a simulated *ménage a trois* where she lay in bed sandwiched between two photographers (Mert Alas and Marcus Piggott) for *Vogue*, both of whom had snapped her earlier that month.

The interview proved equally outrageous, seeing Miley admit to loving weed, but hating children, who she regarded as "fucking mean". This admission was shocking to some as yet again it saw her challenge traditional female roles that depicted womankind as loving, nurturing and selfless. Perhaps the most shocking thing of all about her revelations was that after all this time, the public continued to be shocked.

However this time, she had a definitive answer to the inevitable cry of, "What would the parents say?" Presenting a united front with his daughter, Billy Ray had teamed up with rapper Buck 22 for a raunchy rap version of 'Achy Breaky Heart'. Naturally it featured lyrical references to Miley – and abundant twerking.

The song attracted almost as much judgment as her liberal shoot for *W* magazine, but while she could have drowned in the sea of disapproval, her own voice lost and over-powered by those of millions of enraged parents, she'd instead made a defiant commitment to being herself.

What was more, after years of playing the role model, behaving according to who she believed people wanted her to be, she felt it was long overdue. She'd realised that, regardless of what she did, someone, somewhere, would hate it and the realisation was liberating, as it prompted her to live her life for herself – not for perpetually disapproving other people.

"If I have sex, I'm a slut [but] if I don't have sex, I'm a loser," she told one interviewer of the never-ending battle to please a nation. "If I lose weight, I'm anorexic. If I gain weight, I'm fat. I've learnt that it's irrelevant what I do – somebody will take offence anyway."

That knowledge had given the confidence to understand that she had nothing to lose by unleashing the real Miley – a colourful 21-year-old multimillionaire with a penchant for rebellion. By now seemingly adored and reviled in equal measure, she clarified that she had no intention of deferring to her foes. "Be who you are, do what you do, be who you wanna be, live your life and don't worry what other people have to say about it," she declared. "I feel like the best way of fighting my haters is just keep letting them do what they do and don't let them faze you – just keep doing what you do."

The words of Rihanna's 'Pour It Up', which her producer Mike Will Made It had worked on, were surprisingly apt – the Barbadian beauty had taunted that she didn't care how the haters felt, as she still had more money. It was the ultimate put-down – a signature showing she knew she was on top of the world – and Miley was about to emulate it. As she would point out, "Success is the best revenge" – and, by all accounts, she'd certainly had no shortage of that.